Advanced Grammar

For Academic Writing

Richard Stevenson

Published by *Academic English Publications* 2010
http://www.eurekaenglish.com/aepublications.htm
Academic English Publications is a subsidiary of *Eureka Language Services*. Please contact us for information or sample copies.
Email: admin@eurekaenglish.com

ISBN: 978-1-4457-7122-9

Printed by Lulu Press 2010

Lulu Enterprises
860 Aviation Parkway
Suite 300
Morrisville, NC 27560
United States

Table of Contents

Chapter 1

Clauses 6

Independent clauses vs. Dependent clauses 7

Dependent Clauses 9

Types of Finite Dependent Clauses 10

Non-finite Clauses 13

Chapter 2

Word Forms 17

Word Forms 18

The Gerund 18

Participles 20

The finite verb group 22

Verbs as complements of verbs 24

Chapter 3

Verb Types and Complements 28

Types of verbs and their complements 28

Gerund Clauses 35

Prepositional phrases 37

Infinitives 38

Chapter 4

Noun Clauses 45

Noun Clauses 45

Indirect object 47

Writer Voice 50

Passives 52

Wh-word noun clauses 54

If/whether noun clauses 59

Negatives 61

Modals in reported speech 61

Reporting how something should be done using wh - word clauses 61

Noun clauses as complements of nouns 62

Noun clauses as complements of adjectives 64

Noun clauses as complements of prepositions 66

Omission of *that* 67

Reporting orders and instructions 69

Chapter 5

Tense & Aspect..**71**

Tense & Aspect... 72

Construction of the different tenses... 72

States and Events.. 75

Repeated Events and Duration.. 76

Tenses and Aspects used in English.. 77

Future tense back-shifted in adverbial clauses 86

Tense and Conditionals 88

Some other issues with tense.. 90

Chapter 6

Non-finite tense, Modals, & Hedging **92**

Infinitive, gerund, and participial tenses 92

Modals 94

Hedging.. 100

Chapter 7

Adverbial Clauses..**102**

Adverbial clauses... 102

Time 103

Place 109

Manner 111

Distance and frequency 113

Result.. 114

Purpose... 116

Reason.. 117

Concession 118

Contrast 120

Conditionals 1 121

Conditionals 2 126

Comparison... 129

Chapter 8

Language Patterns **131**

Cause and effect language... 131

Grammar of cause and effect language 133

Compare & Contrast Language... 138

As and Like 140

Argument and refutation language 143

Chapter 9

Relative Clauses **147**

Position of relative clause 149

Restrictive/Defining & Non-restrictive Relative clauses.. 150

Describing *things* 152

Describing people 153

Whose... 154

That & which as objects of prepositions (in which / which...to / that...to) 155

Describing places (Where*)* 156

Describing *time* (When) 158

Describing quality or quantity... 159

Describing whole clauses 161

Infinitival Relatives 162

Relative clauses using subjects of noun clauses 163

Transitivity and relative clauses... 164

Chapter 10

Participial Clauses, Absolute Clauses, and Appositive Phrases....................................**167**

Participles 168

Continuous Aspect in Participial Clauses 172

Perfect Aspect and Participial Clauses... 172

Changing adverbial clauses to participial clauses 173

Absolute clauses.. 175

Appositive Phrases 176

Chapter 11

Cohesion **177**

Cohesion.. 177

Passive voice & Cohesion 179

Adverbial clauses & Cohesion 184

Transition words and cohesion... 186

Pronouns & Cohesion 189

Gerund Clauses, Noun Clauses and Cohesion 191

Topic sentences.. 193

Appendix **195**

Appendix 1: Finite tense and aspect 195

Appendix 2: Infinitive and gerund tense and aspect.. 196

Appendix 3: Types of verbs 198

Appendix 4: Reporting verbs, indirect objects, and types of complements 199

Appendix 5: Coordinators, Conjunctive adverbs, and Subordinators.. 202

Appendix 6: Intransitive Verbs 204

Answers **208**

Chapter 1

Clauses

What is a clause?

In every language, meaning is constructed from sounds, letters, words, the endings of words, and by clauses.

A clause is a building block of language; it is as important as the letters, words, and endings of words to make meaning.

Actually, clauses can be more important than these things. If you spell a word incorrectly, forget to change the tense, or use the wrong word, the reader or listener can usually still understand what you mean. However, an incorrect clause can be impossible to understand.

For example, if you said *I look the telivizon yesterday*, it is easy to understand that you mean *I watched television yesterday*.

However, if you said *I television yesterday* or *watched television yesterday*, it is not so easy to understand what you mean. In the first case, what did you do to the television; did you buy a television, watch a television, or eat a television? In the second case, who watched the television? You? Me? Him? We call these kinds of sentences *fragments*.

The importance of a subject

This brings us to the basic building blocks of a clause. In the case of *watched television yesterday*, the writer (or speaker) has left out the **subject**. All finite clauses in English **must** have a subject (except in the imperative); otherwise, they do not make sense. (For explanation of 'finite' see pages 9-10.)

Note that sometimes in English we use a 'dummy' (pretend) subject. This will either be the word *it* or the word *there*. When we use these words, they have no meaning, but are there to fill in the subject space of the sentence. Note that *there* **does not mean location when it is the subject of a clause**.

> **Examples**
>
> *It* is said that this will be a problem.
> (*It* has no meaning in this sentence; we do not know who has spoken, but this is not important.)
>
> *There* is a problem.
> (There has no meaning. These types of constructions usually indicate that something exists.)
>
> *There* is a tree *there*.
> (The first *there* has no meaning; the second *there* shows location.)

The importance of one verb phrase in each clause

In the case of *I television yesterday*, the writer (or speaker) has left out the verb. Again, this doesn't make any sense. **All** English clauses **must** have a finite verb.

However, the clause should only have **one** verb phrase in the clause. We refer to this as a verb **phrase** because, confusingly, the verb phrase is often created by the combination of two or even three verbs. For example, *I have gone, it has been eaten,* and *it has been being used*. In each of these sentences, there is one subject and one *verb group*.

Sometimes, however, you may want to say that one verb causes another action or that it somehow relates to another action. In this case, you will have two *verbs* in the clause, **but** the second verb will always be *infinitive* or *gerund*. For example, *I want to go*. Here the *verb in the clause* is *want*. *Go* is complement to *want*.

> **Note**
>
> Some verbs are complemented by the infinitive, others by gerunds, and others by the bare infinitive. These are explained in Chapter 2 and 3 in detail.

Sometimes the clause may centre around **two verbs**. These events must be joined by the words *and, but*, or *or*. Sometimes there will be an object after each verb; sometimes a prepositional phrase, sometimes an object and a prepositional phrase, and sometimes even clauses can be objects of each event or can describe the object of each event. However, in each case, the verbs are still joined by the words *and, but*, or *or*. **We do <u>not</u> use commas** before *and, but,* and *or* in this situation.

> ### Examples
> He **researched and wrote** about the issue.
> James **claims** that this is a serious issue **and has written** many books on the issue.
> Symmons also **writes** about an issue which has been a hot topic in newspapers lately **and claims** that there is much yet to be done to resolve it.

Independent clauses vs. Dependent clauses

Now that we know what a clause is, we can distinguish between an independent and a dependent clause.
An **independent clause** is a clause that is complete with a subject and finite verb, and can stand alone, while a **dependent clause** cannot stand alone. (For explanation of 'finite verb', see pages 9-10.)
A better way of recognising dependent clauses, is to know that they always begin with a subordinator. (The exception is when the subordinator is omitted, but in these cases there will be two subjects and two finite verbs making it clear that it is another clause.)

Subordinators include words like *because, that, although, when, where, while, which, since, as, if, whether, who, whom, whose*. More complete lists of subordinators are given in the chapters on noun clauses, adverbial clauses, and relative clauses.

Exercises

1.1 Decide which of these clauses are independent and which are dependent.

1) Although television has been blamed for violence amongst children.
2) Yet, computer games have also been blamed.
3) Then again, parenting has too.
4) Since some children play computer games all day.
5) That children can have serious behavioural problems from playing games too much.
6) For example, 75% of children in Korea play computer games for at least 3 hours a day more than in the USA.
7) However, violence amongst children in the USA is higher than amongst children in South Korea.
8) Wherever children have access to computer games.
9) Smith argues that this debate has its roots in the nature versus nurture dichotomy of psychology.
10) As Gorgons claims that more studies need to be done on the issue.

Coordinators

When we join two or more independent clauses together, we use a **coordinator**. There are seven coordinators in English. They are *for, and, nor, but, or, yet,* and *so*. Clauses joined with a coordinator are called *compound sentences*. **Coordinators always have a comma** before them.

> ### Example
> He wrote about global warming, *and* he wrote about global politics.

> ### Example
> The author does not support American foreign policy, *nor does he defend* it.

When using the word *nor*, **we use question word order**. (This may seem strange, but it is correct!)

Exercises

2.1 Complete the following sentences using the coordinators given. Punctuate them correctly.

1) A lot of people study English for _____

   _____

2) A good understanding of English can help you get a good job and _____

   _____

3) A degree in English cannot guarantee you a good job nor _____

   _____

4) The English language can be used for international communication but _____

_____

5) It is best to use English for international trade or _____

_____

6) Many people think that Chinese may overtake English as the international language yet _____

_____

7) For now English remains the international language so _____

Semicolons and conjunctive adverbs

A second way of joining two independent clauses is by putting a semicolon. We tend to use a semicolon when the clauses are very closely related.

> **Example**
>
> The author claims that global warming is a serious problem; he gives several examples of these problems in his work.

Note that putting a comma between two independent clauses is a common error that even native speakers tend to make. This error is called a comma splice.

> **Example**
>
> **Wrong:**
> The author thinks that the Gulf Stream will **stop, he** thinks that Europe will become much colder than it is today. X
> **Correct:**
> The author thinks that the Gulf Stream will **stop; he** thinks that Europe will become much colder than it is today. ✓

A third way of joining two independent clauses is by using a **conjunctive adverb**. These are words such as **therefore, moreover, nevertheless**, and **thus**.

Students commonly confuse conjunctive adverbs with subordinators. They are, however, very different. Conjunctive adverbs are more like coordinators than subordinators. (A comprehensive list of conjunctive adverbs is given in Appendix 5, page 201.)

> **Examples**
>
> **Beginning a new sentence**
> The author thinks that the Gulf Stream will stop. **Therefore,** he thinks that Europe will become much colder than it is today.
>
> **Following a semicolon**
> The author thinks that the Gulf Stream will stop*; therefore,* he thinks that Europe will become much colder than it is today.

Conjunctive adverbs can either begin a sentence, or follow a semicolon. They are **always** followed by a comma. Conjunctive adverbs can **add information**, can show **result**, can **compare and contrast**, and can show **cause**. They are used to create cohesion in a text. See Chapter 11, page 186 for more information on how to use conjunctive adverbs to create cohesion.

> **Examples**
>
> **Adding information**
> Global warming will lead to cooler weather in Europe*; moreover,* it will lead to cooler weather in North America.
>
> **Showing result**
> Ice in Greenland is melting*; as a result,* the water in the Atlantic Ocean is becoming less salty.
>
> **Comparing**
> Global warming is melting the ice in Greenland*; likewise,* it is causing ice to melt in the Arctic Ocean.
>
> **Contrasting**
> Global warming will heat equatorial areas of the world*; in contrast,* it will cool the northern areas of Europe.

Exercises

3.1 Complete the following sentences using the conjunctive adverbs given. Punctuate them correctly.

1) Internet traffic has increased incredibly over the last decade accordingly _____

_____

2) The size of information being sent across the internet has increased furthermore _____

_____

3) Internet service providers have attempted to increase the size and speed of their network centres nevertheless

_____

_____

4) The amount of storage space on the internet needs to be increased otherwise _____

_____

5) The size of e-mails has increased dramatically in recent years hence _____

_____

6) People are using the internet for more and more new uses for example _____

_____

7) These days many people are using the internet for social networking therefore _____

_____

Dependent Clauses

Independent clauses can stand alone; they make sense by themselves.
Dependent clauses cannot stand alone. This is because they start with **subordinators** or because they do not contain **finite verbs**.

Subordinators are words like **because, although, when, while, where, that**, and **whose**. There are too many subordinators to list them all here, but a complete list can be found in Appendix 5, page 201.

A dependent clause must be joined to an independent clause to make sense (except in spoken English).

> **Example**
> **Dependent clauses**
> ...which he likes.
> ...liking her.
> **Independent clause**
> He likes her.

Finite and Non-Finite Dependent Clauses

Verbs have four functions in English. A verb can function as a **verb**, a **noun**, an **adjective**, and as a **complement**. Thus, not all verbs are functioning as verbs. Some have the job of adjective, and some have the job of noun. For example *he has an important calling in life*. *An important calling* is clearly a noun. It has an article and an adjective before it. Although *call* is a verb, in this sentence, its job is to be a noun. Another example is the verb *bore*. *The bored students listened to the boring teacher*. In both cases the verb *bore* is functioning as an adjective, not as a verb. It is modifying the nouns *student* and *teacher* in the same was as adjectives *nice* or *ugly* might. This is important to understand when it comes to clauses.

Finite verbs change for tense and subject agreement (I go, he goes, they went, we have gone). These verbs are found in all independent clauses and in all finite dependent clauses.

Non-finite verbs are gerunds, participles, and infinitives (going, gone, to go). These forms of verbs can act as nouns and adjectives, but they can also be the verb in non-finite dependent clauses.

Sometimes the non-finite gerund and infinitive forms can act like the verb in a clause. Consider the examples below. In each sentence the underlined part is a clause. In 1) it is a finite clause (it is a **noun clause**); in 2) and 3) it is a non-finite clause. Notice how each clause has a **subject,** a **verb,** and an **object**. We need to look at finite and non-finite clauses separately. (Note that some books refer to *non-finite clauses* as *phrases*.)

> 1) The problem is **that** plagiarism **is** not **considered** a crime in all cultures.
> Subject / Verb (finite) / Object
>
> 2) This has resulted from plagiarism not **being considered** a crime in all cultures.
> Subject / Verb (non-finite) / Object
>
> 3) This has caused plagiarism **to** not **be considered** a crime in all cultures.
> Subject / Verb (non-finite) / Object

9

Chapter 1

Verb	Form	Example
Finite		
	V V~s V~ed Is/am/are V~ing Have/has V~ed Is/am/are V~ed Modal V Do/does not V	Plagiarism often **happens** by mistake. Plagiarism **is being investigated**. Many cultures **do not consider** plagiarism to be a bad thing.
Non-Finite		
Gerund (noun)	V~ing	I like **studying**.
Participle (adjective)	Active: V~ing Passive: V~ed or irregular past participle	The **singing** bird is prettier than the **swimming** bird. This **tried** method works well.
Infinitives	To V (or 'bare infinitive': V)	Their universities make them **do** this.

Types of Finite Dependent Clauses

We can divide finite dependent clauses up in many ways. One useful distinction is between **embedded clauses** and **extra information clauses**.

The doctor *inquired* <u>**where the next operation would be done**</u>.
Subject   Verb   Object

The doctor *wrote down* the room <u>**where the next operation would be done**</u>.
Subject   Verb   Object

Compare the two sentences on the right. In the first sentence the dependent clause is the object of independent clause; in the second sentence the dependent clause is extra information. The first sentence contains an 'embedded clause'. The second sentence contains an 'extra information clause'.

1. Embedded clauses

Embedded clauses are noun clauses.

In this example **Thompson** is the subject; **claims** is the finite verb, and <u>***that babies will develop the ability to recognise their parents by three to four months***</u> is the object of the sentence. Because the noun clause is the *object* of the independent clause, we say that this clause is *embedded*. This makes noun clauses very different from other dependent clauses.

> **Example**
>
> Thompson *claims* <u>that babies will develop the ability to recognise their parents by three to four months</u>.
> Subject   Verb   Object (noun clause)

It is important to remember that noun clauses **function as nouns**. It is also important to remember that **not** all verbs can have a noun clause as their object. (See Chapter 4 for more detail on noun clauses.)

2. Extra information clauses

These clauses give extra information about a noun or a verb. They can be further divided into three types:

a) Adverbial

b) Relative (Also called adjective clauses)

Remember, adverbial clauses *describe verbs* and Relative clauses *describe nouns*.

> **Examples**
> **Adverbial Clause**
> He lives in Mexico *because he likes the climate*.
>
> **Relative Clause**
> English, *which is an international language*, is very useful.

Notice that adverbial clauses and relative clauses function quite differently from noun clauses. Adverbial and relative clauses *add extra information*. Noun clauses *are nouns; they can be the subject or object of another clause*.

c) Noun

Confusingly, some noun clauses can be extra information clauses. This is an advanced point that is covered in chapter 4, pages 63-64 on noun clauses.

> **Note**
>
> *When* and *where* can be used in all three types of clauses. *That, which, whom, whose*, and *why* can be used in relative *and* noun clauses. *What* and *if* can be used in both noun and adverbial clauses; however, they have a different job in each type of clause. *What* and *how* can be used in a special kind of reduced relative clause. In these types of clauses, *what* means *the thing that* and *how* means *the way that*.

Subordinators

Each type of dependent finite clause has a different list of subordinators to choose from. The following list divides some of the subordinators between the types of clauses they are used in. A full list of subordinators can be found in Appendix 5, page 201.

Noun clauses commonly use these subordinators:		
how	*what*	*where*
if	*when*	*which*
that	*whether*	*who*

Relative clauses commonly use these subordinators			
that	*where*	*who*	*whose*
when	*which*	*whom*	*why*

There are a large number of **adverbial clause** subordinators. Some commonly used subordinators are:			
after	*before*	*so that*	*what*
although	*how*	*than*	*when*
as	*if*	*though*	*where*
because	*since*	*until*	*while*

Each type of clause and their subordinators are dealt with in more detail in separate chapters.

Telling the difference between noun clauses, adverbial clauses, and relative clauses.

Consider the following sentences:

The dependent clause in each sentence begins with the same subordinator, but the first sentence contains a **noun clause** and the second a **relative clause**.

> He reports **that Janos test drove this type of vehicle.**
>
> The type of vehicle **that Janos test drove** was a Porsche.

Noun clauses can look a lot like **object** relative clauses, but they are not. Firstly, a noun clause is the object of a verb; a relative clause describes a noun or, perhaps, a clause. Secondly, a noun clause follows a different pattern:

Adverbial clauses can also look like relative clauses, but adverbial clauses describe the verb, not the noun.

Look at the examples on the right.

> Noun Clause: **Subordinator – subject – verb – object**
> Relative clause (*Obj*): **Subordinator – subject – verb**
> Relative clause (*Sub*): **Subordinator – verb – object**
>
> ---
>
> **Example**
> Noun clause: He said **that – he – drove – the car**
> Relative clause (*Obj*): This is the car **that – he - drove**
> Relative clause (*Sub*): This is the person **that – drove – the car**

In the first example, the clause is describing the verb (**live**). It is an adverbial clause. In the second example, the clause is describing the noun (**house**). It is a relative clause.

> I live **where I can see the sea.**
>
> I live in a house **where I can see the sea.**

Exercises

4.1 What types of finite dependent clauses are these? Circle *noun*, *adverbial*, or *relative*.

1) He went to the pub when he had finished his homework. *(noun/adverbial/relative)*
2) She said that she was hungry. *(noun/adverbial/relative)*
3) 1986, when they finished high school, was the year of the Chernobyl nuclear disaster.

(noun/adverbial/relative)

4) That it was wrong was a serious problem. *(noun/adverbial/relative)*

5) She lived where she could see the sea. *(noun/adverbial/relative)*

6) Pirates who worked in the Caribbean made lots of money. *(noun/adverbial/relative)*

7) The idea is that students will demonstrate how well they speak English.

   A *(noun/adverbial/relative)* **B** *(noun/adverbial/relative)*

8) A dictionary is a book that contains meanings. *(noun/adverbial/relative)*

9) Dale Gribble works in a place where he can have fun. *(noun/adverbial/relative)*

10) She wanted to know if it was a problem. *(noun/adverbial/relative)*

11) I will do it now if you want me to. *(noun/adverbial/relative)*

12) I told him that he shouldn't have done it. *(noun/adverbial/relative)*

13) He wondered who the killer was. *(noun/adverbial/relative)*

14) This is the pen that I bought yesterday. *(noun/adverbial/relative)*

15) Global warming is raising sea levels, which means that many islands will soon be underwater.

    A *(noun/adverbial/relative)* **B** *(noun/adverbial/relative)*

16) 1986 was when I started high school. *(noun/adverbial/relative)*

17) I went to high school when I had finished primary school. *(noun/adverbial/relative)*

18) I went to high school in 1986, when I had finished primary school. *(noun/adverbial/relative)*

19) If an accident happens, don't go near the car until you are sure that there will not be a fire.

    A *(noun/adverbial/relative)* **B** *(noun/adverbial/relative)* **C** *(noun/adverbial/relative)*

20) The fact that Homer Simpson is funny is the main reason why '*The Simpsons*' is such a great TV show.

    A *(noun/adverbial/relative)* **B** *(noun/adverbial/relative)*

4.2 Write your own sentences. Include two of each type of dependent clause.

1) _____

_____

2) _____

_____

3) _____

_____

4) _____

_____

Parallel structures

It is important to repeat grammatical items either side of **and, but,** *or* and **nor**. This can be confusing to students, but can be easily explained by the following two sentences:

These two sentences have quite different meanings. In the first sentence, he said that he laughed, and then, after that, he started to cry.

> 1) He said *that* he laughed, and he cried.
> 2) He said *that* he laughed and *that* he cried.

In the second sentence he said that he laughed and he also *said* that he cried. Thus, the meaning is completely different.

It is important to remember this when you are reporting information that has been written, as it can change the meaning. See Chapter 4, page 57 on noun clauses for more on parallel structures.

> **Example**
>
> Hughes argues *that* World War One was caused by Germany **and** *that* Germany needed to pay for the damage they caused.

Exercises

5.1 Combine these clauses into parallel structures.

1) Kapetanos claims that Einstein's theories of relativity are wrong. Kapetanos claims that long distance space travel is, therefore, possible. _____

_____

2) Others argue that long distance space travel is not possible because the nearest galaxy is one million light years away. This is because Einstein's theory of relativity dictates that it would take at least a million years to travel there. _____

_____

3) Some experts have argued that living in the long term without gravity in a spaceship would be bad for the body. But, they point out this problem could be resolved by spinning the space ship as it travels though space to generate a gravitational field.

_____

_____

4) There are two remaining problems with such an expedition. One is that we don't have the technology for such an expedition. The other is that we don't have the finance.

_____

_____

5) Finally, if we were to send an expedition to another galaxy, there are two questions. One is should we send humans? The other is should we send robots?

_____

_____

Non-finite Clauses

While finite dependent clauses begin with a subordinator and contain a finite verb (e.g. **that he did not believe this**), non-finite clauses do not always have a subordinator and do not contain a finite verb.

There are five main types of non-finite clause, each acting much like a finite dependent clause.

Five types of non-finite clauses	
Gerund clause Caust has investigated <u>students using plagiarised sources</u> in some detail.	**Non-finite relative clause** She is the best person <u>to whom to confide</u>.
Infinitival Clause This has caused <u>some students to work harder to paraphrase their sources</u>.	**Non-finite noun clause** The students asked the lecturer <u>how to improve their writing skills</u>.
Participial Clause Some students <u>working hard to finish their theses by the due date</u> become careless about plagiarism.	

Gerund Clause

Gerund clauses are much like noun clauses. They can act as subjects or objects of verbs or as objects of prepositions.

The verb in a gerund clause is expressed in *gerund form.* An example might be:

> **Finite Clause:** *The US exports sheep to Saudi Arabia.*
> **Gerund Clause**: *The US exporting sheep to Saudi Arabia.*

The gerund clause can then be inserted into another clause in the same way as a noun clause can be (except that gerund clauses can be used in many more situations than noun clauses).

> **Examples**
> **Two clauses:** The US exports beef to Japan. This is important for the US economy.
> **Combined with Gerund Clause →** *Exporting beef to Japan* is important for the US economy.
>
> **Two clauses:** Global warming is causing sea levels to rise. This does not make people worried.
> **Combined with two gerund clauses →** *Global warming causing sea levels to rise* is *not making people worried.*

Prepositional phrases

> **Note**
> Some unusual looking prepositions include: **according to, as a consequence of, because of, due to, such as, despite,** and **in spite of.**

Chapter 1

Prepositional phrases are much like adverbial clauses. They give extra information about when and where and why an event happened.

Prepositional phrases begin with a preposition. Prepositions are always followed by noun-like structures. They can be followed by **nouns, noun phrases, gerund clauses,** or **noun clauses.**

Examples

Prepositional phrase + noun
Global warming is caused <u>by humans</u>.

Prepositional phrase + noun phrase
Global warming is a consequence <u>of human activity.</u>
<u>accelerating</u>.

Prepositional phrase + gerund clause
Global warming is a consequence <u>of humans burning</u>
<u>CO$_2$</u>.

Prepositional phrase + noun clause
Robins talked about <u>how global warming is</u>

Participial clauses

Some participial clauses are similar to relative clauses; they describe nouns. They can be restrictive or non-restrictive. Other participial clauses are similar to adverbial clauses. Participial clauses must have the same subject as the independent clause. They are made from either the present or past participle of the verb. Detail is given in Chapter 10.

Examples

Active
Relative clause: The instructor who teaches this class is very smart.
Participial clause: The instructor teaching this class is very smart.

Passive
Relative clause: The lessons which are taught by Gene are lots of fun.
Participial clause: The lessons taught by Gene are lots of fun.

Adverbial
Adverbial clause: Because I want to do well in the IELTS exam, I study hard.
Participial phrase: Wanting to do well in the the IELTS exam, I study hard.

Infinitive clauses and non-finite noun and relative clauses

Infinitive Clauses are clauses constructed from infinitives. Remember that the infinitive is the **to + verb** form of a verb. Examples include: **to do, to sing, to eat, to swear.**

Examples

They agreed <u>to look into the problem</u>.
Johnson asks <u>us to consider this problem carefully</u>.

This caused them <u>to reconsider the problem</u>.
He has come <u>to consider this to be wrong</u>.

Sometimes infinitive clauses can begin with a wh-word. These phrases are either **non-finite relative clauses** or **non-finite noun clauses**. (For more information on these types of clauses see Chapter 3, pages 38-44, for still more on non-finite noun clauses see Chapter 4, page 69; and for still more on non-finite relative clauses see Chapter 9, page 162.)

Examples

Non-finite Noun Clause
Smith does not clearly explain <u>how to solve these</u> problems.

Non-finite Relative Clause
Maria is the worst person <u>with whom to discuss this</u>.

Infinitive clauses can be used in a variety of different ways.

One meaning is **purpose**.

Example

Purpose
I came to Canada *to learn how to speak English.*

Another use is to give **more information** about a noun that has an ordinal number, a superlative, or the words **last, next,** or **only** before it.

Examples

| **Ordinal number** | **Superlative** | **Last** |
| Carter was the *first* person *to make this an issue.* | Johnson is the *best* person *to consult.* | The *last* person *to research this claim was Kraich.* |

They can be used after some nouns such as **ability**, **attempt**, **chance**, and **failure** formed from verbs to extend the noun.

Example

His *failure to produce* solid evidence for his claims is the reason why his ideas don't have much support.

And finally, infinitive clauses can be used after reporting structures in passive voice (See Chapter 3, pages 38-44 for more, also see Chapter 4, page 52).

Example

James is thought to have done the most comprehensive research on the issue.

Exercises

6.1 Decide if the underlined parts of the following sentences contain:

1) Noun clauses	4) Gerund clauses	7) Prepositional phrase
2) Adverbial clauses	5) Infinitive clauses	
3) Relative clauses	6) Participial clauses	

1) <u>Because English is used in so many fields</u>, it is <u>an essential language to use</u>.

   a) _____   b) _____

2) David Crystal suggests <u>that English will be the world's permanent lingua franca</u>.

   a) _____

3) English, <u>which is spoken in North America, the United Kingdom, and Australia</u>, is taught in almost every country in the world.

   a) _____

4) The rise of English arose from <u>Britain and America winning World War II</u>.

   a) _____

5) Some linguists wonder <u>when the rest of the world will stop using English</u> as a lingua franca.

   a) _____   b) _____

6) In the 1950s, <u>when the USA and Britain first started promoting English</u> as a lingua franca, there were fears of <u>Russian or French becoming the world language</u>.

   a) _____   b) _____   c) _____

7) The USA and Britain joined forces <u>to promote English</u> as the world language <u>when they realised the financial benefits</u> <u>of English being the lingua franca</u>.

   a) _____   b) _____   c) _____

8) <u>Before World War II started</u>, Germany tried <u>to promote German</u> as a world language.

   a) _____   b) _____

9) <u>Before 1900</u>, French was used in all diplomatic correspondence.

   a) _____

10) <u>Long before being used as an international language</u>, French was actually used <u>as the language of government</u> in England too.

   a) _____   b) _____

11) English is said <u>to be going to be spoken even more widely in the future</u>.

   a) _____

12) If you decide to learn English, try to avoid using phrasal verbs at first.

    a) _____   **b)** _____   **c)** _____

13) Some researchers wonder if English will suffer the same fate as other past international languages such as Latin.

    a) _____   **b)** _____   **c)** _____

14) However, English will probably remain the world language if nothing happens to change world power structures in the near future.

    a) _____   **b)** _____

15) This is in part due to China having invested large amounts of money in the education of its students in English.

    a) _____

16) There are no languages that are particularly easier to learn than English.

    a) _____   **b)** _____

17) Crystal argues that all languages are as hard as each other to learn.

    a) _____   **b)** _____

18) Languages such as Chinese can be difficult as they do not have a phonetic writing system.

    a) _____   **b)** _____

19) That Chinese has such a difficult writing system makes Chinese unlikely to surpass English as the international language.

    a) _____   **b)** _____

20) English, having a difficult spelling system, is a hard language for some students to learn.

    a) _____

21) Because of English having such a difficult spelling system, many people have promoted the simplification of English spelling.

    a) _____

22) The problem is that nobody can agree on how we should simplify it.

    a) _____   **b)** _____   **c)** _____

23) Linguists have suggested that we should not simplify the spelling until we better understand how languages are learned.

    a) _____   **b)** _____   **c)** _____

6.2 Join the clauses on the left with the phrases on the right.

1) The first person	a)	To be as important as their genetic makeup.
2) The next thing	b)	To prevent CO_2 emissions.
3) Carlos stopped	c)	To finish can go home early.
4) Yesterday, they failed	d)	To do is the reading exercise.
5) Computers have the ability	e)	To take a longer English course.
6) There is a serious need	f)	To Look in the shop window.
7) Hyoung Ju has chosen	g)	How to do the exercises.
8) The instructions explain	h)	To process information very quickly.
9) Global warming is known	i)	To finish the homework.
10) The way children are brought up is said	j)	To be causing sea levels to rise.

6.3 Write four sentences of your own containing gerund clauses.

1) _____

   _____

2) _____

   _____

3) _____

4) _____

6.4 Write four sentences of your own containing prepositional phrases.

1) _____

2) _____

3) _____

4) _____

Word Forms

Revision

What is a clause?

Clauses are the building blocks of languages.

A clause has a subject (unless it is in the imperative), a verb (finite, gerund, or infinitive), and sometimes a complement. The verb is the most important part of a clause; without a verb, a clause does not make sense.

There are two types of clauses: independent and dependent. All sentences need to contain an independent clause. Without one, what you have said doesn't make sense (except sometimes in spoken English).

All clauses must have an a verb

Whether the clause is independent or dependent, it must have a verb. This is the single most important thing in order to be understood in a language. Including a verb in every clause will increase the ability of native speakers to understand what you have said or written by 200%. *All other grammar mistakes are trivial in comparison to this!*

Word Forms

We have learnt that all clauses must have a verb; it is important to remember that verbs can have many word forms. They can be **verbs, adjectives, nouns,** or **infinitives**.

Let's look in more detail at some of the forms that verbs can have.

The verb forms we will look at are in the table below.

Verb	Form	Example
Finite		
Verb	V V~s V~ed Is/am/are V~ing Is/am/are V~ed Have/has V~ed Modal V Do/does not V	Plagiarism often <u>happens</u> by mistake. Plagiarism <u>is being investigated</u>. Many cultures <u>do not consider</u> plagiarism to be a bad thing.
Non-Finite		
Gerund (noun)	V~ing	I like <u>studying</u>.
Participle (adjective)	Active: V~ing Passive: V~ed or irregular past participle	The <u>singing</u> bird is prettier than the <u>swimming</u> bird. This <u>tried</u> method works well.
Infinitives	To V (or 'bare infinitive': V)	Many students come to Britain <u>to study</u> English because their universities make them <u>do</u> this.

> *Note*
>
> **The infinitive** is used when we talk about the name of the verb. For example, we often talk about the verb **to go** or the verb **to be.** This is just a convention for naming verbs.
>
> When the infinitive is used in a clause it is not the verb in the clause; usually it is the complement of a verb.
>
> (For more on the infinitive, see page 38.)

The Gerund

The gerund is the noun form of the verb. It is the *–ing* form of the verb (actually there are two –ing forms of verbs; we will come to the other one in the next section).

The gerund often acts like a noun in a clause. This means it can be the subject or the object of a verb. The gerund can be pluralised and can be preceded by an article, a number, or an adjective.

It is important to remember that if you make a sentence like *He going*, you have put two nouns together (the pronoun *he* and the gerund *going*), thus this sentence does not usually make sense (*He is going* does, however, make sense).

Examples

1. Subject	**2. Object**	**3. Article, adjective**	**4. Number, plural**
Singing is fun.	I went *fishing*.	*The racing* led to *fun celebrating*.	*Two beatings* were enough for him.

Note that we tend to prefer noun forms when they exist to the gerund. Thus, the third example above might also read ***The races** led to fun **celebrations***.

Gerunds can also act like verbs in some non-finite clauses. Take the following sentence for instance:

The president paying a bribe to the police **led to** him being arrested for corruption.
Subject   Verb   Object

In this independent clause, the finite verb is ***led to***. The subject is a clause, and the object is a clause. Note how the verb in the subject clause is in gerund form, and the verb in the object clause is in object form. Most cause and effect type verbs can take a gerund clause as their subject. Not all verbs can have a gerund clause as their complement.

The following table shows some different types of verbs and what kind of complement they can have.

Type of verb	Example verb	Type of complement(s) allowed	Example
Linking verb	be	Adjective, noun phrase, noun clause, gerund clause, prepositional phrase	The problem is him being incompetent.
Reporting verb	state	Noun clause, noun	She stated that he is incompetent.
Motion verb	move	Prepositional phrase	They moved closer to him being removed.
Other verb (1)	result in	Noun phrase, gerund clause	This resulted in him being removed.
(2)	cause	Noun phrase, infinitive clause	This caused him to be removed.
(3)	make	Noun, Noun+adjective, bare infinitive clause	This made him angry.

Exercises

1.1 Circle the finite verbs and underline the gerunds.

1) We have postponed looking into this.
2) Preparing for writing tests is important when students are failing writing classes.
3) Carlo rejects investigating the possibility of reworking this.
4) The reading that the students were given yesterday was not interesting to them.
5) Shipping times are being reduced resulting in customers gradually becoming less dissatisfied.
6) Intending to do your homework is not the same as doing your homework.

1.2 Write these verbs as gerunds in sentences.

1) Write an essay _____

_____

2) Jump to conclusions _____

_____

3) Anticipate _____

_____

4) Ask questions _____

_____

5) Do _____

_____

Chapter 2

Participles

Participles are adjective forms of verbs. You will be familiar with these from lower level English lessons in which you learned the difference between for example, *interesting* and *interested*. As you can see from this example, there are two adjective (participle) forms of verbs: the **present participle** and the **past participle**. The **present participle** is used for active voice adjectives and the **past participle** is used for passive voice adjectives.

Present participle

The **present participle** is the *–ing* form of a verb used to make an adjective. Using the present participle, we can make sentences like ***The boring teacher talked to the interesting and fascinating student***.

> **Example**
> **Present participle**
> The *screaming* child had *worrying* psychological problems.

The present participle and the gerund look exactly the same. However, it is important to remember that the present participle is an adjective.

You can tell the difference between the gerund and the present participle because the gerund will either be the object or the subject of a verb and the present participle will usually be followed by a noun.

Another way to tell if you're the ~ing form being used is a gerund or an present participle is to rewrite it as a relative clause. If it can be done, it is a participle; if it can't be done, it is a gerund.

> **Example**
> **Present participle**
> The <u>screaming child</u> had <u>worrying psychological</u> problems.
> The <u>*child who was screaming*</u> had <u>*psychological problems that were worrying*</u>. (Rewritten as relative clauses)
> **Gerund**
> This essay justifies <u>disciplining children</u> with psychological problems. (Cannot be rewritten as a relative clause)

Remember that the present participle cannot be the finite verb of the clause. Thus, if you have a sentence like ***The boring teacher*** you have no finite verb in the sentence, and it does not make sense (***The teacher <u>is boring</u>*** does, however, make sense because ***is boring*** is a finite verb).

Past participle

The ***past participle***, like the ***present participle*** acts like an adjective, but it is a passive voice adjective. The past participle is the *PP* 'tense' of the verb. For example, you will have learned ***go - went - gone, see - saw - seen***, and ***have - had - had***. In these cases, the past participles are ***gone, seen***, and ***had***.

For a regular verb, the past participle is the same as the past tense of the verb, for example: ***played, killed, loved***.

> **Example**
> **Irregular passive participle**
> The *chosen* student was happy.

> **Example**
> **Regular passive participle**
> The *bored* student was unhappy.

Remember that the past participle of an irregular verb cannot be the *finite verb*. The past participle of a regular verb, however, is identical to the past tense of a regular verb. This means that the '–ed' form of a verb can sometimes be the verb in the sentence depending on the word order and also depending on whether or not there is already a verb in the clause.

> **Example**
> **-ed form as past tense of verb**
> He *liked* school.
> (In this case, the subject and object either side of the verb clearly indicate that the *liked* is a verb.)

> **Example**
> **-ed form not past tense of verb due to word order and due to there being another verb in the clause.**
> The *liked* boy was unhappy.
> (In this case, it is clear that *liked* is not a verb. *Liked* has no subject, it is followed by a noun (which is the subject of the clause) and there is another verb (*was*) in the clause.

Choosing between the present (active) and past (passive) forms of the participle can be difficult for students. Thus, it is important to remember the following rule.

The person or thing 'giving' the adjective will have an ~ing adjective, and the person or thing 'receiving' the adjective will have an ~ed adjective. This means that ~ed adjectives generally apply to humans and other living things. ~ing adjectives, on the other hand, are used for either living or not living things

Consider the following example:

The bored man told the interesting news to the entertained children.

He the man is receiving boredom from something; the news is making other people receive interest, and the children are receiving entertainment from the man and the news.

The only problem with following this rule is that learners need to know what the verb actually means. For example, *to bore* means to make a person receive boredom; *to bare* means to have a baby; *to marry* means to have a wedding, *to addict* means to make addicted, and *to locate* means to find. Thus, *an addicted person* finds it hard to quit, and *a located object* is an object that has been found. But note that *it is located in the garden* means that the object *can be found* in the garden.

Notice also that intransitive verbs cannot have past participles. For example, *to happen* can't have an object; it is intransitive. Thus, although we can make the participle *happening* (it is a happening nightclub), we cannot make the participle *happened*. Other similar verbs include: *disappear*, *occur*, *last*, *fluctuate*, and *emerge*.

Exercises

2.1 Circle the verbs, underline the gerunds, and double underline the participles.

1) The interesting teacher explained grammar to the disinterested students.
2) Some complicated aspects of writing include paragraphing and breaking up sentences into clauses.
3) Reading books can be an exciting way of entertaining yourself.
4) Working on a troubling problem is what a dedicated student does.
5) A student who studies all night is being a hardworking student.
6) The worrying effects of global warming are causing concern.

2.2 Write sentences using the following verbs as active participles.

1) Entertain _____

_____

2) Bore _____

_____

3) Understand _____

_____

4) Correspond _____

_____

5) Result _____

_____

2.3 Write sentences using the following verbs as passive participles.

1) Interest _____

_____

2) Plan _____

_____

3) Love _____

_____

4) Require _____

_____

5) Perceive _____

_____

2.4 Choose between the present and past participle (~ing and ~ed) forms of the adjectives in the following passage.

Africa is suffering from many _____ *(alarm)* problems. First, some African countries are governed by

_____ *(disgust)* governmental systems which are totally corrupt and which destroy their _____

(complicate) economies. For example, Zimabawe's _____ *(trouble)* economy is being destroyed

because of such a corrupt dictatorial governmental system (Stewart 2004, p2). This _____ *(bewilder)* government has sent Zimbabwe into a _____ *(disturb)* bankruptcy, rendering Zimbabwe's _____ *(distress)* people even more poor (Stewart 2004, p3). _____ *(Exasperate)* poverty has accompanied Africans for a long time. In Sub-Saharan Africa, GDP per capita is $US790 (Collins 2005, p67). The _____ *(alarm)* percentage of Africans who live in _____ *(shock)* poverty increased from 42% to 47% across the last two decades (Stewart 2004, p4). Moreover, Africa has experienced several _____ *(confound)* humanitarian crises. For instance, in Sudan 50,000 people have died, more than 1.4 million have been forced from their homes, and up to 10,000 people, most of them _____ *(exhaust)* children, were dying each month because of _____ *(sicken)* violence and _____ *(devastate)* disease (Stewart 2004, p1). Disease strikes Africans daily, causing many to die. It has been estimated that 130,000 Africans die from _____ *(debilitate)* disease every week (Laberge 2008, p21). AIDS itself kills about 44,000 Africans weekly, and unsafe water kills another 14,000 (Laberge 2008, p21).

The finite verb group

There are **three tenses** (past, present, and future) in English and **two voices** (passive and active). We can also change the verb from simple form to continuous form or perfect form or even perfect continuous. We call these forms **Aspects**. English has four aspects

The **finite** form of the verb changes for all of these. Tense, aspect, and voice can be combined for **finite** verbs in a variety of different ways. (For more detail, see Chapter 5.)

Simple

The simple uses the base form of the verb. In present tense the ending must agree with the subject, in past tense, -ed is added to regular verbs; the future tense is achieved by putting **will** or **be going to** at the front.

> **Example**
>
> | **Simple** | (Regular) | (Irregular) |
> |---|---|---|
> | (Past) | I played. | He went. |
> | (Present) | I play. | He plays. |
> | (Future) | I will play. | I am going to |

Continuous

The continuous is formed by the verb *to be* and the active participle. Tenses are achieved by changing the tense of the verb **be**. The active participle cannot change tense.

> **Example**
>
> **Continuous**
> (Present)   They *are playing*.

Perfect

The perfect is formed by using the verb **have** with the passive participle. Tenses are achieved by changing the tense of the verb **have**.

> **Example**
>
> | **Perfect** | (Regular) | (Irregular) |
> |---|---|---|
> | (Present) | I *have played*. | He *has gone*. |

Passive Voice

The passive is formed by using the verb **be** with the passive participle. Again, tenses are formed by changing the tense of the verb **be**. Occasionally, the verbs **get** and **make** can also be used with the passive participle to make passive voice.

Combinations of these aspects and tenses are also possible.

> **Example**
>
> | **Passive** | (Regular) | (Irregular) |
> |---|---|---|
> | (Present) | The piano is played by me. | He got drunk. |

Note that a full list of regular and irregular examples of each tense of each aspect and the combinations are given in the appendix.

> **Example**
>
> **Passive Perfect Continuous**
> (Past)   The piano had been being played by me.

Thus, the only possible ways to create a finite verb in English are by using the base form of the verb (the simple tense), by adding –ed to the end of a verb, by putting the verb 'to be' at the front of a verb *and* either –*ing* or –*ed* (with a regular verb; the past participle with an irregular verb) to the end, or by using *have* and –*ed* to the end (for a regular verb; the past participle for an irregular verb).

Do

The auxiliary verb **do** is used in negatives and questions. **Do** and the verb it is working with can together be considered the finite verb of the clause. **Do** is just another verb such as **be** and **have** which is used to construct grammatical meaning. **Do** changes tense and reflects subject-verb agreement. It is actually complemented by the

> **Examples**
>
> **Negative:**   I do not understand.
> **Question:**   Why do you sing?

bare infinitive. Remember to delete it when you no longer want to construct a negative or a question.

Modals

Modals are used in front of verbs to show *probability, ability,* or *permission*. There are two types of modals. True modals such as **must**, **should**, and **can**, and modals formed from verbs such as **have to**, **ought to**, and **be able to**.

> **Example**
> I *can* <u>speak</u> English.
> She *might* <u>sing</u> a song.

Modals are followed by the *bare infinitive*, which does *not* change for tense or subject-verb agreement.

Verbs preceded by modals are still considered to be *the finite verb of the clause*.

> **Examples**
>
> **Future**
> He should be going to do it tomorrow.
>
> **Past**
> He should have done it yesterday.

Modals can show tense; however, it is important to note that future tense can only be formed using **be going to** and past tense by using the present perfect. Note that **can** only has past and present tenses.

A full list of examples of all the tenses of the infinitive is given in Appendix 2, page 195. More explanation of modals is given in Chapter 6, pages 94-100.

> **Note**
> *I think that…* is also a modal-like structure. The meaning is not that the person is thinking, but that they believe it to probably be true.

Exercises

3.1 Put the correct verb form into the gap; pay attention to word form, tense and aspect.

Viking success in the pre-mediaeval period can _____ *(be attributed)* to four factors. Firstly, the Vikings _____ *(establish)* long distance _____ *(trade)* routes, the profits from which _____ *(be used)* to finance the vast armies and navies that were raised by the Scandinavian kings during this period. Secondly, the Vikings _____ *(maintain)* naval superiority. Thirdly, their _____ *(frighten)* appearance and methods of attack _____ *(encourage)* the peasants of Europe to believe, at least at first, that they _____ *(be attacked)* by demons. The peasants believed that they could _____ *(not fight)* them; as a result, they _____ *(not fight)* them. And, lastly, _____ *(advance)* battle techniques and _____ *(interest)* tactics helped the Vikings _____ *(overwhelm)* their _____ *(select)* enemies. The decline of the Vikings after their rapid ascent to power _____ *(be brought about)* by _____ *(change)* weather patterns, by the conversion of Viking _____ *(occupy)* areas and Scandinavia itself to Christianity, and by the gradual assimilation of the Vikings into 'Western' culture.

3.2 Find 15 mistakes in the following passage (all are with *verbs*).

Throughout history, the country that has control the seas and oceans has became a major super power. The Portuguese built their empire from their position as the leading sea-faring nation in Europe in the Fifteenth Century. The Spanish Empire, too, was create from control of the seas; control which leading to the discovery of America. The British Empire becames the largest in the world through naval superiority. The Vikings, too, came to dominate most of Europe and parts of America because they control the seas. Except for pirates, who have outlawed Vikings anyway, the Norsemen had almost complete control of the seas of northern Europe and the Atlantic Ocean. Since none of the northern European countries of England, Ireland, Scotland, France, or Germany been threatened from the north seas before, their naval defences were poor. Thus, the Vikings were able sail out of the oceans at high speeds right up the rivers, before any warning could to be given and could completed their raids with lightning speed. The Vikings had an ancient history of sea-faring, dating back to pre-historic times. They had developing the art of sea-faring to powerful levels, they were not afraid to take to the sea during storms, and they had good methods of navigation, which included using the altitude of the sun to calculate their latitude. Some Viking raids are conduct over land, especially later, when Viking forts and colonies had establish, and particularly in Russia. But, apart from Russia, such colonies and forts could not had been established without first gaining control of the seas.

Verbs as complements of verbs

Verbs are often complemented by other verbs. Some verbs can be complemented by the gerund, some by the infinitive, some by either the gerund or the infinitive, and some just by the bare infinitive. There is no rule determining this, it is simply something that you have to remember.

Examples
Gerund
The author *denies claiming* that global warming is not happening

Infinitive
Drey *hastened to disclaim* responsibility for these statements.

Gerund or infinitive
Gerund: Authors often *hate admitting* that they are wrong.
Infinitive: Authors often *hate to admit* that they are wrong.

Bare infinitive
The author *helped* the readers *understand* the importance of Russell's 'teapot' analogy.

Remember that in these cases, the infinitive, the gerund, or the bare infinitive are not the verb in the independent clause; they are complement to it.

Verbs that must complemented by gerunds or gerund clauses

acknowledge	end up
advocate	evaluate
anticipate	finish
avoid	hypothesise
consider	ignore
debate	insist on
define	justify
delay	keep on
deny	propose
describe	postpone
discuss	question
dislike	reject
document	risk
emphasise	spend time

Verbs that must be complemented by infinitives or infinitive clauses

appear	manage
attempt	neglect
choose	object
claim	offer
convince	plan
deserve	refuse
expect	resolve
fail	seek
forget	seem
grow	send
guarantee	tell
happen	threaten
hasten	vow
help	want
hope	
know	

It is also important to note that when the infinitive or gerund is the verb in a non-finite clause, it can reflect different aspects. A list of some of the possible aspects of infinitives follows. See Appendix 2, page 195 for a complete list.

Infinitive Aspects (Using the verb *to do* as an example)

Past:	To have PP	To have done	*Perfect:*	To have PP	To have done
Present:	To V	To do	*Passive:*	To be PP	To be done
Future:	To be going to V	To be going to do	*Perfect continuous*:	To have been V-ing	To have been doing
Continuous:	To be V-ing	To be doing			

As stated above, the gerund can also show aspect. A few possible constructions are listed in the examples below. See Chapter 6, page 92 for more and Appendix 2, page 195 for a complete list.

Gerund Aspects (Using the verb *to do* as an example)

Present:	V-ing	Doing
Future:	Being going to V	Being going to do
Past or perfect:	Having PP	Having done

Common errors

The following are a list of things that you *cannot* do with verbs (using the verb *speak* as an example). If you make these constructions, they are probably wrong. It is a good idea to check through your writing before you submit it to see if you have made any of these types of mistakes.

Wrong	Correct
I am speak	I speak *or* I am speaking
It is spoke	It is spoken
I have spoke	I have spoken *or* I spoke
I have speaking	I have spoken *or* I am speaking (Unless a gerund is the object of the verb *to have*).
I can to speak	I can speak
I can speaking	I can speak *or* I can be speaking
To spoke	To speak *or* To have spoken
To spoken	To speak *or* To have spoken *or* to be spoken
To speaking	To be speaking *or* To speak (Note, that *to* followed by the gerund can be correct in some fairly rare instances in which *to* is a preposition. When *to* forms the infinitive, the –ing form is never used).
Do not spoke	Do not speak *or* Have not spoken
Do not spoken	Do not speak *or* Have not spoken *or* Be not spoken
Do not speaking	Do not speak *or* Is not speaking
Do you spoke	Do you speak *or* Did you speak
Does it spoken	Is it spoken *or* Has it spoken
Do you speaking	Do you speak *or* Are you speaking

Exercises

4.1 Change the verb complements to gerunds or infinitives.

In the 960s Erik the Red, a fiery Norwegian, was sent from his home in Norway _____ *(explore)* the oceans. He chose _____ *(go)* to Iceland, where he convinced Thjodhildur _____ *(marry)* him. He later ended up _____ *(be)* banished from there for three years. Erik kept on _____ *(go)* west and spent his time _____ *(explore)* a land with inviting fjords and fertile green valleys. He described _____ *(be)* greatly impressed by the land's resources, and he hastened _____ *(return)* to Iceland and convinced some Icelanders _____ *(come)* with him to this land, which he called "the green land". In 986 he planned _____ *(take)* 25 ships out from Iceland back to Greenland. He convinced 500 men and women _____ *(join)* him. Of the 25 ships, the Greenlanders documented only 14 _____ *(reach)* their destination. The Vikings evaluated _____ *(settle)* in several locations, before founding Brattahlid and the two hamlets of Vesterbygden and Østerbygden. Viking records around the year 1000 claim 3,000 people _____ *(be living)* in 300-400 farms on Greenland. This small community managed _____ *(survive)* for 500 years. Why they failed _____ *(survive)* beyond that time is still a great mystery.

(adapted from http://www.greenland-guide.gl/leif2000/history.htm viewed 12/7/09)

4.2 Put the correct verb form into the gap; pay attention to word form, tense (including 'aspect'), and to what kind of verb complement you use.

It was not just control of the seas that _____ *(lead)* to the Vikings _____ *(dominate)* northern Europe. The Vikings also _____ *(use)* their frightening appearance _____ *(help)* them. When they first _____ *(arrive)* on the shores of England, Ireland, and Normandy, the troubled locals _____ *(think)* that they _____ *(be)* demons in league with the devil and _____ too _____ *(scare)* _____ *(fight)* and _____ *(offer)* them gifts _____ *(be left alone)*. The _____ *(appal)* methods of *attack* which _____ *(be used)* by the Vikings _____ *(help)* them _____ *(believe)* that these warriors _____ *(be)* supernatural beings. The Vikings _____ *(rape)* the women and _____ *(cut)* the throats of all the children, women, and priests. They _____ even _____ *(be known)* _____ *(gather)* entire townships together in their cathedrals and _____ *(burn)* them. They particularly _____ *(hate)* monasteries, and _____ *(raid)* and _____ *(burn)* every church building they _____ *(come across)*, making sure they _____ *(kill)* the monks and nuns. It _____ *(be thought)* that the attacks on monasteries and cathedrals _____ *(be)* revenge for the Catholic Church's denunciation of the Viking Gods such as Thor. Nevertheless, the brutality of _____ *(kill)* _____ *(unarm)* monks and nuns, as well as their other uncivilized tactics _____ *(scare)* the local folk into _____ *(believe)*, at least at first, that these men were receiving help from the devil whom no ordinary man could _____ *(fight)*. Thus, resistance was probably weaker than it might _____ *(be)*, which _____ *(allow)* the Vikings _____ *(gain)* control of large parts of northern Europe and Russia. The Vikings _____ *(have)* other advantageous tactics. For example, they always _____ *(attack)* by surprise, and quickly. Due to their ships _____ *(be)* speedy, the Vikings could _____ *(attack)* before any warning could be given. They regularly _____ *(attack)* on wet stormy nights when everybody _____ *(be)* inside, and visibility _____ *(be)* low. They _____ *(have)* little regard for the promises that they _____ *(make)*. For example, they _____ *(accept)* gifts and peace treaties, then _____ *(rebuild)* their armies and _____ *(attack)* again when the enemy let down their guard. These were such highly _____ *(develop)* battle tactics, that the Germans, one thousand years later, _____ *(use)* these same tactics in their blitzkrieg attacks during World War II. Scandinavia _____ *(be)* a battle ground for many centuries and the art of battle _____ *(develop)* there, more than anywhere else in Europe. It _____ even _____ *(be thought)* that the knights of mediaeval Europe _____ *(learn)* their art from the Vikings. The rise of the power and wealth of the Vikings thus can _____ *(be attributed)*, amongst other reasons, to battle skills that were far more _____ *(advance)* than those _____ *(employ)* by other Europeans.

4.3 Find 19 mistakes with verb word forms in the following passage.

The Viking conquests were fund not only by plunder from previous expeditions, but also from to trade. Just as naval superiority has always be a key ingredient in establishing global power, so too has trading. The far-reaching Islamic empires of the mediaeval times building on trade, as were the Dutch, British, French, and American Empires. The Vikings had a vast trading pattern; they trade with such far away places as Tashkent in central Asia, Baghdad, Jerusalem, Alexandria, Byzantium, Russia, France, Germany, Poland, Britain, Iceland, Greenland, and America. The revenues from this trade must had contributed greatly to the financed of the voyages of conquest.

Thus, the Vikings were able to spreading out across the knowing world. They established trading posts at Novograd and Kiev in modern day Russia, and in fact, the modern day Russian state owes, at least in part, its establishment to the Swedish Vikings. As well, the Vikings gained control in all of England, in Normandy, parts of Germany, Ireland, Scotland, Wales, Iceland, and Greenland. Viking settlements have also been discover in Newfoundland in North America, and less certain evidence has found in Massachusetts, Florida, and even Brazil. Attacks were made on Spain and northern Africa, and attempts were made to captured Rome and Byzantium. The colonies of Greenland and America were eventually abandoned as the strength of the Vikings declining.

The colony in Newfoundland was attacked by Eskimos and since the settlers were too far from Greenland to receive speedy assistance, and due to be out-numbered, the colony was abandoned, and the colonists returned to Greenland. The Vikings had spreading out too far. The Greenland colony fell to change weather patterns. Europe, and indeed all of the north Atlantic suffered from a mini ice age between about 1350 AD and 1800 AD. The colder weather meant that Greenland was no longer inhabitable and the colony there died out. It is probable too, that this colder weather played some part in the decline of the power of the Scandinavian countries themselves . Colder weather implies that less food could produced; hence, there being a smaller population, which meaning less young men to fill the Viking armies. Thus, it can being argued that to at least some small extent, the change in weather patterns was responsible for the decline of the Vikings.

Verb Types

and Complements

Types of verbs and their complements

Verbs can be complemented by noun phrases, gerunds, infinitives, adjectives, gerund clauses, infinitive clauses, noun clauses, or in some cases prepositional phrases or noun phrase + adjective; other verbs cannot have complements. Unfortunately, there are no easy rules to help decide what kind of complement a verb should have, but it is still important as the wrong kind of complement can make your writing very hard to understand.

To help us decide what kind of complement a verb can have, it is useful to divide verbs into different types. There are many ways of dividing up verbs, but the following list is useful for considering their complements.

> **The types of verbs we will consider are:**
>
> | | | |
> |---|---|---|
> | *linking verbs* | *intransitive action verbs* | *ditransitive action verbs* |
> | *reporting verbs* | *transitive action verbs* | |
> | *motion verbs* | *ambitransitive action verbs* | |

Before continuing, we need to know what the following words mean:

Noun phrase: A noun phrase is a noun and its modifiers. The modifiers usually come before the noun and include adjectives, quantifiers, qualifiers, pronouns, and articles.

> ***Example:***
> ...the two very big student apartments.

Gerund clause: A gerund clause is a clause in which the verb is in gerund form. This type of clause is called a non-finite clause. The subject can often be left out of a gerund clause. Gerund clauses are found as subjects and objects of many types of verbs. They are also found in prepositional phrases.

> ***Example:***
> ...two of my friends <u>eating</u> all of the delicious food.

Infinitive clause: An infinitive clause is a clause in which the verb is in infinitive form. This type of clause is called a non-finite clause. The subject can often be left out of an infinitive clause. Infinitive clauses are found as objects of some types of verbs. They can also act like adverbial or relative clauses, acting as 'extra information' clauses, providing more information about the action. Often infinitive clauses start with the subordinator 'for'.

> ***Example:***
> ... <u>for</u> two of my friends <u>to eat</u> all of the delicious food.

Noun clause: a clause that can be either the object or the subject of a verb. Noun clauses are usually the objects of reporting verbs. Note that a finite clause must contain a finite verb.

Prepositional phrase: A prepositional phrase is a preposition followed by either a noun group or a noun phrase. Prepositional phrases can also contain wh-word noun clauses.

The table on the next page shows a summary of these different functions of verbs.

Linking verbs			Reporting verbs		
Subject		**Complement**	**Subject**		**Object**
Dummy	**(linking verb)**	Adjective	Noun phrase	**(reporting verb)**	Noun phrase
Noun phrase		Noun phrase	Dummy (*it*)		Noun clause
Gerund clause		Gerund clause			Infinitive clause
Noun clause		Noun clause			Quoted speech
Infinitive clause		Infinitive clause	**Intransitive action verbs**		
		Adverb	**Subject**		**Object**
		Prepositional phrase	Noun group	**(intransitive verb)**	*(no object)*

Motion verbs (prepositional phrase as complement)			Ambitransitive		
Subject		**Object**	**Subject**		**Object**
Noun phrase	**(motion verb)**	Prepositional phrase	Noun phrase **(ambitransitive verb)**		Noun phrase
		Adverb	Noun clause		Gerund clause
					Infinitive clause

Transitive action verbs			Ditransitive action verbs		
Subject		**Object**	**Subject**	**Indirect Object**	**Direct object**
Noun phrase	**(transitive verb)**	Noun phrase	Noun phrase **(ditransitive verb)**	Noun phrase	Noun phrase
Gerund clause		Gerund			
clause		clause			
		Infinitive			
clause					

Now lets look at each type of verb in a little bit more detail.

Linking Verbs

Linking verbs are the most complicated types of verbs. They can be divided into five types

Five types of linking verbs

1. *be*
2. *appear, seem, tend*
3. *make, find*
4. *tend, become, grow, turn, prove, remain*
5. *feel, look, smell, sound, taste*

Each has interesting properties that are not shared by other verbs. Their individual properties can be as follows:

1. TO BE

Subjects: noun phrase, dummy subjects (*there* & *it*), noun clause, gerund clause, infinitive clause
Complements: adjectives, noun clause, gerund clause, infinitive clause, prepositional phrase

Examples
There are several problems with this. **Or** It is very cold today. **Or** The solution is in this book.

Note
To be is transitive, but it is not used usually in passive voice.

2. APPEAR/SEEM/TEND (TO BE)

Subjects: noun phrase, dummy subjects (*there* & *it*), infinitive clause
Complements: adjectives, noun clause, gerund clause, infinitive clause

> **Examples**
> It **appears** *that Steffan Welsh has lost the election*.
> Steffan Welsh **appears** *to have lost the election*.

> **Note**
> When we use the dummy subject *it*, we follow these verbs with noun clauses. When we use a real subject, we use infinitive phrases or adjectives. When we use the dummy subject *there* we complement this verb with an infinitive clause.

> **Note**
> *Tend* must have *to be* after it to follow these patterns.

3. MAKE, FIND, CONSIDER

> **Subjects:** noun phrase
> **Complements:** noun phrase + adjective (*find*, *make*, or *consider*), noun phrase + bare infinitive clause (*make* only)

> **Note**
> These are the only verbs that have a noun phrase and an adjective together as the verb complement.

Notice that only *make* can be used in both patterns. *Find and Consider* can only be used with a noun phrase + adjective complement. The structure noun phrase + adjective is sometimes called a **small clause** because it has some similar properties to a clause.

> **Example**
> The beautician **made** the girl beautiful. **Or** She **made** me laugh.

4. BECOME, GROW, TURN, PROVE, REMAIN

> **Subjects:** noun phrase, gerund clause
> **Complements:** adjective, noun phrase, infinitive clause (except *become*)

> **Example**
> The weather **grew** *wet and windy*.

> **Note**
> *Turn* can only be complemented by adjectives that can change (e.g. colour). *Prove* can only be complemented by abstract adjectives (e.g. *interesting* and *nice* (which you can't see), not *beautiful* or *pink* (which you can see).

5. FEEL, LOOK, SMELL, SOUND, TASTE

> **Subjects:** noun phrase
> **Complements:** noun phrase + bare infinitive clause, adjective, prepositional phrase beginning with *like*, adverbial clause beginning with *like*.

> **Examples**
> They **felt** it happen.   This water **tastes** like sea water.
> It **sounds** terrible.   It **feels** like it is going to rain.

> **Note**
> *Look* and *sound* cannot be complemented by noun phrase + bare infinitive.

Exercises

1.1 Find nine errors in the following text

The fact that hamburgers make fat is true, but they also appear us addictive. If there was proved for this, it seems to be fast food companies would prove liable. Are fast food companies purposely making their hamburgers addict? If so, seems to be no reason why we should not treat them in the same way as we treat cigarette companies who knowingly made cigarettes addictive despite the health hazards. We know that fast food companies have teams of scientists making hamburgers tasting perfect; they add food colouring to the food to make it to look delicious. Studies have shown that if you eat fast food, you will grow obesity. They have also shown that food high in fat and sugar actually alters the brain, harnessing natural pleasure systems in the brain to make us want to eat more. Thus, it is becoming obviously that altering fast food to make it smell appetizing, taste delicious, and look mouth-watering, is not so different from what cigarette companies are doing.

1.2 Now write sentences of your own with a variety of subject and object types using the suggestions given below.

1) to be (subject: dummy, complement: noun phrase) _____

_____

2) appear (subject: dummy, complement: adjective) _____

_____

3) seem (subject: noun phrase, complement: infinitive clause) _____

_____

4) tend (subject: dummy, complement: infinitive clause) _____

_____

5) make (subject: noun phrase, complement: noun phrase + adjective) _____

_____

6) sound (subject: noun phrase, complement: adjective) _____

_____

7) become (subject: noun phrase, complement: noun phrase) _____

_____

8) grow (subject: noun phrase, complement: infinitive clause) _____

_____

9) look (subject: noun phrase, complement: adverbial clause)_____

_____

10) feel (subject: noun phrase, complement: noun phrase + bare infinitive clause)_____

_____

Reporting verbs

Reporting verbs can also be divided into several categories including

1. **transitive**
2. **ditransitive**

> **Note**
> Chapter 4 covers reporting verbs and noun clauses in detail.

and

1. **reporting verbs that can have a *that noun clause* as their complement**
2. **reporting verbs that can have *wh-word noun clauses* as their complements**
3. **and reporting verbs that can have *if/whether noun clauses* as their complements**

TRANSITIVE

'**Transitive**' means that a verb has an object. Not all verbs can have objects, as you will see below. The following table shows the types of complements that transitive reporting verbs can have. (See pages 181-182 for more on 'transitive' verbs.)

> **Subjects:** noun phrase
> **Complements:** noun phrase + bare infinitive clause, adjective, prepositional phrase beginning with *like*, adverbial clause beginning with *like*.

1. DITRANSITIVE

'**Ditransitive**' means that a verb can have two objects. (An example is ***give***: I ***gave*** her a present.) Some reporting verbs, such as ***tell*** are ditransitive. The following table shows the types of complements that they can have.

> **Subject:** noun phrase
> **Complement:** noun phrase + noun phrase (not all verbs), noun phrase + that noun clause (not all verbs), noun phrase + wh-word noun clause (not all verbs), noun phrase + if/whether noun clause (not all verbs)

> **Note**
>
> Ditransitive reporting verbs *must* have an indirect object. Note that some transitive reporting verbs can also have an (optional) indirect object. We use the preposition *to* before the indirect object. There are also a few reporting verbs that can have an optional indirect object without the preposition *to*. A full list of these verbs is given in Appendix 4, page 201.

See Appendix 4, page 198, for a list of reporting verbs and information about whether they can be followed by a *that, wh-word,* or *if/whether* noun clause, or an infinitive phrase.

Passive voice

In passive voice, transitive (but not ditransitive) reporting verbs can have a real subject or a 'dummy' subject using the word *it*. With a real subject, we report the information using an infinitive clause. With a dummy subject, we report the information with a noun clause.

> **Subject:** dummy (***it***), noun phrase
> **Complement:** direct object (not all verbs), that noun clause (not all verbs), wh-word noun clause (not all verbs), if/whether noun clause (not all verbs)

> ***Examples***
>
> 1. **Broadbent** *argues* that the human body cannot survive without important vitamins and minerals that can only be found in meat.
> 2. **The human body** *is argued* to be unable to survive without important vitamins and minerals that can only be found in meat.
> 3. **It** *is argued* that the human body cannot survive without important vitamins and minerals that can only be found in meat.
> 4. **Walker** *has decided* to reconsider.
> 5. **Davies** *denied* the claims.
> 6. **Carson** *tells* us that humans evolved on a vegetarian diet.
> 7. **We** *are told* that humans evolved on a vegetarian diet.

Exercises

2.1 Write the following sentences in reported speech using the information given. Use either a noun clause or infinitive clause as the complement to the reporting verb. Use Appendix 4, page 198 to help you with these exercises.

1) (Subject: Bognar, Verb: believe) If we look at the carbon footprint of each human on earth, we can see some interesting statistics.

   _____

   _____

2) (Subject: Borzillo, Verb: maintain) Interestingly, the size of the carbon footprint generated from car use is considerably smaller than the carbon footprint generated by food production.

   _____

   _____

3) (Subject: it, Verb: have been revealed) On average, each person in the western world generates about 4 tonnes of carbon a day from car use, and about 6 tonnes a day from the production of the food they consume.

   _____

   _____

4) (Subject: we, Verb: point out) We can do more to stop global warming by eating more environmentally friendly foods than by stopping driving cars.

   _____

   _____

5) (Subject: Richards, Verb: explain) Which food products generate the largest carbon footprint?

   _____

   _____

6) (Subject: we, Verb: be told) The largest carbon footprint is from meat and dairy products, chicken products, and greenhouse grown vegetables.

   _____

   _____

7) (Subject: The reason that dairy and meat products generate such a large carbon footprint , Verb: be suggested) The reason that dairy and meat products generate such a large carbon footprint is that firstly, cows consume a large amount of food and water, and secondly, that cows produce a large amount of the global warming gas methane in their excrement.

   _____

   _____

8) (Subject: it, Verb: have been noted) Organic foods require more energy and must be produced in larger quantities to feed the same number of people, so they are actually worse for the environment than non-organic foods.

   _____

   _____

Motion verbs

Subject: noun phrase
Complement: <u>none</u>, prepositional phrase, infinitive clause, adverb.

Motion verbs are verbs that describe motion. **They cannot be used in passive voice.** Motion verbs do not usually have an object; they are intransitive. This means that they cannot be used in passive voice. Usually verbs of motion require a prepositional phrase to show the direction of the movement. Sometimes we can complement them with infinitives to show the *purpose of the motion*.

Chapter 3

> **Examples**
> Abdullah went into the house. **Or** Abdullah has come to study. **Or** Abdullah arrived yesterday.

Intransitive action verbs

> **Subject:** noun phrase
> **Complement:** <u>None</u>

Action verbs describe things that happen including causes and effects. Some action verbs can have an object, others cannot. Action verbs that cannot have an object are called 'intransitive'. **They cannot be used in passive voice.** These verbs do not have complements. Usually they involve actions that we do to ourselves such as *smiling*. You smile yourself; the action does not affect an object. This is usually true in all languages. That is, *smile* is usually intransitive in all languages. It can, of course, be followed by a prepositional phrase showing the direction or purpose; however, unlike motion verbs, the prepositional phrase is not needed.

Examples of these verbs include: *benefit, cry, excel, happen, immigrate, laugh, listen, sigh, yawn* (see Appendix 6, page 203 for a complete list)

Transitive action verbs

> **Subject:** noun phrase, gerund clause
> **Complement:** noun phrase, gerund clause, infinitive clause.

Transitive verbs are verbs that need an object. They do not make sense without an object. **These verbs can be used in passive voice. Note that they cannot have an object in passive voice.**

Transitive verbs are not always actions, they can also be states such as: *contain, have, involve, lack, own,* and *require*.

These verbs need to be divided into three groups: those that can have gerund clauses or infinitive clauses as their complements, those that can only have gerund clauses as their complements, and those that can only have infinitive clauses as their complements. (For more examples and exercises see page 39)

> **Examples**
> Many scientists fear that global oil supplies have already **started** <u>falling</u>. *Or* Many scientists fear that global oil supplies have already **started** <u>to fall</u>.
> Several scientists have **spent time** <u>researching the probable outcomes of this eventuality</u>.
> However, most governments have **attempted** <u>to ignore the problem</u>.

Ambitransitive action verbs

Ambitransitive verbs are verbs that can either have an object or not have an object (for example, *I drove home* or *I drove <u>my car</u> home*).

> **Subject:** noun phrase, gerund clause
> **Complement:** noun phrase, gerund clause, infinitive clause

> **Examples**
> She **played**. *Or* She **played** <u>a game</u>.

These verbs can be used in passive voice as long as they have an object in active voice. Note that they cannot have an object in passive voice.

This is by far the most common type of verb in English. These verbs can either have no object or can have an object.

These verbs need to be divided into three groups: those that can have gerund clauses or infinitive clauses as their complements, those that can only have gerund clauses as their complements, and those that can only have infinitive clauses as their complements.

Ditransitive action verbs

Ditransitive verbs are verbs that can have two objects - for example: *I gave <u>her</u> <u>a present</u>*. In this example, the verb *gave* has two objects: **1)** *her* and **2)** *a present*. The following table shows the possible complements for these types of verbs.

> **Subject:** noun phrase, gerund clause
> **Complement:** noun phrase + noun phrase, noun phrase + gerund clause, noun phrase + infinitive clause.

These verbs can be used in passive voice. These are the only type of verbs that can have an object in passive voice.

> *Examples:*
> She wrote me a letter. **Or** They keep us guessing. **Or** This is causing us to worry.

> **Note**
> *Deny, wish, write*, read are not ditransitive when they are reporting verbs followed by a noun clause, but are ditransitive when followed by a direct object.

These verbs can have two objects. The first object is called the indirect object because it is indirectly affected by the verb. The second object is called the direct object.

Examples of this type of verb include: *allow, assign, bet, bring, build, buy, call, cause, deny, do, get, give, keep, make, permit, read, send, take, wish*, and *write*.

> **Note**
> Several reporting verbs are also ditransitive.

Ergative verbs

> **Subject:** noun phrase,
> **Complement:** noun phrase.

> **Example**
> The good news cheered us up. *Or* We cheered up.

Ergative verbs have the special property that you can switch the subject and object without using passive voice. Generally, you can also use them in passive voice if you want.

Examples of these verbs include: *bake, blow up, burn, burst, calm down, cheer up, combine, end,* and *shut down*.

Exercises

3.1 Complete these verbs with logical complements (if they can have a complement).

1) Everybody laughed _____

2) This evidence lacks _____

3) The reporters went _____

4) This allowed _____

5) Next, the explosion happened _____

6) At first, they always assign _____

7) The terrorists blew up _____

8) Several scientists arrived _____

9) Finally, the computer shut down _____

Gerund Clauses

Aside from linking verbs, which can have adjective complements, most verbs either have a noun phrase or a clause as their object. Noun phrases as objects are straightforward, but sometimes you need to put a whole clause as the object.

Take the following example.

*The president **is** hopeless. Nobody **wants** to vote for him.* Suppose we want to join these two clauses using the verb **_resulted in_**, we need to change the form of these clauses. In this case we will have to use **gerund clauses**. We change the verb in each clause to a gerund.

This means that we say: [*The president **being** hopeless*] **_resulted in_** [*nobody **wanting** to vote for him*].

However, English is considerably more complicated than this. Some verbs require a gerund clauses as their complement, others an infinitive clause, and yet others a noun clause.

In the next section, we will study when we should use infinitive clauses instead of gerund clauses. The following chapter is devoted to noun clauses.

Constructing gerund clauses from finite clauses

Chapter 3

The main difference between a finite clause and a gerund clause (and other non-finite clauses) is that finite clauses contain *finite verbs* and gerund clauses do not. A *finite verb* is a verb that is acting as a verb. Consider the following clause: **The bored student enjoyed walking home with his interesting friends.** Each underlined word is a verb. We have the verbs **bore, enjoy, walk,** and **interest**. However, in this sentence only **enjoy** has the function of verb in the sentence. We say it is a **finite verb**. The verbs *bored* and *interesting* have the function of adjective in this sentence. The verb **walking** is a gerund. It is the **noun** form of the verb. (Notice that the *noun* form and *adjective* form can both end in ~ing. This causes students a lot of confusion.

Gerund clauses **must** contain the **gerund** form **not** the **finite** form of the verb. Actually, the gerund form has the same function as a finite verb in a finite clause; however, we **must** change the form to gerund (and sometimes infinitive) form when the clause is the subject or object of a finite verb.

Example

Johnson observed <u>Battersby attempting the experiment</u>. (The subject of the gerund clause is given.)

Examples continued

Johnson has considered <u>beginning the experiment again</u>. (The subject of the gerund clause is omitted, but is clearly *Johnson* from the independent clause.)

Johnson suggested <u>beginning the experiment again</u>. (The subject could be Johnson, but Johnson could have been making this suggestion to some students who should begin again. The subject needs to be guessed from the context.)

They observed <u>him attempting the experiment again</u>. (In these two cases the subject is a pronoun. Note
They described <u>his attempting the experiment again</u>. how the pronoun is in object or possessive form.)

Notice that we often leave out the subject of a gerund clause. When the subject is left out, it can either be interpreted from the independent clause or from the context. Note that some verbs will always be followed be a gerund clause with no subject; for other verbs, the subject of the gerund clause is often optional. Notice also, that pronouns will either take the possessive (**my, his, her, their**) or the object form (**me, him, her, them**) when they are *subject* of a gerund clause.

Remember, a clause **cannot** have two finite verbs in (unless coordinated by **or, but**, or **and**).

Example

Clause 1: Transportation costs <u>are becoming</u> higher.

Clause 2: Food prices <u>are going up</u>.

We want clause 1 to be the subject and clause 2 to be the object of the verb **give rise to**:

*Transportation costs **becoming** higher* **is giving rise to** *food prices **going up**.*

Note that when a verb has a noun form (e.g *argue / argument*), we prefer the noun form unless the verb clearly forms a part of a clause.

Example

Battersby considered <u>the arguments</u>.

Battersby considered <u>arguing his case</u>.

In the first sentence, Battersby considered the arguments that somebody had given him. We have no subject and object, we are just considering the *noun*. In the second sentence, Battersby considered the clause '**Battersby will argue his case**'; this has a clear subject (omitted because it is the same as in the independent clause) and a clear object. In this case, we use the *gerund*.

Exercises

4.1 Combine the following clauses using the verb given. Remember to change the clause that will be the object of the verb to a noun phrase.

1) Many people. (like) Many people go out and have fun. _____

_____

2) My wife. (enjoy) My wife washes the clothes._____

_____

3) The government. (contemplate) The government will make health care reforms. _____

_____

4) The government. (finish) The government have been working on these problems. _____

_____

5) The incoming government. (question) The government has stopped its aid programme for the poor.

_____

6) The government. (put off) The government have not got involved in the debate over abortion. _____

_____

7) People are burning fossil fuels. This will cause global temperatures to rise. _____

_____

8) The president acted crazily. (resulted in) The party lost the election. _____

_____

9) A person is a good president. (Involve) A person listens to others. _____

_____

Prepositional phrases

Prepositional phrases are a *preposition* + *a noun phrase* **or** a *preposition* + *a gerund clause*. It is also possible to have *preposition* + *wh-word noun clause*.

Prepositional phrases are sometimes the complement of some verbs of motion.

Circumstances

However, usually prepositional phrases add extra information to a clause about *when, where, why*, and *how* the action happened. We call these the **circumstances**.

Example
He walked to school.

Examples

As a result *of petrol prices going up*, many families are struggling to make ends meet.

The outcome *of the current economic crisis* will be a huge restructuring of the way banks manage bad debt.

The outcome *of how the company reacted to the crisis* was many people loosing their jobs.

Some of this information can also be added using adverbs, adverbial clauses, or relative clauses. There is no limit to the number of prepositional phrases that can be added to a clause.

Notice that if the prepositional phrase comes before the clause, we put a comma after the prepositional phrase. We do not usually put a comma before a prepositional phrase if it comes after the clause.

Examples
When: He came *at three o'clock*.
Where: He works *in the city*.
Why: He went home *because of the rain*.
How: He walks *like a monkey*.

Note
Circumstances can also be added through adverbial clauses of time, place, reason, and manner, and occasionally through relative clauses. Here, we are only interested in circumstances using prepositional phrases. For adverbial clauses, see chapter 6. For relative clauses, see chapter 9.

Exercises

5.1 Use the information in brackets to add extra information about time, place, and reason to these clauses. In some cases you can also add a prepositional phrase of manner.

1) Commodity prices rose. (many countries) (the last year) (increased transportation costs)._____

_____

2) This led to lower consumer spending. (those countries) (the current financial year) (consumer could not afford to buy many products) (the way that they have in the past)_____

_____

3) Lower spending led to layoffs. (March and April) (The United States) (companies could not afford to keep their employees) _____

_____

4) Lower spending has also led to lower profits. (the beginning of this crisis) (even the largest companies) (Lower revenue) (this is like what happened in 1929). _____

_____

5) Unlike in 1929, the crisis has not led to countries increasing trade tariffs. (2008) (the world) (increasing trade tariffs is seen as unhelpful these days) _____

_____

5.2 Now write sentences of your own including as many prepositional phrases as possible, adding information about circumstances.

1) _____

_____

2) _____

_____

3) _____

_____

4) _____

_____

Infinitives

Infinitives can be complement to verbs, nouns, and adjectives, and have a range of functions. These functions are listed on the next few pages.

Infinitives can be used to *show purpose, result, more detail about adjectives and abstract nouns, the situation causing an emotion, somebody's opinion about someone,* and *that something needs to be done.* They can be used instead of *some noun clauses, relative clauses, and adverbial clauses.* They are also used with *modal like structures,* and *in predictions about the future.*

Constructing infinitive clauses

We construct infinitive clauses in exactly the same way that we construct gerund clauses. Infinitive clauses do not contain finite verbs, they contain infinitive verbs. If we want to change a finite clause to be the object of a finite verb, we change the finite verb in the clause to the infinitive.

> ### Example
> Finite Clause: The government <u>lost</u> the election. We want to make this clause object of the verb **to cause**.
> → The president's crazy antics **caused** the government <u>to lose</u> the election.

Infinitives and gerunds as complements of verbs

When a verb is complement to another verb, we must either use the gerund form, the infinitive form, or the bare infinitive form. (Notice, however, that reporting verbs and the verb *be* can also be complemented by noun clauses.)

We can divide verbs into the following groups depending on what type of verb complement they will take:

1. Gerund clause only

2. Gerund or infinitive clause with different meaning

> ### Examples
> **Gerund clause only**
> They discovered *her playing in the corner.*
> She kept on *playing in the corner.*
>
> **Gerund clause or infinitive clause with different meaning**
> She forgot to do her homework. (She didn't do it because she didn't remember to do it.)
> She forgot doing her homework. (She couldn't remember if she did it or not.)
>
> | **Infinitive clause only** | **Bare infinitive clause** |
> |---|---|
> | She convinced *me to play with her.* | She made me do it. |
> | She chose *to play with me.* | |
>
> **Gerund or infinitive clause with same meaning**
> She continued to play in the corner.
> She continued playing in the corner.

3. Infinitive clause only
4. Bare infinitive clause
5. Gerund clause or infinitive clause with same meaning

The following are some verbs that can only be complemented by gerund clauses

describe	*discuss*	*enjoy*	*imagine*	*practice*
discover	*dislike*	*finish*	*keep on*	*suggest*

Note that *imagine* and **suggest** are reporting verbs and can also take that clauses as their complements.

The following are some verbs that can only be complemented by infinitive clauses

agree	*ask*	*convince*	*help*	*pretend*	*refuse*
appear	*choose*	*expect*	*plan*	*promise*	*want*

Note that **ask** and **promise** are reporting verbs. Although reporting verbs tend to have infinitives as their complements if they do not have noun clauses, they can also sometimes have gerunds as can be seen with *imagine* and **suggest** above.

The following are some verbs that can be complemented by gerund or infinitive clauses with the same meaning

attempt	*hate*	*propose*
begin	*love*	*regret*
continue	*prefer*	*start*

The following are some verbs that can be complemented by gerund or infinitive clauses but the meaning changes

forget	*go on*	*remember*	*stop*	*try*

The following are some verbs that can be complemented by bare infinitive clauses

hear	*let*	*make*	*see*	*watch*

These clauses *must* have a subject. Notice that these verbs mostly relate to sense.

The Differences in meaning amongst verbs that can have an infinitive or gerund complement are as follows:

Forget

I forgot to do it. – I didn't do it because I didn't remember about it.

I forget doing it. – I don't remember if I did it or not.

Stop

He stopped to look at her. – He stopped what he was doing, and he looked at her.

He stopped looking at her. – He was looking at her, and then he stopped looking at her and started to do something else.

Go on

He went on to finish first. – After that, he finished first.

He went on running. – He continued to run.

Remember

I remembered to do it. – I did it (I didn't forget it).

I remember doing it. – I have a memory of doing it.

Regret

I regret to say that this is true. – Unfortunately, I have to tell you that this is true.

I regretted saying that. – I wish I hadn't said that.

Try

I tried to eat it. – I made an effort to eat it.

I tried eating it. – I ate a little bit of it so I would know if I liked it or not.

Chapter 3

> **Note**
>
> *Help* can either be followed by an infinitive phrase or a bare infinitive phrase. For example: *she helped me to do it*, and *she helped me do it*. There is no difference in meaning.

A list of verbs that can be followed by infinitives or gerunds is given in Appendix 3 on page 200.

Exercises

6.1 Put the verbs into the correct form (gerund or infinitive) to complement the finite verbs in the following passage. Note that you may also need to alter the voice of the complement. (Check Appendix 3, page 197)

The American diet of fatty meats is helping _____ (ruin) the environment and is making people in the third world _____ (starve). This is because we keep on _____ (eat) mostly meat that comes from cows, and cows are helping _____ (do) three things to the environment. Firstly, cows spend their time _____ (create) an incredible amount of the global warming gas methane through their excrement. Their excrement also manages _____ (create) a lot of pollution by being washed into rivers and lakes. Secondly, they happen _____ (consume) a massive amount of water. In fact, the main reason why the Murray River, Australia's largest waterway, appears _____ (die), is not the on-going drought, but over-farming of cattle. Thirdly, cattle in Australia and North America are causing deserts _____ (spread). The Australian outback cannot endure hard hoofed feet of cattle _____ (walk) all over it, slowly killing the grasses. Without grasses, the good topsoil tends _____ (blow) away and nothing is left but infertile bottom soil. Thus, when rains come, the grass struggles _____ (grow) back. Lastly, cattle continue to consume a massive amount of food. It is estimated that for every meal we get from a cow, we have _____ (feed) that cow eight meals. It is also estimated that in 1900, 95% of the world's crops went to feeding humans. Today. 45% of the world's crops have been demonstrated _____ (feed) cows. This, in turn, is guaranteeing food prices throughout the world _____ (rise). Demand for grain has increased and thus so have prices. This has lead to people who are surviving on two dollars or less a day being now unable to buy enough food.

Infinitives showing purpose

Infinitives are also used to give extra information about events and even about nouns and adjectives. One use of infinitives after nouns or verbs is to show our *purpose* or *intention* (especially after verbs relating to motion). Notice that the infinitive clause has the same subject as the independent clause.

> **Examples**
>
> I stopped <u>to kill him</u>.   I came to Ireland <u>to study English</u>.
> I am writing <u>to try to stop him</u>.   They did it <u>to surprise us</u>.

Infinitives are also used after some nouns to show purpose.

> **Example**
>
> We met to make an agreement <u>to stop the killing</u>.   Guns <u>to protect people</u> are needed.
> There was a meeting <u>to discuss this</u>.

These infinitive clauses can usually be replaced with *adverbial clauses of purpose* using the subordinators **so that** or **in order to**.

> **Example**
>
> I stopped <u>to kill him</u>.   I stopped **so that** I could kill him.
> There was a meeting <u>to discuss this</u>.   There was a meeting **in order to** discuss this.
> I am writing in order to try to stop him.   I am writing to try to stop him.

Infinitives showing result

When you want to show that something is a result of there being *too much* of something, we often use the word *too* in combination with an infinitive.

> **Example**
> He was too stupid to understand.

We also use this pattern when there is a sufficient amount of something (When there is *enough* of something).
These clauses can usually be rephrased using the coordinator *so*.
They are similar in meaning to the adverbial subordinator *so...that....*
(See Chapter 7, page 116 for more.)

> **Example**
> He was smart enough to understand.

Infinitives showing that something needs to be done

Sometimes we use infinitives to show that something needs to be done. In the following example, the speaker means '*he <u>must</u> do the homework that I have given him.*' It could be rewritten as '*I gave him some homework which I want him to do.*'

> **Example**
> I gave him some homework to do.

Exercises

7.1 Rewrite the following clauses with infinitive phrases

1) They plugged in the computer so that they could test it. _____

   _____

2) They had several jobs that needed to be done before they could relax. _____

   _____

3) She drove the car very fast in order to see how it performed at high speeds. _____

   _____

4) We were so upset that we could not speak. _____

   _____

5) He is fairly crazy, so he will probably be able to do it. _____

   _____

6) There is a new law; it was made so that young people would be protected. _____

   _____

7.2 Write sentences of your own using infinitive phrases to add extra meaning

1) (purpose) _____

2) (purpose) _____

3) (result) _____

4) (result) _____

5) (needs to be done) _____

Infinitives instead of reported speech and noun clauses

Some reported speech and noun clauses can be said using infinitives. Some examples of reporting verbs that can be followed by infinitives include *agree, learn, choose, mean, decide, intend,* and *hope.*

> **Example**
> He decided to do it.
> In other words: He decided *that he would do it.*

Some other reporting verbs such as *advise, ask, expect, teach,* and *tell* require an indirect object before the infinitive clause. The indirect object is the subject of the infinitive clause.

> **Example**
> He told me to do it.

When we report information using noun clauses, and the reporting verb does not require an indirect object, we have two options for creating passive voice. Take the sentence:
he claims that learning about infinitives is fun. This can be reported in passive voice as: *it is claimed that learning about infinitives is fun*; however, it can also be reported as: *learning about infinitives is claimed <u>to</u>*

**be fun.** Thus, we use infinitives when we use passive voice to report a fact and the subject of the reported information is the same as that of the independent clause.

Examples

Many people claim that being the president is a fun job. → Being the president is claimed to be a fun job.

Cunningham reports that he is a dangerous fugitive. → He is reported to be a dangerous fugitive.

Note

When you want to put an infinitive phrase into past tense (as we have done in the second example here, we use present perfect.

We also use infinitives to report information in the situation when a noun clause is embedded in a relative clause and the independent clause and noun clause have the same subject. Consider the following sentences.

1. _**Bush, whom James knew, was happy.**_ (A relative clause describing _**Bush**_.)

2. _**James knew that Bush was his foe.**_ (A noun clause that is object of the verb _**know**_).

We can combine these two sentences, making the noun clause the object of _**knew**_ in sentence one. There are two ways to do this. We can either say: _**Bush, whom James knew was his foe, was happy**_ (notice that we can not use the subordinator _**that**_ in this situation), or we can say: _**Bush, whom James knew to be his foe, was happy**_.

Examples

The US presidency, which many people claim is a fun job, is actually not much fun at all. → The US presidency, which many people claim to be a fun job, is actually not much fun at all.

Coffee, which historians tell us originated in northeast Africa, is a delicious drink. → Coffee, which historians tell us to have originated in northeast Africa, is a delicious drink.

Some nouns which are related to reporting verbs such as _agreement, decision, hope, order_, and _promise_, can be followed by either a noun clause or an infinitive phrase.

Example

His decision that he would retire surprised us all. → His decision to retire surprised us all.

Some reporting verbs can be followed by a wh-word and an infinitive phrase when they report _the way that (how)_ something should be done, _when_ it should be done, or _where_ it should be done.

Example

He explained what we should do. → He explained what to

Infinitives with linking verbs such as seem and appear

When we use the verbs _**seem**_ and _**appear**_, we can either have a real subject or a dummy subject. If we use a real subject, the verb that is complement to _**seem**_ and _**appear**_ will be in the infinitive. If we use the dummy subject _it_, we must follow these verbs with a noun clause; however, if we use the dummy subject _**there**_, we follow these verbs with _to be_ in the infinitive clauses.

We can also use the verbs _**prove**_ and _**look**_ followed by the infinitive form _to be_ in much the same way.

Examples

He seems to like being president.

It seems _that he likes being president._

There seems to be a problem.

Example

There proved to be too many problems with that method, so we abandoned it.

Infinitives showing more detail about adjectives and abstract nouns

When we use the dummy subject _it_ to introduce an adjective, we often follow it with an infinitive phrase that explains the circumstances of the adjective. For

---

Examples

It was interesting to meet him. (Meeting him was interesting).

It will be fabulous to find out. (Finding out will be fabulous).

---

example: **seeing you is good** would usually be said as **it is good to see you**.

Some adjectives such as **able, ready, unlikely, likely,** and **prepared** are always followed by an infinitive giving more information about the adjective. These adjectives have real subjects.

> **Examples**
>
> He was able to understand the whole book. **Or** She is unlikely to understand English.

Some abstract nouns such as **willingness** and **ability** are also followed by infinitive clauses to give more detail about them. We also follow some adjectives describing emotions with infinitives to show what is causing that emotion.

> **Example**
>
> He showed a willingness to find a solution.

> **Examples**
>
> She will be difficult to convince. **Or** He is hard to like.

We also use infinitives after adjectives such as **difficult, easy, hard, right,** and **wrong** to show an opinion about someone.

> **Examples**
>
> I am sorry to have to say this. **Or** I was upset to have to say goodbye.

Infinitives instead of relative clauses

After some verbs such as **appeal, arrange, ask, long, pay, wait,** and **wish**, we can add a prepositional phrase beginning with **for**. This can be

> **Example**
>
> He longed for a book to read. (He longed for a book which he could read)

followed by an infinitive phrase that gives more information about the **for** prepositional phrase. In most cases, it is also possible to use a relative clause in these cases.

After nouns that have ordinal numbers before them, we use the infinitive to describe the noun.

> **Example**
>
> He was the first person to go to the moon. (He was the first person who ever went to the moon).

Similarly, we use infinitive clauses to describe nouns that have a superlative adjective before them. We do not use a relative clause in this situation.

> **Example**
>
> She is the best person to ask for help. (She is the best person to whom you can ask for help.)

However, we can also use a relative subordinator followed by an infinitive clause. We call these infinitive relative clauses.

> **Example**
>
> She is the best person to whom to ask for help.

Infinitives showing the future

We often use infinitives after verbs such as **hope, intend,** and **be going** to talk about the future. Note that a general difference between infinitives and gerunds is that infinitives tend to focus on the future, while gerunds tend to focus on the past.

> **Examples**
>
> I hope to do it some day.   I intend to do it someday.   I am going to do it some day.

We can see this same difference in tense or time with the verbs discussed above on page 39. We discussed how **stop doing** and **stop to do** have different meanings. **I stopped doing** discusses the past. (**I was doing something, but I stopped doing it.**) **I stopped to do** discusses the future. (**I stopped doing something, and then I did something else.**)

Chapter 3

Infinitives after semi-modals

True modals such as **must**, **should**, **can**, and **can't** are always followed by the bare infinitive. However, semi-modals (verbs that do the same job as a modal are followed by infinitives, including **have to**, **ought to**, **want to**, **need to**, **allowed to**, and **managed to**.) are followed by infinitives.

> **Examples:**
> You ought to do your homework.   We want to finish class early today.   He managed to finish his essay a week early.

Exercises

8.1 Rewrite the following sentences with infinitive clauses.

1) In a democracy, we all have the freedom. This freedom lets us say whatever we want as long as it does not harm others.

   _____

   _____

2) It seems that the global economy is headed for total meltdown. (Subject: the global economy)

   _____

   _____

3) The economy, which some analysts believe is going to improve in about 12 months, is currently in a downward spiral.

   _____

   _____

4) Major car companies have asked for a government bailout, which they will use to improve sales and to help with fiscal restructuring.

   _____

   _____

5) Stevenson has argued that cycles of economic depression and boom are inevitable in capitalist democracies. (Subject: Cycles of economic depression and boom)

   _____

   _____

6) It seems like there are going to be many more layoffs before this crisis is solved. (Subject: there)

   _____

   _____

7) Surpassing previous stock market losses was scary. (Subject: it)

   _____

   _____

8) Many governments have agreed that they need to work together to solve this current crisis.

   _____

   _____

9) I was sad because I saw so many people lose their jobs.

   _____

   _____

10) The economist Ashley Davis is interesting when we listen to her.

   _____

   _____

Chapter 4

Noun Clauses

Revision

What is a finite clause?

A finite clause is a building block of a sentence. It must contain a subject and a finite verb. Very often it contains a complement (often an object).

What is a finite dependent clause?

A dependent clause begins with a subordinator. It cannot stand alone and must be attached to an independent clause.

What are the three types of finite dependent clauses?

There are three types of dependent clauses; each has a different function.

> **Three types of finite dependent clause:**
> 1. noun clause 2. adverbial clause 3. relative clause

What does a noun clause do?

A noun clause acts like a noun. It functions as the subject or object of a verb. It can either be the subject of the verb **be** or **become** or it can be the object of **be** or it can be the object of a reporting verb.

> **Example**
> He said *that he didn't agree with this opinion.*

What does an adverbial clause do?

An adverbial clause describes the verb in the independent clause (though this is not always obvious). Unlike a noun clause, an adverbial clause gives *extra information* about the verb in the clause.

> **Example**
> I went home *after I finished school.*

What does a relative clause do?

A relative clause describes either a noun in the independent clause, or it describes the whole clause. Like an adverbial clause, a relative clause gives extra information about a noun. Sometimes this information is essential (restrictive); sometimes it is not (non-restrictive).

> **Example**
> Maki, *who is a great teacher,* has a very cute black dog, *which is very smart.*

Noun Clauses

We can divide dependent noun clauses up in several ways. One division is into embedded noun clauses and adjunct noun clauses. Another division is by the type embedded noun clause (*that, wh-word,* or *if/whether*).

1. Embedded & Adjunct Noun clauses

Embedded noun clauses are clauses that are either the subject or the object of an independent clause. In this example, the subject is the clause **that it is a problem**, the verb is **is** and the object is the clause **what I did not want to hear**.

> **Example**
> *That it is a problem* is *what I did not want to hear.*

Adjunct noun clauses, like relative clauses and adverbial clauses, add extra information about the clause or a part of the clause. We will return to these at the end of the chapter.

> **Example**
> It is necessary *that you answer all of the questions.*

2. Noun clauses with the verb to be & noun clauses with reporting verbs

Embedded noun clauses can be divided up between noun clauses that are used as the subject or object of the verb **be** and noun clauses as objects of reporting verbs.

> **Example**
> *What he wants to know* is *when the reaction began.*

Chapter 4

Be

Noun clauses can be used as either the subject or the object of the verb **be** and other closely related verbs such as **become, tend to, seem,** and **appear**.

Reporting verbs

Noun clauses can be the *object* of reporting verbs. Reporting verbs are verbs that are used to report what people say, think, and learn, as well as the way that they speak. Examples of such verbs include: **state, consider, realize,** and **whisper**. A complete list is given in Appendix 4, pages 198-200.

> *Example*
> Jansen reports that eastern Africa was a haven for wildlife.

It is important to note that not all reporting verbs can be used with noun clauses. For example, the verb **speak** reports what people say, but it cannot be followed by a noun clause. A list of which reporting verbs can be followed by noun clauses is given in Appendix 4, pages 198-200.

3. Types of Embedded Noun clauses

Embedded noun clauses can be divided into three types.

> **Three types of noun clause**
> 1. that noun clauses
> 2. wh-word noun clauses
> 3. if/whether noun clauses

> **Note**
> Noun clauses never have commas before them or after them.

> **The subordinators that can be used for these three types of noun clauses are listed below.**
> | how | if | that | what | when | whether | where | which | who |

That noun clauses

That noun clauses report facts, thoughts, knowledge, and ideas.

Not all reporting verbs can be followed by *that* noun clauses. A list of which reporting verbs can be followed by *that* noun clauses is given in Appendix 4, pages 198-200.

Some of the verbs that can be complemented by a *that* noun clause include **state, claim, assert, maintain, point out, argue,** and **insist**.

Tense

We usually report written information in present simple; this might not make sense, but it is an accepted convention in English. However, if the reporting verb is in past tense, we often report the event in the noun clause in past tense, but note that if the verb in the noun clause is a state or a repeated event that is still true today, we may use present tense instead of past tense. If the reporting verb is in any other tense, the noun clause can be in any tense. More on tense with reporting verbs can be found in Chapter 5, pages 84-85.

> *Examples*
> Johnson <u>reports</u> that Homo Neandethal remains <u>are found</u> in several locations across Germany.
>
> At last year's conference, Johnson <u>reported</u> that in 1986, he <u>found</u> the remains of an almost intact mammoth 800 kilometres east of Novosibirsk.
>
> At the 1987 conference, Johnson <u>admitted</u> that he <u>enjoys</u> the challenge of interpreting how ancient creatures might have died.

Location of reporting verb

The reporting verb can either come before or after the noun clause, but in academic writing, it always comes before.

> *Examples*
> **Academic**
> Johnson states that this tower will be the tallest in the world.
>
> **Newspaper**
> This tower will be the tallest in the world, stated Johnson.

According to

A common mistake that students make is to put *according to* before a reporting structure.

They might write: ***According to Johnson, Johnson states that this tower will be the tallest in the world***. However, this means that ***Johnson <u>said that Johnson said that this</u> tower would be the tallest in the world***. ***According* to** means '***states that***', it is a <u>preposition</u>.

> ### Example
> *In the article*, Kraich argues that animals are happier on farms than in the wild.
> Or
> *According to Kraich*, animals are happier on farms than in the wild.
>
> But **not**
> *According to the article, Kraich argues* that animals are happier on farms than in the wild.

You may want to use this structure if you want to write about an author's quote. For example, if Kraich writes: ***Tibor Machan argues that animals don't have rights***. You may report this as: ***<u>According to Kraich, Machan argues that</u> animals don't have rights***.

> ### Note
> It is acceptable to use the preposition *in* with a reporting verb.

As

We use ***as*** to show that we agree with an author.

However, it is important to remember that ***as*** is an adverbial subordinator of manner. Clauses starting with ***as*** are dependent clauses. This means that the information that is reported is the independent clause. (In the example on the right, the independent clause is '***animals are happier on farms than in the wild***'.)

It is not possible to have a noun clause after an *as* clause.

> ### Example
> **As** Kraich argues, animals are happier on farms than in the wild. (This means that you, the writer, agree with this statement.)

Indirect object

Some reporting verbs require an indirect object; for others they are optional, and for others an indirect object is not allowed. To explain indirect objects, we need to know what a *ditransitive verb* is. An *intransitive verb* is a verb that cannot have an object, while a *transitive verb* is one that needs an object. A *ditransitive verb*, on the other hand, is a verb that can have *two* objects. One of these objects is called the *indirect object*.

In the first example, it is not possible to put an object after the verb ***walk***. In the second example, the object is ***cars***. In the final example, the object is ***a present***, and ***<u>the girl</u>*** is the *indirect object*.

> ### Examples
> **Intransitive**
> The boy walks.
> <small>Subject   Verb (No object)</small>
>
> **Transitive**
> The boy likes *cars*.
> <small>Subject Verb Object</small>
>
> **Ditransitive**
> The boy gave <u>the girl</u> *a present*.
> <small>Subject Verb   Object   Object</small>

> **Reporting verbs fall into 5 categories**:
> **Category 1**: no indirect object allowed; examples: *know, learn, maintain*
> **Category 2**: indirect object *optional* with preposition *to*; examples: *illustrate, indicate, respond*
> **Category 3**: indirect object *optional* with preposition *with*; examples: *argue, confirm, debate*
> **Category 4**: indirect object *compulsory*; examples: *assure, convince, tell*
> **Category 5**: indirect object *optional* with *no preposition*; examples: *ask, believe, question*

See Appendix 4 on page 198 for a complete list of reporting verbs and whether they require indirect objects.

Chapter 4

Examples

Category 1

Gregory maintains that Hitler suspected himself to have Jewish ancestry.

Category 2

Gregory indicates that this may be why he ordered his family cemetery to be destroyed.

Or Gregory indicates *to his readers* that this may be why he ordered his family cemetery to be destroyed.

Category 3

Historians debate whether Hitler tried to hide his Jewish ancestry.

Or Historians are debating *with each other* whether Hitler tried to hide his Jewish ancestry.

Category 4

Gregory assures *us* that the only Jewish life Hitler knowingly spared was that of his mother's doctor.

Category 5

Gregory believes that the reason Hitler hated Jews so much was because his father's doctor had been a Jew.

Or Gregory believes *other historians* that the reason Hitler hated Jews so much was because his father's doctor was a Jew.

Exercises

1.1 Match the reported speech on the left to the quotes on the right

a) He acknowledged that this was a serious problem.

b) Stevens asserts that we should give it serious consideration.

c) Johnson assures his readers that there is nothing to be concerned about.

d) James believes that there are more important issues than this.

e) Davis concedes that considerable work still needs to be done to increase sales

f) Gribble & Gribble have declared that they will no longer be aggressively trying to increase their market share.

g) James disputes that this was really the cause of the increase in sales.

h) Copper Star emphasise that the recent rise in their sales was unrelated to their recent advertising campaign.

i) Smith explains to his readers that there are two forces driving prices upwards.

1) 'One thing we know for sure, is that the sales increase was not a result of recent spending on commercials.'

2) 'This is not a matter for panic or undue worry.'

3) 'What needs to be understood is that inflation is being pushed upwards by two separate causes.'

4) 'It is correct to think that this is a worry.'

5) 'This is only one of many concerns, several of which have much greater significance.'

6) 'This is a matter that we should think carefully about.'

7) 'Despite what some people have argued, this is clearly not the reason for the larger number of transactions.'

8) 'We have stopped our campaign to actively attempt to increase sales.'

9) 'It has been successfully argued in the past that enlarging our market share will require a large amount of time and effort.'

1.2 Insert the following words into the correct definitions:

hold   imply   indicate   inform   insist   maintain   mean   agree   contend respond

1) To _____ means to tell or share knowledge.

   We are _____ that Marge Simpson's character is based on the mother of the creator of the show.

2) To _____ means to suggest indirectly.

   The producers of the Simpsons have _____ to viewers that the show will continue to be produced next year.

3) To _____ means to argue a position.

   Christian groups have _____ that the Simpsons is anti religious; the creators deny this.

4) To _____ means to maintain your position.

   Jones _____ that the Simpsons is the greatest TV show of all time.

5) To _____ means to signify or to convey a significance.

   Homer Simpson's relaxed attitude _____ that he has had many jobs.

6) To _____ means to not be opposed to an opinion.

   The creators of the Simpsons _____ with critics that it is ridiculous that Bart and Lisa Simpson have stayed in the same class at school for over twenty years.

7) To _____ means to answer a challenge or a question.

   To criticisms of declining quality, the creators of the Simpsons have _____ that their show is still the number one rating cartoon on US television after over 20 years of episodes.

8) To _____ means to direct someone's attention to something.

   The creator of the Simpsons has _____ that the character 'Bart' is based on himself.

9) To _____ means to make a claim or a statement. This word is often used negatively to show that you disagree with the person making the claim.

   Grandpa Simpson _____ that he knew Thomas Edison.

10) To _____ means to continue to make a claim even though others may disagree.

   The creators of the Simpsons _____ that the town of Springfield, where the Simpsons live, is a fictional town.

1.3 Insert the following reporting verbs into the blanks so that the sentences are grammatically correct and are logical.

state	*agree*	*inform*	*tell*	*write*	*disclose*
assure	*contend*	*convince*	*remind*	*reassure*	*observe*

1) The creators of the TV show King of the Hill _____ us that the show is not based on real people.

2) They have _____ their viewers that the show is not based on real life characters.

3) They _____ that rivalry between their show and the Simpsons does not exist; however, outsiders _____ us that this simply isn't true.

4) They have _____ to media sources that the show will continue to be produced next year.

5) Viewers have _____ that the show is not set in any real town.

6) Most viewers _____ with critics that the coolest character in the show is Boomhauer.

7) The producers of the show have tried to _____ the viewers that the lead character, Hank Hill, cannot show any emotions, except to his dog.

8) Differences between Hank Hill and his son, Bobby Hill, _____ us that a father and a son can be quite different from each other.

9) Christian groups have _____ viewers that the show is not anti religious.

10) Critics have _____ that the shows continued popularity is due to its excellent script and fine acting.

11) Hank Hill once _____ that he could never vote for George Bush.

1.4 Write 5 sentences using reported speech. Use the word in brackets

1) (as) _____

   _____

2) (according to) _____

   _____

3) (Conclude) _____

   _____

4) (claim) _____

   _____

5) (mention) _____

   _____

1.5 Put the following sentences into reported speech using the prompt given. Change the tense if needed.

1) "Unlike height or weight, which can be measured, intelligence is not an absolute."

Carlson stated that _____

_____

2) 'The new building will be named after the entrepreneur who donated money for it to be built.'

The reporter said that _____

_____

3) 'One point two million people live in Auckland.'

In yesterday's paper, it was stated _____

_____

4) 'I frequently got lost when I went out when I was young.'

She mentioned that _____

_____

5) 'I am considering the situation and will get back to you tomorrow about it.'

He said that _____

_____

1.6 Find the errors in the following statements:

1) In the article modern humans suffer much more stress than their ancient ancestors did (Wallis, Thompson & Galvin 1983).

2) In the article 'Stress and its affects on modern society' (Wallis, Thompson & Galvin 1983), ancient humans had to worry about where to find each day's food, about wild animals, and about keeping their sleeping place safe.

3) According to Linden (1984), she states that modern humans have considerably more to stress about.

4) According to Peterson (1988) state that modern humans have to worry about the traffic on their way to work, about being late, about meeting deadlines, about doing a good job, and about the cost of living.

5) According to Linden (1984) that modern humans also have to worry about family stresses, more complex friendship stresses, and the pressures of conformity to an increasingly complex web of interrelated cultures and subcultures.

6) According to the article 'Stress: Can we Cope?' (Peterson 1988), the author states that all of these pressures are taking an increasing toll on our society.

7) As Wallis, Thompson and Galvin (1983) state that what was originally evolved as a mechanism to assist us in our fight for survival in the wild has become one of the biggest health problems in a world that we have created ourselves but from which we cannot escape.

Writer Voice

Writer voice does **not** refer to active and passive voice, it refers to the way that the author presents their opinion and the way that they present other people's opinions. Often in academic writing, we are asked to give our position. It is not really necessary to include the words *'my opinion is...'* or *'I believe that...'* in these situations. Instead, it is often the reporting structure (Or absence of a reporting structure) that makes it clear what your opinion is. Consider the following sentences; whose opinions are they? (Levack, the writer, or someone else's)

1. *Levack states that there is a link between obesity and genes.*

2. *It is stated that there is a link between obesity and genes.*

3. *As Levack states, there is a link between obesity and genes.*

4. *It is clear that there is a link between obesity and genes.*

5. *I believe that there is a link between obesity and genes.*

6. *There is a link between obesity and genes.*

7. *Levack states that <u>there is a link between obesity and genes</u>(a) and that <u>this view leads us to the conclusion that banning fast food will not assist in reducing obesity rates</u>(b).*

8. *Levack states that <u>there is a link between obesity and genes</u>(a), and <u>this view leads us to the conclusion that banning fast food will not assist in reducing obesity rates</u>(b).*

1 & 2: In **1 & 2** it is obvious that the statement is **Levack's** view.

3: In **3**, the word *as* indicates that the writer agrees with **Levack**. So in **3**, the opinion is both **levack's** and the **writer's**.

4, 5, & 6: In each of these sentences, the sentence is the **author's** opinion. In **5**, the author has stated that this is their opinion, but in **6**, they have not. The author **does not need to state that it is their opinion** because generally the absence of a reporting structure will indicate that the position belongs to the author.

7 & 8: **7a** and **8a** are both clearly Levack's opinion, but **7b** and **8b** are different. **7b** belongs to Levack; the repetition of *that* indicates that this is also something said by Levack. In **8b**, *that* is missing after *and*. This means that it is very unclear whether this second statement is Levack's statement or the author's statement. Generally it will be presumed that **8b** is the author's opinion.

Reporting verbs

Choice of reporting verb can also make an indication about the author's feelings towards what is being said and can sometimes even show whether the author agrees or disagrees with the statement. Reporting verbs can generally be put on a scale ranging from those that show that the author disagrees with the statement to those that show that the author agrees.

Reporting verbs showing agreement or disagreement:

Disagree	Doubtful	Neutral	Agree
claim	believe	argue	demonstrate
forget	guess	discuss	explain
insist	ignore	propose	illustrate
maintain		state	point out

Examples

Author disagrees with claims
Robert Jones *claims* that Labradors are the most intelligent dogs in the world.

Author doubts claims
Robert Jones *believes* that Labradors are the most intelligent dogs in the world.

Author is neutral about claims
Robert Jones *argues* that Labradors are the most intelligent dogs in the world.

Author agrees with claims
Robert Jones *demonstrates* that Labradors are the most intelligent dogs in the world.

Note that the writer will often go on to explain why they disagree, using a contrasting clause. Note also that we cannot use a word showing agreement (such as *as*) together with a reporting verb showing disagreement (such as *claim*).

Exercises

2.1 Make corrections to statements of the writer's position in the following sentences.

1) Therefore, I believe that understanding the effect of fast food on humans is crucial.

    _____

    _____

2) I think that movies can make the world a better place.

    _____

    _____

3) I disagree with Szalavit's article; I believe that fast food causes addiction.

_____

_____

4) I disagree with Szalavitz's (2003) claims that people misunderstand what fast food addiction is because they misunderstand the word 'addict' and we cannot regard fast food as addictive.

_____

_____

5) In conclusion, I agree with Stewart's (2004) claims. Africa has many problems that need to be blamed on African leaders not on the West or on colonialism.

_____

_____

6) I do not agree with Johnson when he argues that we can treat animals however we want. I think that Kraig is right when she says that the way we mistreat animals on farms is unethical and immoral.

_____

_____

7) What she states is that the research that has been done recently is superficial and not accurate and that this statement is based on two general issues: changes in the brain when fast food is consumed and the evolution of humans to desire fat.

_____

_____

Passives

It is common to report information in passive voice in both academic writing and in newspapers. Two common reasons for using passive voice include *not wanting* to state whom the author is or *not knowing* whom the author is. For this reason, we do not usually include the author in a *by* prepositional phrase (although we can if we want to). However, **the most common reason for using passive voice is to create cohesion**. See Chapter 11, page 181 for more on passive voice and cohesion.

Passives can be constructed from most reporting verbs, but note: if the reporting verb must have an indirect object (e.g. *tell*), then the only passive possible is as follows:

> *Example:*
> *Reporting verb that must have an indirect object*
> **Active voice:** He tells <u>us</u> that global warming is a serious issue.
> **Passive voice:** <u>We</u> are told that global warming is a serious issue.

For all other reporting verbs, there are two types of passives that can be constructed from noun clauses.

Real subject

In real subject relative clauses, we report the information in an infinitive clause. These types of clauses are usually constructed to improve cohesion (see Chapter 11, page 181).

> *Example*
> **Active Voice**
> Robert Jones claims that Labradors are the most intelligent dogs in the world.
> **Passive voice**
> Labradors are said to be the most intelligent dog in the world.

Dummy subject

These passives start with the dummy subject *it*. *It* has no actual meaning in these sentences; it just exists to fill in the subject slot in the clause. In dummy subject noun clauses, we report the information in a noun clause. These types of clause are usually constructed to hide information about the subject, not for cohesion.

> *Example*
> **Active Voice**
> Robert Jones claims that Labradors are the most intelligent dogs in the world.
> **Passive voice**
> It is said that Labradors are the most intelligent dogs in the world.

Dummy subject passives with noun clauses contain a lot of information about the subject and the tense. Much of this information, including tense, can also be included in the infinitive phrases that complement real subject passives.

Infinitive tenses follow these patterns	Passive infinitive tenses follow these patterns
Present	**Passive Present**
To + V	To be + Past participle
To sing	To be sung
Present continuous	**Passive Present continuous**
To be + Active participle (~ing form of a verb)	To be being + Past participle
To be singing	To be being sung
Past	**Passive Past**
To have + past participle	To have been + Past participle
To have sung (Note: we use present perfect to show passive present tense in infinitives)	To have been sung (Note: passive past and past perfect are the same)
Present perfect	**Passive Present perfect**
To have + past participle	To have been + Past participle
To have sung (Note: this is the same as the simple past)	To have been sung (Note: passive past and passive present perfect are the same)
Future	**Passive Future**
To be going to + V	To be going to be + Past participle
To be going to sing (Note: we can only use *be going to* to form future tense in infinitives; we cannot use *will*.)	To be going to be sung.

Examples
Present
Active: This graph shows that some dogs are better at understanding human language than others.
Passive: Some dogs are shown to be better at understanding human language than others.
Past
Active: In his TV show, Jones specified that some of his dogs were more aggressive than others.
Passive: In Jones' TV show, some of Jones' dogs were specified to have been more aggressive than others.
Future
Active: Jones states that some dogs will make better companions than others.
Passive: Some dogs are stated to be going to make better companions than others.
Present Perfect
Active: Jones stipulates that many dogs have been bred for specific purposes.
Passive: Many dogs are stipulated to have been bred for specific purposes.

Exercises

3.1 Rewrite the following active voice noun clauses in passive voice using both real and dummy subjects.

1) Trelaur alleges that smoking causes cancer.

Smoking _____

It _____

2) He argues that 80% of people who got cancer last year smoked.

_____

_____

3) He claims that the tobacco companies are not helping the situation.

_____

_____

4) He suggests that tobacco companies have been covering up the effects of nicotine on cigarette addiction.

_____

_____

5) He mentions that tobacco companies are covering up this issue.

_____

_____

6) He states that high paid lawyers had a vested interest in protecting these companies last year.

_____

_____

7) He warns that new laws to be introduced next year will have some effect.

_____

_____

3.2 Rewrite the following Dummy subject passives as real subject passives

1) It has been noted that smoking amongst teenagers has declined in recent years.

Smoking amongst teenagers _____

2) It has been observed that during the same period mobile phone use has increased

_____

3) It has been pointed out that mobile phones and smoking have much in common.

_____

4) It has been proven that the cost of mobile phones has led to a lower rate of smoking.

_____

5) It is believed that this could be the reason for recent declines in rates of smoking.

_____

3.3 Rewrite the following real subject passives as dummy subject passives.

1) Games and messaging are reasoned to be more important to teenagers than smoking.

It _____

2) Independence has been remarked to be another reason for the popularity of the mobile over smoking.

_____

3) This information is reported to be important for planning future anti-smoking campaigns.

_____

4) Mobile phone use is stated to be going to be important for future anti-smoking campaigns.

_____

5) Smoking was shown to have been the cause of countless deaths last year alone.

_____

Wh-word noun clauses

Wh-word noun clauses report *wh-word* questions. Note that **what** and **how** can also be used to create reduced relative clauses, for example: **this**

> **Example**
>
> Wh-word question: *What time is it?* → He asked **what time it was**.

caused *what I thought was a small problem*. **Cause** cannot be followed be a noun clause. Here, **what** means **the thing that**. Similarly, **how** means **the way that**. See Chapter 9, page 147 on relative clauses for more.

Not all reporting verbs can be used with *wh-word* noun clauses.

Reporting verbs that can be used include:

ask	discuss	imagine	question	say	tell	wonder
decide	explain	inquire	realise	see	think	
describe	forget	know	remember	suggest	understand	
discover	guess	learn	reveal	teach	want to know	

All of these verbs except for *describe*, *discuss*, and *wonder* can be used with *that* clauses too.

See, *imagine*, *say*, *suggest*, and *think* are usually used in negative clauses.

> **Example**
>
> He could <u>not</u> **think** *what time it was.*

Word order in wh-word clauses

Question word order

Sometimes the word order changes with *wh-word* clauses. We always use statement word order in noun clauses, and we **never** use a question mark. There are always two questions that can be made about any statement; a question about the subject and a question about the object.

Consider the following sentences and the way that the question is formed. Notice how when the word order changes or an auxiliary verb is used to create a question, the reported speech reverts to the statement word order.

Also, notice how the reported speech does not contain a question mark. It is no longer a question.

English question patterns and the way that they are reported

There are three patterns for questions in English: those using the verb 'be', those using auxiliary verbs (do, have, be, modal), and all other verbs. We can also divide the type of question into 5 types: a subject question; an object question; a question about circumstances; a question about intensity, quality, or classification; or a yes/no question. We will look at each type of question and how we report them below. Yes/no questions are covered in the following section on if/whether noun clauses on page 59.

Subject questions

In a subject question, we do not know the subject. For example: *Someone did an experiment.* → *Who did an experiment?*
Subject questions are easy to construct. No matter which verb is used, we simply change the subject of the clause to a question word.

The table below demonstrates this using a variety of different verbs as examples.

Subject Questions		
All other verbs	**Be**	**Auxiliary verbs**
??? hurt her? → ***What hurt her?*** ??? did it? → ***Who did it?*** ??? has one? → ***Who has one?***	??? is interested? → ***Who is interested?***	??? is hurting her? → ***What is hurting her?*** ??? has hurt her? → ***What has hurt her?*** ??? was damaged? → ***What was damaged?*** ??? does not change anything? → ***What does not change anything?*** ??? can not be harmed? → ***What cannot be harmed?***

Subject wh-word noun clauses

When we report these types of questions, we simply make the question the object of a reporting verb. We do not use the subordinator *that* in these circumstances.

> **Example**
>
> The report described **what was hurting her**.
> **Not**: The report described ~~that~~ **what was hurting her**. X

Object questions

In an object question, we do not know the object of a clause. For example: It caused ???? → What did it cause? In this type of question, there are three possible questions. We can construct questions using *be*, using *auxiliary verbs*, and using *any other verb*.

Any other verb

With these verbs, we use the auxiliary verb *do* to make the question. *Do* comes after the question word and changes for tense and subject-verb agreement. The actual verb in the question remains in its base form. **The object is deleted**. (See table below for examples).

Chapter 4

Be

With this verb, we do not use the auxiliary verb *do*, instead we change the word order. The verb *be* comes after the question word and **before the subject**. **The object is deleted.** (See table below for an example.)

Auxiliary verbs

When the verb in a clause is in the continuous, perfect, or in passive voice, or when a modal is used, or when the verb is negative, we use the following pattern: we move the auxiliary verb (or modal) before the subject. The actual verb does not change form. **The object is deleted.** (See table below for examples.)

Object Questions		
All other verbs	**Be**	**Auxiliary verbs**
It hurt ??? → *Whom **did** it hurt?* You did ??? → *What **did** you do?* You have ??? → *What **do** you have?*	Her job is ??? → *What **is her job**?*	**This is** hurting ???? → *Who **is this** hurting?* **This has** hurt ??? → *What **has this** hurt?*

Object wh-word noun clauses

When we report these types of questions, we use statement word order; we delete the question verb *do* or we change the word order back. The object remains missing.

> **Examples**
>
> Whom did it hurt? → The report described ***whom it hurt.***
> What is her job? → The report described ***what her job is.***
> Whom is this hurting? → The report described ***whom this is hurting.***

Circumstance

Questions of circumstance can ask about the way that something is done, the reason that something is done, the place that something is done, or the time that something is done.

> **Example**
>
> The experiment was done because ???? → Why was the experiment done?

Making this kind of question is very similar to making an object question, except that we include the object in the question. We use *how* to ask about **the way that something is done**; we use *why* to ask about **the reason that something is done**; we use *when* for the time, and *where* for the place.

All other verbs.

With these verbs, we use the auxiliary verb *do* to make the question. *Do* comes after the question word and changes for tense and subject-verb agreement. The actual verb in the question remains in its base form. (See table below for examples).

Be

With this verb, we do not use the auxiliary verb *do*, instead we change the word order. The verb *be* comes after the question word and **before the subject**. (See table below for an examples.)

Auxiliary verbs

When the verb in a clause is in the continuous, perfect, or in passive voice, or when a modal is used, or when the verb is negative, we use the following pattern: we move the auxiliary verb (or modal) before the subject. The actual verb does not change form. (See table below for examples.)

Circumstance Questions		
All other verbs	**Be**	**Auxiliary verbs**
It resulted in this in ??? → ***When did it result in this?*** They did this by??? → ***How did they do this?***	It is true because???? → ***Why is this true?***	They are doing this in??? → ***Where are they doing this?***

Wh-word noun clauses reporting circumstances.

To make this kind of question, we keep the question word, but change the clause back to statement word order.

> **Examples**
>
> How did this happen? → The report described **how this happened.**
> Why did this happen? → The report described **why this happened.**
> Where did this happen? → The report described **where this happened.**
> When did this happen? → The report described **when this happened.**

Classification/Possession/Intensity/Quantity

With verbs other than **be**, we can ask about the type of noun (classification), we can ask about the adverb or adjective related to the verb or noun (intensity), and we can ask about the amount of the object that was affected (quantity).

Classification

We use **which/whose + noun + do** + the rest of the clause or **which/whose + noun + be + subject.**

> **Examples**
>
> He succumbed to the disease, Malaria. → Which disease did he succumb to?
> This is the disease, Malaria. → Which disease is this?
> This is cause by the disease, Malaria. → Which disease is this caused by?
> This is Stevani's report on Malaria. → Whose report on Malaria is this?

Intensity

We can ask about the intensity of an adverb, we use **how + adverb + do** + the rest of the clause.

> **Example**
>
> He succumbed to the disease **very** quickly. → How quickly did he succumb to the disease?

Similarly, we can ask about the intensity of an adjective related to a noun when we have used the verb **be**. In this case, we use **how + adjective + be + subject.**

> **Example**
>
> The problem is **very** serious. → How serious was the problem?

Quantity

We can also ask a question about the quantity of an object affected by a verb using the pattern **how + quantifier + do + clause** or **how + quantifier + is there**. Quantifiers are words like **much, many,** and **few.**

> **Examples**
>
> She consumed **a lot of** water. → How much water did she consume?
> There is **not a lot of** water. → How much water is there?

Classification/Possession/Intensity/Quantity Questions		
All other verbs	**Be**	**Auxiliary verbs**
Which disease does she have?	How serious is it?	Which disease has she had?
Whose water did she drink?	Whose drink is this?	Whose water is she drinking?
How quickly did she succumb to the disease?	Which person was she?	How quickly are they doing it?
How much water did she drink?	How much water is there?	How much water is she drinking?

Wh-word noun clauses reporting questions of classification, quantity, or quality.

To report this kind of question, we retain the question word and its complement (e.g. Which disease, how quickly, how serious, how much) but the rest of the clause is in statement word order.

> **Examples**
>
> Which disease did he succumb to? → The report described **which disease he succumbed to**.
> Whose water was drunk? → They stated whose water was drunk.
> How serious is the disease? → The report described **how serious the disease is**.
> How much water did she consume? → The report described **how much water she consumed**.

Chapter 4

Polite language questions

Sometimes when we want to be more polite, we use *wh-word* and if/whether noun clauses. This rarely happens in academic writing, but it is still an aspect of noun clauses that you need to be aware of.

> ### *Examples*
> Excuse me; I wonder if I could ask you *what time it is*. **Or** Could I just ask you *what time it is*?
> I wonder if you could tell me *what time it is*. **Or** I would appreciate it if you could tell me *what time it is*.

When reporting these types of questions, **it is not necessary to include the polite language clause**. Similarly, it is not necessary to report **please**.

> ### *Example*
> I wonder if you could please tell me where the police station is.
> Jennifer asked *where the police station was*.

Parallel Clauses

Grammar structures often need to be repeated after **and, but**, and **or**. Such clauses are called **parallel**. Take the following two sentences for instance:

> *Jane said that she was sad, and she cried.*
> *Jane said that she was sad and **that** she cried.*

In the first sentence, Jane said that she was sad; after she had said this, she cried. In the second sentence, Jane said that she was sad, and Jane said that she cried.

So, it is important to include **that** in the second sentence because it changes the meaning.

> ### Note
> We never omit the **that** from parallel noun clauses.

> ### *Example*
> The Doctor asked two questions: Where does it hurt? How much does it hurt?
> The doctor asked **where** it hurt <u>and</u> **how much** it hurt.

Exercises

4.1 Report these Wh-word questions

1) What is the only word in the English language that begins and ends with und?

   She asked _____

2) How much money is there in the world?

   They wonder _____

3) Where is the city of Ouagadougou?

   George wants to know _____

4) Why do so many people in the world feel sad?

   We were just discussing _____

5) How much wood could a woodchuck chuck if a woodchuck could chuck wood?

   She explained _____

4.2 Complete these polite questions.

1) Excuse me, I don't suppose you know how often _____

2) Would we just be able to enquire what time _____

3) I wonder if you can tell us where _____

4) Excuse me, if you don't mind, can I ask how _____

5) I really wonder which _____

4.3 Report these 'polite language' questions

1) I wonder if you could tell me why you are wearing that silly hat.

She asked _____

2) I'd really like to know whom you went to the party with.

   I inquired _____

3) Could you tell me when the next bus comes?

   He wondered _____

4) Would you mind telling me how many people went to class today?

   I wanted to know _____

5) Could you tell me how much that dog in the window is?

   David asked _____

4.4 Make sure that the following questions and statements are reported as parallel clauses

1) Which is the best university in the world? How much does it cost to attend?

   The student enquired which _____ and how much _____

2) Where will you spend your next holidays? How will you get there?

   Audrey asked _____ and _____

3) The Gobi desert is in Asia. I have been to the Gobi desert.

   The explorer stated _____

4) How do you get to school? How do you get home again?

   _____

5) Why are you studying English? What do you hope to use English for in the future?

   _____

If/whether noun clauses

If/whether noun clauses report yes/no questions. An example of a yes/no question is: ***Do you like grammar?*** The only possible answers to these questions are ***yes*** or ***no***. We report yes/no questions like this: ***I asked <u>if</u> you like grammar.***

Not all reporting verbs can be used with *wh-word* noun clauses. All of the following verbs can be used with *wh-word* clauses. All except *wonder* can be used with *that* clauses.

(***Know***, ***say***, ***see***, and ***remember*** are usually used in negative clauses)

Reporting verbs that can be used with if/whether clauses include:								
ask	discover	inquire	know	question	remember	say	see	wonder

Word order in English yes/no question varies in the same was as wh-word questions do. In a yes/no question, there are three possible questions. We can construct questions using *be*, using *auxiliary verbs*, and using *any other verb*.

Any other verb

With these verbs, we use the auxiliary verb *do* to make the question. *Do* comes before the subject and changes for tense and subject-verb agreement. The actual verb in the question remains in its base form. (See table below for examples).

Be

With this verb, we do not use the auxiliary verb *do*, instead we change the word order. The verb *be* comes **before the subject**. (See table below for an example.)

Auxiliary verbs

When the verb in a clause is in the continuous, perfect, or in passive voice, or when a modal is used, or when the verb is negative, we use the following pattern: we move the auxiliary verb (or modal) before the subject. The actual verb does not change form. (See table below for examples.)

Chapter 4

Yes/no Questions		
All other verbs	**Be**	**Auxiliary verbs**
It hurt her → Did it hurt her?	She is hurt → Is she hurt?	It was damaged → Was it damaged?

Reporting yes/no questions in if/whether noun clauses

When we report these types of questions, we use statement word order; we delete the question verb *do* or we change the word order back.

> *Examples*
>
> Did it hurt her? → The report described *whether it hurt her.*
> Is her job demanding? → The report described *whether her job was demanding.*
> Is this hurting the community? → The report described *whether this was hurting the community.*

If or Whether?

We use *whether* more often when there is a choice of options.
We use *if* more often when there is only one possibility.

> *Example*
> I was asked whether global warming was good or bad.
> She asked him if global warming was a problem.

Or not

Or not can be used with *if* and *whether* in the following ways:

> **Whether or not....:** He asked *whether or not* the data was valid.
> **Whether.... or not:** He asked *whether* the data was valid *or not*.
> **If.... or not:** He asked *if* the data was valid *or not*.
> **But _not_:** He asked *if ~~or not~~* the data was valid.

Reporting uncertainty

Whether can also be used with the reporting verbs *choose, debate, decide, know,* and *wonder* to report that a person is uncertain about doing an action. This is done either by following whether with an *infinitive*, or by following it with a clause that includes a *modal*.

> *Example*
> **Infinitive**
> He debated whether to do it.
> **Modal**
> He debated whether he should do it.

Exercises

5.1 Write the following conversation in reported speech.

    Dr. Minogue: Do you have any pain? *Patient*: Yes, quite a lot.

    Dr. Minogue: Where is the pain? *Patient*: It's on the left, around my heart.

    Dr. Minogue: Is it in the chest? *Patient*: Yes.

    Dr. Minogue: What part of the chest? *Patient*: In the upper part, I think.

    Dr. Minogue: Could you describe to me what kind of pain it is? *Patient*: It is a bit hard to describe.

    Dr. Minogue: Is it a sharp kind of ache, or is it a dull kind of ache? *Patient*: It's pretty dull.

    Dr. Minogue: How did the pain start? *Patient*: When I was coughing.

    Dr. Minogue: Does it hurt a lot when you breathe in deeply? *Patient*: Yes, quite a lot.

    Dr. Minogue: Is the pain always there, or does it come and go? *Patient*: It comes and goes.

First, Dr. Minogue asked the patient _____; the patient replied that ____

_____

_____

_____

_____

_____

Negatives

With some reporting verbs, the negative is often expressed in the independent clause rather than in the noun clause.

Here is a list of these verbs:

> **Example**
> I do not think that she suspects me.
> **Not**: I think that she does not suspect me. **X**

believe	feel	intend	propose	suppose	wish
expect	imagine	plan	reckon	think	

Modals in reported speech

Modals are used for a range of different reasons in speech. When we report modals, we must include them in the reported speech. Modals are explained in detail in Chapter 6, pages 94-100.

> **We use modals in the following situations:**
>
> to report ability
> to report possibility
> to report that a person has to or must do something
> to report permission
> to report a question about the future, or a promise, an expectation, or a prediction
> to not fully commit ourselves to a statement.

(This last point is covered in Chapter 6, page 100, in the section on *hedging*.)

When you need to report that a person said that they had the ability to do something, use the modal **could**.

> **Example**
> He said that he could drive a car.

To report that there was a possibility that they might do something use **might, could**, or **may**.

> **Example**
> He said that he might come tonight.

To report that a person said that someone might have to or must do something, use **must** or **have to**.

> **Example**
> My teacher said that I must do my homework.

To report that somebody gave permission use **could** or **might** (more formal).

> **Example**
> My teacher said that I could go home.

To report that a person made a statement about the future, but that that point in time is now in the past, use **would**. (See Chapter 4, page 46, and Chapter 5, pages 84-85, for more on this.)

> **Example**
> He said he would come yesterday. (Last week, he was talking about the future. The future is now yesterday.)

Reporting how something should be done using wh - word clauses

Wh-word clauses can also be used to report information about how something should be done. When used in this way, *wh-words* can either be followed by the **infinitive** or by a **clause including a modal**.

Examples of verbs that can be used in this way include:

Chapter 4

describe	guess	remember
discover	imagine	say
discuss	know	suggest
explain	learn	tell
forget	realise	understand

Examples
Infinitive
He told me *what* **to do**.
Modal
He told me *what* **I should do**.

Exercises

6.1 Report the following statements in the negative using the reporting verbs given

1) He cannot be the president. (believe)   I _____

2) Do you know what time it is? (suppose)   I _____

3) What have you been through? (imagine)   I _____

4) It was done. (intend)   We _____

5) He won. (expect)   They _____

6.2 Put these words in order to form reported speech using modals

1) we / our / should / homework / she / do / explained / that

_____

2) crazy / kill / might / the / somebody / indicated / he / that / man

_____

3) be able / will / it / guess / I / I / to do / that / probably

_____

4) tomorrow / whether / she / it / rain / would / wondered

_____

5) the / whether / he / might / boy / home / early / go / enquired

_____

6.3 Rewrite the following noun clauses. If the clause uses the infinitive, rewrite it using a modal; if the clause uses a modal, rewrite it using the infinitive.

1) I guessed how to do it. _____

2) He suggested how it should be done. _____

3) I understood what to do. _____

4) He revealed what we should be doing. _____

5) He did not say which way we should do it. _____

Noun clauses as complements of nouns

Consider the following two sentences:

The Questions <u>that Preshad raises in his latest article</u> are very interesting.
The fact <u>that Preshad asked these questions in his latest articles</u> is very interesting.

The first sentence contains a **relative clause**; the second contains a **noun clause**. The most obvious difference is that the relative clause is missing its object (or subject); the noun clause contains subject, verb, and object. There are two other key differences; the first is that the subordinator **which** can be used instead of **that** in the relative clause, but not in the noun clause. The other is that the relative clause can be restrictive or non-restrictive and that they **can** have commas; the noun clause never contains commas.

These kinds of noun clauses are called '**adjunct**' noun clauses; they look like relative clauses, but they are not. They provide more information about the noun in the same way that an infinitive clause might. They do **not** **describe** the noun like a relative clause does. **That** is never omitted in these cases. They are different from embedded noun clauses because they are not the object (or subject) of the clause; they are extra information.

There is a similarity between these kinds of noun clauses and some infinitives. Compare the following two sentences:

The agreement <u>that we should continue</u> was made by the director.
The agreement <u>to continue</u> was made by the director.

There is very little difference in the above two sentence; unfortunately, not all nouns can be followed by noun clauses, and not all by infinitive clauses.

The following sections look at the types of nouns that can be complemented by this type of noun clause.

Nouns formed from reporting verbs

Not all nouns can be followed by noun clauses; some nouns related to reporting verbs can be followed by noun clauses.

The following nouns (made from reporting verbs) can be followed by adjunct noun clauses:

admission	claim*	knowledge	sense
advice	conclusion	order	statement
agreement*	decision*	promise*	thought
announcement	dream	reply	threat*
answer	expectation	retort	understanding
argument	feeling	response	warning*
assertion	guess	rule	wish*
assumption	hope*	rumour	worry
belief	information *	saying	

*The nouns followed by an asterisk can also be followed by an infinitive clause.

> **Example**
>
> It is his conclusion *that global warming is a part of the psychological phenomenon of the belief that the end of the world is coming soon*.

It is important to remember to include a verb in the independent clause that accompanies these noun clauses, since the noun clause is not object of a verb.

Thus, the following sentence is a fragment.

The conclusion *that global warming is a part of the psychological phenomenon of the belief that the end of the world is coming soon*. X (Wrong)

To correct the fragment, include a verb.

The conclusion *that global warming is a part of the psychological phenomenon of the belief that the end of the world <u>is coming soon is held by some professors</u>*.

Nouns formed from adjectives

Some nouns formed from adjectives can be followed by *that* noun clauses.

The following nouns (made from adjective) can be followed by adjunct noun clauses:

awareness	confidence	inevitability	possibility	sorrow
certainty	eagerness	likelihood	probability	willingness

> **Example**
>
> The possibility *that global warming will become a serious problem* is very low.

Facts, ideas, & beliefs

Noun clauses can also be complements of nouns related to facts, ideas, and beliefs.

> **Example**
>
> The fact **that students at Prince Sultan University study hard** is well known.

These nouns include:

Chapter 4

> **The following nouns (about facts, ideas, & beliefs) can be followed by adjunct noun clauses:**
>
> | | | | | |
> |---|---|---|---|---|
> | advantage | effect | impression | prospect | vision |
> | benefit | evidence | news | risk | word |
> | chance | experience | opinion | sign | |
> | confidence | fact | possibility | story | |
> | danger | faith | principle | tradition | |
> | disadvantage | idea | proposition | view | |

Exercises

7.1 Rewrite the following sentences using the noun forms of the verbs.

1) The author admits that television is partially responsible for violence amongst children.
    _____

2) Karlsson claims that because difficult children are often put in front of the TV to quieten them down, it seems as though the TV is making them violent.
    _____
    _____

3) Gribble correctly asserts that there are many quality TV shows for children that contain little violence.
    _____

4) Lee argues that by the time a child is 10 years old in America, the child has seen over 10,000 murders on television.
    _____

5) Uchiro assumes, perhaps incorrectly, that TV desensitises children to violence.
    _____

7.2 Find the errors in the following sentences

1) The media gives the impression that TV responsible for all crime in America.
    _____

2) A logical response is often given is that many children's fairy tales also contain violent story lines but that fairy tales are rarely blamed for violence amongst children.
    _____
    _____

3) There is evidence that violence on TV causes violent children is limited.
    _____

4) Recent news that violence in America has decreased in recent years suggestion that TV is not making Americans more violent.
    _____

5) The likelihood that violence on TV will be reduced in the near future very low.
    _____

6) Cunningham's reason that TV appears to make children violent because violent children like to watch violent TV shows.
    _____
    _____

Noun clauses as complements of adjectives

Adjectives are often followed by infinitive clauses when an opinion is expressed, for example: **it was hard <u>to kill</u> <u>him</u>**, but other adjectives can be followed by *that* noun clauses.

Consider the following two sentences:

It is important <u>to begin the survey immediately.</u>
It is important <u>that we begin the survey immediately</u>.

There is very little difference in meaning between these two sentences. Notice that we use the *dummy subject it* in both cases.

Adjectives that can be followed by noun clauses in this way include:

apparent	essential*	funny*	likely	possible
appropriate	evident	good*	luck	probable
awful*	extraordinary	important*	natural*	sad*
bad*	fair	inevitable	obvious*	true*
clear	fun*	interesting*	plain	unlikely

*Adjectives with asterisk * can also be complemented by infinitive clause.*

Example

He believes that <u>*it*</u> is **essential** <u>that we immediately begin to curb greenhouse gases</u>.

Adjectives followed by *that* noun clauses can also be used to show **the cause of a feeling**. These adjectives can have *real* subjects.

Example
<u>**The students**</u> were **worried** <u>that they would not pass the test</u>.

Adjectives that can be followed by noun clauses to show the cause of a feeling:

afraid	conscious	happy	sorry
angry	eager	hopeful	sure
anxious	fearful	positive	surprised
aware	frightened	pleased	thankful
certain	glad	proud	upset
confident	grateful	sad	worried

A very small number of –ed adjectives can be followed by a that noun clause (a few others are followed by an infinitive or a prepositional phrase). They usually come after verbs such as *be*, *become*, or *feel*. These –ed adjectives are usually related to a transitive verb. These adjectives also have a *real* subject.

Adjectives that can be followed by noun clauses to show the cause of a feeling:

amazed	determined	pleased	upset
amused	disgusted	scared	worried
annoyed	distressed	surprised	
convinced	disturbed	touched	
delighted	irritated	thrilled	

Example
<u>**The government**</u> is **scared** <u>that there will be a major voter backlash if they move to curb greenhouse gases</u>.

Chapter 4

Exercises

8.1 Join these clauses to create noun clauses. You may need to change the word form in some sentences.

1) Most people find this interesting: Australia has so many poisonous creatures.

   _____

2) Many new migrants to Australia are fearful. They fear being bitten by a poisonous creature.

   _____

3) Australian spiders are unlikely to kill an adult human, but it is not impossible.

   _____

4) Most people are conscious of this: the Redback is deadly poisonous.

   _____

5) Many people also believe this is true: the Whitetail is deadly poisonous.

   _____

6) These people are often amazed to find out the following: there is little evidence supporting this claim.

   _____

7) Nevertheless many people are still afraid. They fear being bitten by a White tail.

   _____

Noun clauses as complements of prepositions

Some but not all prepositions can be followed by noun clauses. Prepositions can be divided into the following groups:

1) **_Intransitive prepositions_** (preposition can not have an object (E.g. **_He went out_**.).)

2) **_Transitive prepositions_** (preposition must have an object (E.g. **_He stood by the house_**.).)

   a. Complemented by noun phrase only (E.g. **_He studied with his friends_**.)

   b. Complemented by noun phrase or gerund clause (E.g. **_He studied without his friend_** or _He completed the assignment **without anyone helping him**_.)

   c. Complemented by noun phrase, gerund clause, or **noun clause**

In this chapter, we are concerned with this last group. Note that this group is generally only complemented by _wh-word noun clauses_ or _whether noun clauses_. **They are generally not complemented by _that_ noun clauses.** If you want to complement a preposition by a statement of fact rather than a question, you should use the subordinator **_how_**. Note also that _if_ is **not used** after a preposition, only **whether** is used.

Note also that in most cases, it is also acceptable (and more normal) to use a gerund clause instead of a noun clause.

> **_Examples_**
> He talked _about_ **how James couldn't come**. (or He talked _about_ **James not being able to come**.)
> He talked _about_ **whether James could come or not**. (not **_if_**)

> **Prepositions that can be complemented by wh-word noun clauses or _whether_ noun clauses:**
>
> | | | | |
> |---|---|---|---|
> | about | despite | in spite of | on |
> | because of | due to | notwithstanding | than |
> | by | for | of | to |

Examples

They are writing in acknowledgement ***of*** who was said at the interview.

They are worried ***about*** who will and won't do it.

It depends ***on*** how much he barks.

Exercises

9.1 Make the following clauses into noun clauses as object of the preposition given.

1) Cornes told the story of [he became interested in astrophysics]

_____

2) Smithson discussed the question of [who should be in charge of the project?]

_____

3) Gilbert considers the issue of [should everybody in the world be forced to become vegetarian?]

_____

4) Despite [Clayton does not smoke], Clayton advocates a more liberal attitude towards smoking.

_____

5) Due to [the situation is hypocritical], Gilbert advocates making it illegal.

_____

6) Several papers on [what happened during the prohibition period in America?] have highlighted the idiocy of such an approach.

_____

9.2 Write sentences with noun clauses as object of the prepositions given.

1) (Notwithstanding) _____

2) (because of) _____

3) (of) _____

4) (In spite of) _____

5) (By) _____

6) (For) _____

7) (Than) _____

Omission of *that*

That can be omitted in some noun clauses, but not in others. In some cases it must be omitted. There are no easy rules to explain this, so mostly it is better to always include ***that***. When the verb is about saying or thinking, ***that*** is often omitted, but when information about the *way it is said* is included (for example, ***shout***), we often don't omit ***that***.

When omission usually happens

That is often omitted after reporting verbs relating to communication, the mind, or thinking.

We omit *that* after the verbs:

admit	*complain*	*insist*	*say*
agree	*decide*	*mention*	*warn*
claim	*deny*	*promise*	

Chapter 4

Also, omission often happens after category 4 indirect object reporting verbs (when we *must* have an indirect object) (see Chapter 4, page 47, for more on indirect objects, also see Appendix 4, page 198).

When omission is unusual

> **We do <u>not</u> usually omit *that* after the verbs:**
>
> answer   argue   emerge   explain   happen   reply

Also, omission is unusual when **that** is followed by a subordinator for another clause.

> **Example**
> She said **that** <u>because she could not do it</u>, **he was angry**.

When omission can't happen

We do <u>not</u> omit **that** when the noun clause is the *subject* of the verb in the independent clause.

> **Example**
> **That** *there was a problem* <u>was</u> obvious.

We do <u>not</u> omit **that** when the noun clause is not embedded (when it is extra information or adjunct). See Chapter 4, pages 63-66 for more on adjunct noun clauses.

> **Example**
> <u>The fact</u> **that** *she was upset* was obvious.

We do <u>not</u> omit **that** when the noun clause is complement to **than**.

> **Example**
> It's better that she comes <u>than</u> **that** *she doesn't*.

We do **not** omit **that** when the reporting verb is a category 2 or category 3 indirect object verb (it is followed by the optional preposition and an indirect object.) See Chapter 4, page 47 for more on indirect objects.

> **Example**
> He illustrates <u>to his readers</u> **that** *nuclear war is inevitable*.

Omission is not possible in parallel structures where the subordinators show that both clauses relate to the reporting verb.

> **Example**
> She said **that** *she was angry* and **that** *she was sad*.

When omission must happen

When a noun clause is the object of a relative clause, and it has the same subject as the object being described by the relative clause, we **must** omit **that**. More on this can be found in Chapter 9, page 163.

> **Examples**
> This is the **book**. You think ***that this book*** is good.
> This is the **book** which ~~**this book**~~ you think ~~**that**~~ is good.

Exercise

10.1 Delete *that* wherever it is possible. If it is possible but unlikely to delete *that*, put brackets around it.

The fact that time has not been decimalised is quite incredible. The way that the current model of time works

is quite antiquated. Firstly, that there are twelve months in a year is quite ridiculous. It has been argued that we could just as easily have ten months. Many people insist that this would not be possible, but they have to admit that there could be five months with 35 days each and 5 months with 36 days each.

Furthermore, that there are 24 hours in a day is extremely odd. Many fans of decimalisation of time agree that we could have ten hours in a day and that we could have 100 minutes in each hour. It would obviously be better that we had 100 minutes in an hour than that we had 60 minutes in an hour. Although this may seem strange, fans of decimalisation of time say that if we had 10 hours in a day, then each of these decimalised hours would be equivalent to 2 hours and 24 minutes of the hours that we currently have. They also say that 1 decimalised minute would equal 1 minute and 24.6 seconds of current time. However, the main obstacle to decimalisation of time is the simple fact that changing all the clocks in the world to a new time system would be too expensive.

Reporting orders and instructions

So far we have looked at reporting statements and questions. Statements have the word order SVO - for example: *He likes George Bush*. Statements, as we have seen, are reported in *that* noun clauses – for example: *Matt said that he likes George Bush*. Questions either have the word order SVO or OVS – for example, *Who does George Bush like?* or *Who likes George Bush?*

Orders and instructions, however, don't have a subject. The word order is VO. Examples of orders and instructions include:

Shut up!	*Do the exercises at the end of the chapter.*
Sit down.	*Please have a cup of tea.*

Infinitive

Orders and instructions can be reported in three ways. One way is to use the infinitive:

> **Examples**
>
> He said *to shut up*.
> They asked us *to sit down*.
> The book instructs the students *to do the exercises at the end of the chapter*.
> The Queen asked me *to have a cup of tea*.

Noun clause + modal

Another way is to use a noun clause with a **modal**.

> **Examples**
>
> He said *that I <u>should</u> shut up*.
> They said *that we <u>should</u> sit down*.
> The book says that the students <u>should</u> do the exercises at the end of the chapter.

Subjunctive

The third way to report orders and instructions is to use a noun clause with the **subjunctive**

The subjunctive is very similar to the bare infinitive; it does not change for subject-verb agreement.

Thus, we say *he advised that she <u>shut</u> up* (not *shut<u>s</u> up*).

> **Example**
>
> He advised that I <u>shut</u> up.

The subjunctive is used only after the following verbs:				
advise	*decree*	*intend*	*propose*	*stipulate*
agree	*demand*	*order*	*recommend*	*urge*
ask	*desire*	*plead*	*request*	
beg	*direct*	*pray*	*rule*	
command	*insist*	*prefer*	*suggest*	

Chapter 4

The subjunctive can also be used after some adjectives when we use **the dummy subject _it_** and the verb **_be_**. These sentences can also use infinitive clauses. Infinitive clauses will use the subordinator **_for_** if the subject is included. If the subject is omitted, the subordinator will be too. See Chapter 3, pages 38-44 for more on infinitive clauses.

> ### _Example_
> **Subjunctive noun clause**: It is crucial <u>that he **reconsider** his position</u>.
> **Infinitive clause (with subject)**: It is crucial <u>to reconsider his position</u>.
> **Infinitive clause (with no subject)**: It is crucial **<u>for him</u>** <u>to reconsider his position</u>.

> ### A subjunctive noun clause (or an infinitive clause) can be used after these adjectives:
> | | | | | |
> |---|---|---|---|---|
> | _best_ | _crucial_ | _essential_ | _important_ | _recommended_ |
> | _critical_ | _desirable_ | _imperative_ | _necessary_ | |

> ### _Examples_
> It is **best** _<u>that I shut up</u>_.
> It is **recommended** _<u>that we sit down</u>_.
> It is **crucial** _<u>that the students do the exercises at the end of the chapter</u>_.
> It is **important** _<u>that I have a cup of tea</u>_.

Negatives

To make a subjunctive verb negative, we simply put **_not_** before the verb in the clause.

> ### _Examples_
> They asked _<u>that we **not** sit down</u>_.
> He requested _<u>that I **not** shut up</u>_.

Continuous and Passive Forms

The Subjunctive can also be used in continuous and passive forms.
Continuous is formed by _be + V ~ing_.
Passive is formed by _be + Past Participle_

> ### _Example_
> They asked _that we <u>be sitting</u>_.
> The Queen urged _that the cup of tea <u>be drunk</u>_.

Exercises

11.1 Report the following instructions from a recipe book using the infinitive

- a) _First, cut up some onion and dice some garlic_
- b) _Put the onion and garlic into a fry pan and fry it for five minutes_
- c) _Next, add a tin of diced tomatoes._
- d) _Then, stir the mixture well and cook for another 5 minutes._
- e) _Lastly, boil some water and cook the pasta for ten minutes._

_____

_____

_____

_____

_____

11.2 Repeat the same exercise using a noun clause and a modal

_____

_____

_____

_____

11.3 Repeat the same exercise again using the subjunctive (note: you will have to use different reporting verbs from the last two exercises)

_____

_____

_____

_____

_____

Tense & Aspect

Tense & Aspect

English has three **tenses**, three **aspects**, and two **voices**

By **tense**, we mean whether the event is located in the past, the present, or the future.

The **aspects** are the simple, continuous, perfect, and continuous perfect forms of the verb. Each can be located in the past, present, and future.

Verbs are either in **Active** or **Passive voice**. Active voice is used to put emphasis on the doer of the action; passive voice is used to put emphasis on the event or to hide the doer. Passive voice can also be used to create cohesion within a text.

Technically, English only has a past and a present tense; it does not actually have a future tense. Future tense is formed by putting a modal of probability before the bare infinitive form of the verb, or by using the phrase **to be going to**. Modals are discussed more fully in Chapter 6.

Construction of the different tenses

Construction of the tenses in English is easy. You should not make any mistakes with constructing the tenses. Using the tenses is much harder. This section will discuss how to construct the tenses. The next section will discuss common uses of the tenses.

You will need to know the following vocabulary to understand this section:

The infinitive: (E.g. *to love* (this form can never change it's ending)). See Chapter 3, pages 44-50 for more on infinitives.

The bare infinitive: This is the dictionary or base form of the verb (E.g. *love* (this form can never change it's ending))

Gerund: Formed by adding *~ing* to the end of the verb. (E.g. *loving*) This is the noun form of the verb. It is not the same as the active participle (although it looks the same)

Present Participle: Formed by adding *~ing* to the end of a verb. This form is not the same as the gerund. See Chapter 2 for full explanation. Note that this is really an 'active' participle.

Past Participle: Formed by adding *~ed* to the end of a verb or by using the irregular passive participle (PP) (E.g. **loved, learned, drunk, gone, sung**). See chapter 2 for full explanation. Note that the words 'past' and 'present' are misleading. These are really active and passive forms of the adjective formed from a verb.

Active voice (E.g. **He loves her**.)

Passive voice (E.g. **She is loved (by him)**) Passive voice takes the object and makes it into the subject.

Modal of probability (E.g. **Might, will, could, may**)

Auxiliary verb A verb which is used to modify the tense, aspect, or voice of a verb, to make the verb negative, or to form a question. Auxiliary verbs include **have, be, get**, and **do**.

Simple Aspect

Simple tenses in active voice are formed from the base form of the verb. The present tense must agree with the subject (**I go**, **He goes**, etc). The past tense is formed either by adding **~ed** to the end of the verb, or by using the irregular past form of the verb. Future tense is formed either by using a modal such as **will** or **might** with the bare infinitive form of the verb. This form of the verb never changes to agree with subject (E.g. **I will go, he will go, they will go, not he will goes**). Modals are explained more fully in Chapter 6.

Simple tenses in passive voice simple are formed from the verb **be** and **the past participle**. With regular verbs, this means adding **~ed** to the end of the verb. For irregular verbs, it means using the past participle. Tense is changed by changing **be** into past, present and future (present: **is**, past: **was**, future: **will be**). The *past participle never* changes form. (E.g. **I am drunk, I was drunk, not I was drunked**). Remember that the verb *to be* needs to change to agree with the subject (E.g. **I am drunk, he is drunk, not he is drunks**).

Simple Aspect

	Active voice	Passive voice
Past	V~ed **or** irregular past tense	was/were PP
Present	V or Vs	am/is/are PP
Future	Modal + V	Modal + be PP

Examples

	Active	Passive
Past	The students <u>studied</u> the case.	The case <u>was studied</u> by the students
Present	The students <u>study</u> cases.	Cases <u>are studied</u> by the students.
Future	The students <u>will study</u> the case.	The case <u>will be studied</u> by the students.

Continuous Aspect (also called the *progressive* aspect)

Continuous aspect is formed with *be* and the **active participle**. Past tense is created by changing *be* into past or future tense. *Be* must also agree with the subject. Passive voice is created by *be* and *being* **and the past participle**. Again, *be* changes tense and subject verb agreement, none of the other parts of the verb change.

Continuous Aspect

	Active voice	Passive voice
Past	was/were V~ing	was/were being PP
Present	am/is/are V~ing	am/is/are being PP
Future	Modal + be V~ing	Modal + be being PP

Examples

	Active	Passive
Past	The students <u>were studying</u> the case.	The case <u>was being studied</u> by the students
Present	The students <u>are studying</u> the case.	The case <u>is being studied</u> by the students.
Future	The students <u>will be studying</u> the case.	The case <u>will be being studied</u> by the students.

Perfect Aspect

Perfect aspect is created by *have* and the **past participle**. *Have* changes tense and subject verb agreement. Passive voice is created by *have* and *been* **and the past participle**. Remember, only the *have* changes tense and subject verb agreement.

Perfect Aspect

	Active voice	Passive voice
Past	Had PP	Had been PP
Present	Have/has PP	Have/has been PP
Future	Modal + have PP	Modal + have been PP

Examples

	Active	Passive
Past	The students <u>had studied</u> the case.	The case <u>had been studied</u> by the students
Present	The students <u>have studied</u> the case.	The case <u>has been studied</u> by the students.
Future	The students <u>will have studied</u> the case.	The case <u>will have been studied</u> by the students.

Chapter 5

Perfect continuous aspect

Perfect continuous aspect is created by **have** and **been** and **the active participle**. Note that this aspect can have 5 auxiliary verbs in the active tense (**be going to have been being...**). Remember, only the first auxiliary verb (**have**) changes tense and subject verb agreement. Passive voice is created by **have** and **been** and **being** and **the past participle**.

Perfect Continuous Aspect

	Active voice	Passive voice
Past	Had been V~ing	Had been being PP
Present	Have/has been V~ing	Have/has been being PP
Future	Modal + have been V~ing	Modal + have been being PP

Examples

	Active	Passive
Past	The students <u>had been studying</u> the case.	The case <u>had been being studied</u> by the students
Present	The students <u>have been studying</u> the case.	The case <u>has been being studied</u> by the students.
Future	The students <u>will have been studying</u> the case.	The case <u>will have been being studied</u> by the students.

Summary

The following table summarises the tenses and aspects that are possible in English. Make yourself familiar with this table. Forming tense and aspect is the easy part. You should not have any trouble with forming it. (Symbols used in this table: V – base form of verb, V~s – verb with 's' on the end, V~ing – verb with 'ing' on the end, PP – past participle)

	Past	Present	Future
Active simple	V~ed / irregular past	V/V~s	Modal + V
Passive simple	Was/were PP	Is/am/are PP	Modal + be PP
Active continuous	Was/were ~ing	Is/am/are V~ing	Modal + be V~ing
Passive continuous	Was/were being PP	Is/am/are being PP	Modal + be being PP
Active perfect	Had PP	Have/has PP	Modal + have PP
Passive perfect	Had been PP	Have/has been PP	Modal + have been PP
Active perfect continuous	Had been V~ing	Have/has been V~ing	Modal + have been V~ing
Passive perfect continuous	Had been being PP	Have/has been being PP	Modal + have been being PP

Exercises

1.1 Change the following verbs to the tense given in brackets. Make sure the verb agrees with the subject given.

1) *Cause* (Passive past simple) It _____

2) *Affect* (Active future continuous) This _____

3) *Disrupt* (Passive past perfect) Services _____

4) *Go* (Active future perfect continuous) I _____

5) *Have* (Active past perfect) We _____

6) *Do* (passive present perfect continuous) It _____

7) *Contrast* (Active past simple) You _____

8) *Corrupt* (Passive past perfect) The disk _____

9) *Upload* (Passive future simple) These programmes _____

10) *Disregard* (Active future perfect)   You _____

11) *Claim* (Active present simple)   The author _____

12) *Consider* (Passive Past Perfect)   They _____

13) *Vary* (Active future simple)   It _____

14) *Restructure* (Passive future perfect)   The company _____

15) *Respond* (Active past continuous)   Johnson _____

16) *Research* (Passive past perfect continuous)   A cure _____

17) *Require* (Passive present perfect)   A payment _____

18) *Occur* (Active past continuous)   These events _____

19) *Sentence* (Active present perfect)   The judge _____

20) *Interpret* (Passive past perfect continuous)   The results _____

21) *Involve* (Passive present simple)   Several researchers _____

22) *Export* (Passive future perfect continuous)   Many products _____

23) *Establish* (Passive present continuous)   This practice _____

24) *Finance* (Passive future continuous)   The project _____

States and Events

Forming tense and aspect is easy in English; the hard part is **using** it. To understand how the English tense system is used, we need to understand the differences between two types of verbs: **states** and **events**. **Events** are things that happen, while **states** are situations that affect people and things. Both **states** and **events** work differently with tense, so we need to understand both of these types of verbs.

Examples of *states* include: Love, *be*, *have*, *know*, *want*, and *feel*. None of verbs actually **happen**. It is quite difficult to answer the questions 'how?', 'where?' and 'why?' about these verbs. For example, '***how do you love her?***' or '***where do you love her?***'

> **Note**
> Be careful about ***have*** because it has four meanings: it can be a state (e.g. *I have a car*); it can be an event (e.g. *I had breakfast at 8.00*); it can be an auxiliary verb (a verb that changes the tense of another verb) (e.g. *I have finished my homework*); and it can be a semi-modal (E.g. *I have to go*).

Examples of events include: *Do, drive, happen, cause, break.* You can usually talk about a start and end time of these verbs. For example, I started driving at 7:50 a.m. and finished at 8:30 a.m.

> **Note**
> This does not work well for states. '*I started wanting a new car at 7:50 am*, *and finished wanting a new car at 8:30 am.*' This doesn't make a lot of sense.

Exercises

2.1 Decide if the verbs in the following sentences are states or verbs.

> *Example*: This position is misguided. a) state_____ (*'is'* is a state not an event)

1) This argument has four main points. a) _____

2) Changes in attitudes towards women over the last 100 years have resulted in a number of changes to their status. a) _____

3) Cultural prejudice is affecting the status of foreigners in this country. a) _____

4) Accidents are often caused by mobile phone use. a) _____

5) The claims that Parks puts forward are very misguided. a) _____   b) _____

6) In his thesis, Watanabe proposed a more active programme of reconciliation. a) _____

7) Many do not understand the affects that the war had on neighbours countries and the feelings that they harbour. a) _____ b) _____ c) _____

8) Because people have noticed this, it has led to a number of changes. a) _____   b) _____

9) Most lecturers prefer to receive student work via e-mail these days because it stops them from having to do paper work. a) _____ b) _____ c) _____ d) _____

Repeated Events and Duration

Events also need to be divided into three groups because each group works differently with tense in English. The three groups of events are: **repeated events, events with no duration, and events with duration.**

Repeated events

Repeated events are events that happen again and again. There is no clear start or end time to this repetition. Consider the following 2 sentences.

1) *I went to school yesterday.*
2) *I went to school when I was young.*

(1) means that I did this action just once yesterday. On the other hand, (2) means that the action happened again and again for a long time. In fact, we don't know when it started or ended. **English tense works the same way for the repeated events in (2) and for states**, so this book will group them together and talk about them as **states/repeated events**.

Events with no Duration

Some events do not really have duration. Examples of **Events with no duration** include: *break, die, recognize,* and *buy*. We cannot (usually) talk about these events as taking time; for example: *While I was recognising him, he said hello.*

These events **can only be complete**; they are **not usually used in continuous forms**; for example: *While the car was hitting the tree* is not really acceptable.

These events **cannot really happen now** because we can't really know as we speak that, for example, the car will hit the tree as we speak. It is more usual for the event to have just finished at the time of speaking, or to be about to happen. In any case, English has never developed a tense for describing an event that finishes as you speak.
(Notice that many of these no-duration verbs might be able to be given duration in some circumstances.)

Events with Duration: complete vs incomplete

Events with duration (for example: *drive, write, sing, watch*) can be either finished or not finished at the time we are talking about. For example, right now *I am typing on my computer*; I haven't finished doing it yet. On the other hand, with '*I ate dinner tonight*', the event has finished. We use the continuous aspects to describe unfinished events.

Example

Complete: *The war caused a massive backlash.*
Incomplete: *The war is causing a massive backlash.*

Obviously, complete events cannot happen *now* because if they were happening now, they would not be finished!

Summary

We have seen that there are four different situations that we need to consider when choosing a tense:

1) Is the verb a state or an event? State: dislike – *He dislikes these arguments.* Event: Write – *He is writing about the arguments.*
2) Is the event repeated or not? Repeated: *I drive a BMW* (always). Not repeated: *I am driving a BMW* (now).
3) Does the event have duration or not? If the event has no duration, it must be **complete**. No Duration: break – *They broke the agreement.* Duration: talk – *They were talking about the agreement.*
4) If the event has duration, is it complete or incomplete? Complete: *I drove my BMW yesterday.* Incomplete: *I was driving my BMW at 3pm yesterday.*

Tenses and Aspects used in English

English has 3 tenses but there are several aspects for each one. Following are the tenses and their aspects:

1) **Location in time**
2) **Showing order of events**
3) **Showing that one event continues until another**
4) **Showing a connection between a past event and a present event**
5) **Showing that an experience has happened**

This is how each aspect might be shown on a timeline.

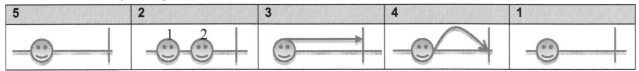

(1) **Location in time** - simply tells us when the event happened. Now, before now, or after now. **Usually a time word is used to help identify this time**. We use simple or continuous aspects depending on whether the event was complete at the time we are talking about.

(2) **Showing order of events** - tells us that one event happened before another. Time words such as **before** and **after** can do the same job.

(3) **Showing that one event continues until another** – tells us that the event continued until the time we are talking about (including now). We can use time words such as since to show when the event started and for to show how long the event has been continuing for.

(4) **Showing a connection between a past and a present event** – tells us that a past event somehow has a result in the present or is in someway connected to the present. This is probably the hardest aspect for students to master because many languages do not have this concept. This aspect is never used with a time word.

(5) **Past experience** – tells us that a person has experienced something at some time in their life. We use this aspect when we are more interested in whether a person has done this at some time in their life than when it happened. **We do not use a time word with this aspect**.

Most aspects can happen in most tenses, but they can't happen in all tenses. Notice also, that depending on whether it is a state, a complete event, or an incomplete event, we might choose from, for example, present perfect or present perfect continuous. The following tables summarise all of the tenses and aspects possible in English. Details of each situation are given after the tables.

Past Aspects	(5) Past experience	(2) Showing that one past event happens before another	(3) Showing that a past event continues until a past time	(1) Located in past
States / repeated events	Present perfect		Past perfect + since/for	Past simple
Complete events	Present perfect	Past perfect		Past simple
Incomplete events			Past perfect continuous	Past continuous

Present Aspects	(4) Showing a connection between a past event and the present.	(3) Showing that a past event continues until the present	(1) Located in present
States / repeated events		Present perfect + since/for	Present simple
Complete events	Present perfect		
Incomplete events		Present perfect continuous	Present continuous

Chapter 5

Future Aspects

	(2) Showing that one future event happens before another	(3) Showing that a future event continues until a future time	(1) Located in the future
States / repeated events		Future perfect + since/for	Future simple
Complete events	Future perfect		Future simple
Incomplete events		Future perfect continuous	Future continuous

(1) Location in time

This aspect shows whether the action happens now, before now, or after now. A time word is often (but not always) used for the past and future in the aspect. Note that a time word might be a word like '*yesterday*', but it could also be a clause like '*when I was 18*'.

States / repeated events use past simple, present simple, and future simple for this aspect.

> ### *Examples*
>
> **Past**: I hated my first car.   **Present**: I hate my car.   **Future**: I will hate my new car.
> **Past**: I drove to work last year.   **Present**: I drive to work.   **Future**: I will drive to work next year.
>
> We can also use the semi-modal *used to* for past tense in this aspect. *I used to drive to work last year* has much the same meaning as *I drove to work last year*.

Complete events can only happen before now and after now. They cannot happen now because if they were happening now, they would not be complete. These events also use past simple and future simple.

> ### *Examples*
>
> **Past**: I drove to work yesterday.   **Present**: *not possible*   **Future**: I will drive to work tomorrow.
>
> Notice that the meaning differs between *I drove to work yesterday* and *I drove to work last year*. The first shows that the event happened once, the second that it happened repeatedly. The time word is important for showing this.
> Note that some verbs that have no duration, must be used like this, e.g. *Recognise*.

Incomplete events use past continuous, present continuous, and future continuous to show that the event had started, but had not finished at the time we are talking about.

> ### *Examples*
>
> **Past**: I was driving to work at 3pm yesterday.   **Present**: I am driving to work.   **Future**: I will be driving to work at 3pm tomorrow.
> Note then that the *time word* (last year, yesterday, at 3pm yesterday) can help you choose the correct aspect.
> Also, notice that *present simple* is used only to show that a *state* is true now, or that an *event repeats* now, not to show that it is happening now.

Summary of location in past, present, and future

	Past	Present	Future
States / repeated events	Past simple	Present simple	Future simple
Complete events	Past simple		Future simple
Incomplete events	Past continuous	Present continuous	Future continuous

Exercises

3.1 The following verbs are all in the simple aspect (they are not perfect). Select between simple and continuous forms depending on the type of verb and whether the event repeats or not and whether it has finished or not at the time that you are talking about.

1) When we _____ (arrive) at the theatre, several subjects _____ (wait) to be tested on. We always _____ (begin) by testing on animals and then _____ (move) on to humans. When we _____ (test) on animals this time, the animals _____ (have) no negative symptoms, so we _____ (be) able to move on to humans.

2) A study which _____ (be done) in 1996 _____ (show) that there _____ (be) a lot of differences between cultures with regard to attitudes towards plagiarism. Western universities always _____ (treat) plagiarism as if it _____ (be) a serious crime. Eastern universities always _____ (not treat) it so seriously. Students who _____ (study) at Hong Kong University at the time of the study _____ (appear) confused. They _____ (not understand) why teachers _____ (want) them to write the same thing in words that _____ (are) not as good as the original.

3) While I _____ (write) this dissertation, I _____ (get) help from a number of different people. The foremost source of assistance _____ (be) my supervisor, who _____ (help) me understand good research methods and _____ (help) me to find excellent resources to back up my arguments. In the future, I always _____ (remember) her help and I hope that some day I _____ (be) able to offer similar help to my own postgraduate students.

(2) Showing order of events

This aspect is very easy to use; it uses the **past perfect** or **future perfect**. It is important to point out at this point that the *past* perfect and *present* perfect are quite unrelated. The *past* perfect is *not* a past form of the *present* perfect; it is a completely different concept. The *past* perfect shows that one event happened before another.

> Take the following story, which happened in the following order:
>
> **[1] *Germany invaded Czechoslovakia.* [2] *Germany invaded Poland.* [3] *Germany invaded France.***
>
> If we are going to tell the story in the same order as the events happened, we might say:
>
> [1]*Germany invaded Czechoslovakia, and* [2]*then they invaded Poland, and* [3]*then they invaded France.* (past simple is used throughout)
>
> However, if we change the order of events, and start with [2], we would use past perfect. Thus:
>
> [2]*Germany invaded Poland;* [1]*they had invaded Czechoslovakia.* [3]*Then they invaded France.*
>
> Similarly, if we start with event [3], we get:
>
> [3]*Germany invaded France.* [1]*They had invaded Czechoslovakia, and* [2]*they had invaded Poland.*

Thus, the **past perfect tells us the order of the events; it tells us which happened first**.

Often however, we use time words like **when, after,** and **before** instead of past perfect. **After** and **before** tell the order of events too.

> Thus, we could also say:
>
> **Germany invaded France *after* they *invaded* Czechoslovakia, and *after* they *invaded* Poland.**

In this sentence we don't need past perfect, because the same meaning is given in the time words. We can, of course, use past perfect, but the meaning is no different from past simple.

On the other hand, **when** does not tell us the order of events, so when we use **when** in the same story, we *have to* use past perfect.

Chapter 5

Thus:
Germany invaded France <u>when</u> they <u>had invaded</u> Czechoslovakia and <u>when</u> they <u>had invaded Poland</u>.

Note
Past perfect *can only* be used for complete *events*; it *cannot* be used for *incomplete events*, or for *states* or *repeated events*.

Future perfect works in the same way to show that one event will happen before another. However, there is one complication. See *Future tense back-shifted in adverbial clauses* on page 86 for more.

Exercises

4.1 Choose between the past perfect and past simple in the following story.

When a UN envoy visited the Darfur region of Western Sudan in 2004, they (found / had found) that several hundred thousand locals (were murdered / had been murdered) and almost a million people (were made / had been made) homeless. The war there started in 2003 when the SLA (attacked / had attacked) an airport in Darfur and (captured / had captured) the head of the Sudanese Air Force. The SLA (was made / had been made) up of Durfurian locals who (were dissatisfied / had been dissatisfied) with their government. They (suffered / had suffered) through many years of drought and (saw / had seen) their land invaded by Arabic nomads who were also escaping the drought. All of this (was ignored / had been ignored) by the Sudanese government. After the attack on the airport, the Sudanese government (organised / had organised) a militia group to control the SLA. This militia group (was called / had been called) the Janjaweed. By the time the UN envoy (visited / had visited) Darfur in 2004, the Janjaweed (ran / had run) riot, killing and murdering the Darfurians. The Sudanese government claimed that they did not sanction the actions of the Janjaweed, but aid workers (told / had told) the UN that they (saw / had seen) Sudanese government helicopters and air force planes supporting the Janjaweed.

4.2 Tell the following stories using past perfect and past simple as needed. Start from the third event.

1. Einstein's life: (a) went to school in Germany and did well (b) was introduced to science by Max Talmund (c) 1894 Moved to Italy (d) went to university in Switzerland (e) in 1903 got a job at the Swiss patent office (d) in 1905 wrote a paper on the theory of relativity

(3) Showing that one event continues until another

The **present perfect** has three main uses. It can show that a past event continued until now; it can show that there is a relationship between a past event and now, and it can show that we have had an experience at some point in our life. A summary of the different uses of present perfect can be found on page 91.

However, in this section, we will concentrate on the meaning that the past event continues until now. Here we use either the **present perfect** (usually with either *since* or *for*) with a **state** or a **repeated event**, or we use the **present perfect continuous** with an **incomplete event**.

Example
I **have loved** my daughter <u>for</u> 10 years.
I **have taught** English <u>since</u> 2001.
<u>How long</u> have you **taught** English?
I **have** <u>always</u> **taught** English.
I **have taught** English <u>all year</u>.
I **have taught** English <u>from</u> the year that I graduated. (Until now.)
I **have owned** it <u>a year or so</u>. (Implied by time word.)

Since a *complete event is finished*, it does not make sense to talk about it continuing until now, so complete events are not used in this aspect. Only **incomplete events**, **states**, and **repeated events** can happen in this aspect.

The time word is very important with states and repeated events. They use the **present perfect** with *for* or *since*, but there are a few other time situations, often implied that will also create this meaning of present perfect; some other situations include the question *how long* and the words *always*, *all*, and

Example
We *have been studying* English tense.
I *have been driving* since 6 am.

from. Notice that sometimes we leave out *for* before a time word with present perfect. Here the 'continuing until' meaning is *implied* because present perfect is not otherwise used with a time word.

Incomplete events use **present perfect continuous**. *For* and *since* are not needed with this aspect because it means continuing until now anyway. Notice that some repeated events such as '*study*' can be treated as one long continuous event or a series of repeated events. Thus you can say '*I have been studying English since 1996*' and '*I have studied English since 1996*' with very little difference in meaning.

Past and Future

Past and future tense of this aspect work exactly the same. **Past perfect +** *since/for* is used for past states/repeated events continuing up until a time in the past, and **past perfect continuous** is used for an incomplete events continuing up until a past time. Future uses **future perfect +** *since/for* and **future perfect continuous**.

> **Examples**
> I *had been* a teacher for five years <u>when it happened</u>.   I *will have been* a teacher for 20 years <u>by 2021</u>.
> I *had been teaching* for an hour <u>when it happened</u>.   I *will have been teaching* for 8 hours <u>by 6pm</u>.

Two uses of past perfect

Thus, we now have two uses for past perfect. The main use is to show the order of events as described in the previous section. The second use, **combined with** *since* or *for* shows that a past event continued until another past event.

Summary of past perfect so far		
Past perfect (Complete events)	I went to the city when I had finished my homework	(First I finished my homework; then I went to the city.)
Past perfect + since for (states & repeated events)	I had loved with her for five years by the time that we got married.	(My loved continued from five years before we got married until we got married.)

Exercises

5.1 Change the verbs in this passage to either show that the verb is located now in time (present simple or present continuous) or that it continued until now (present perfect continuous or present perfect + since/for).

Earth _____ (have) an amazing variety of life on it. There _____ (be) huge trees, tiny bugs, intelligent ocean living creatures, and furry dogs. There _____ (be) living creatures on Earth since 3 billion years ago. Since then, it _____ (evolve) in weird and wonderful ways. For the last millennia, however, homo sapiens _____ (dominate) the Earth. Homo sapiens now _____ (have) the largest brain of all the land creatures. Yet, with that power there _____ (be) responsibility; something that human kind _____ (abuse) since the beginning of the industrial age.

5.2 Change the verbs in this passage to either show that the verb is located in the past in time (past simple or past continuous) or that it continued until a past time (past perfect continuous or past perfect + since/for).

I _____ (be) interested in the subject since I was a teenager. I _____ (have) research tools since my 16th birthday, which I _____ (use) regularly until I was in university. Surprisingly, though, there _____ (not be) very many developments in the field for about 30 years until the publication of my Phd Thesis. People _____ (study) related topics when this influential paper _____ (be published), but did not focus on the exact issue that my paper focused on. I _____ (write) it in 1966 and 1967 when I _____ (study) at Vatalia University.

(4) Showing a connection between a past event and a present event

This is probably the hardest aspect to understand in English and is the one that most students struggle with. Remember that we said that the present perfect has three main uses in English: (1) to show that a state continues until the present, (2) to show a connection between a past event and the present, and (3) to show that we have

Chapter 5

had an experience. Here we are looking at the second use. Notice that **this aspect is only possible with complete events**.

Consider the following two sentences:

> *I __lost__ my passport.*
>
> *I __have lost__ my passport.*

The first sentence indicates that the passport was lost in the past, but it tells us nothing about now. Maybe I have now found my passport.

The second sentence also indicates that I lost my passport in the past, but the important thing is that this is a problem **now**. **Now** it is a problem that I have lost it.

Deciding if the verb should be in past simple or present perfect

There are a couple of rules that you can follow to see whether you should be using past simple or present perfect.

(1) **Look for a time word** (time words can include: *in 1982, yesterday, after I finished, while I was doing it*); if there is a time word, it must be **past simple** because present perfect never has a time word. (The exception to this rule are *since* and *for*; these are usually followed by present perfect to show that the event continued until now.)

> ### Examples
> Twenty years ago, not many people *realised* that computers would become so important.
>
> Many jobs *disappeared* when computers arrived in the work place.

(2) If there is **no time word**, think about whether the verb is true about now. If it is not true about now, it must be past simple. If it is true about now, it is probably present perfect.

> ### Examples
> Workers who *spent* all day working with numbers can now use computers for the same task.
> (They do not spend all day doing this nowadays.)
>
> However, employers complain that these workers *have become* dependent on calculators.
> (They are dependent on calculators nowadays.)

Exercises

6.1 Decide if the following verbs should be in present perfect or past simple.

1) Computers _____ (change) people's lives. In the past, people _____ (have) to do calculations on a piece of paper or with an abacus. Today's children, however, _____ (grow up) without needing to use computers and as a result, often _____ (not learn) to do calculations in their heads.

2) Military conflicts have changed over the last 2000 years. Roman military conflicts _____ (be fought) with swords and wooden shields. Medieval military conflicts _____ (be fought) with swords, metal shields, and catapults. Since the 1500s, conflicts have been fought with guns. Now, however, military leaders _____ (learn) to use a wide array of computer-assisted weaponry. In fact, weapons _____ (be developed) that can remotely send missiles to a target pin-pointed by a satellite.

3) The invention of the automobile _____ (revolutionise) the way of life in many countries. People who _____ (have) to walk for days to reach a city can now reach the city in hours, while people who _____ (live) on the edge of cities can now get to the city in less than an hour. This _____ (lead) to a massive boom in the number of people living on the edge of cities and _____ (lead) to the phenomenal growth of sprawling cities like Los Angeles, Sydney, and Tokyo.

4) Unfortunately, I _____ (be asked) to switch off the wireless router by the university because it _____ (cause) some problems campus wide. I _____ (log) a request for the wired points to

be activated throughout the building, but _____ (not receive) yet a response from them. I _____ (not realise) that this would happen if we used a wireless router as the university _____ (not tell) me that such problems could arise.

(5) Showing that an experience has happened

The final use of present perfect is to show that you have had an experience at some stage in your life. We are not interested in when the experience happened, only in the fact that it happened. We never use a time word with this aspect. Complete events and states can both be experiences.

> **Examples**
> I have been to New York twice. *Or* I have tried sushi.

Summary of present perfect so far		
(A) Present perfect + since/for	The patient has had measles since Monday.	(This means that the measles started on Monday and continued until now.)
(B) Present perfect (result)	The patient has caught measles.	(This means that the patient caught measles in the past and that this is an issue now.)
(C) Present perfect (experience)	The patient has had measles twice.	(This means that the patient caught measles twice at some time in their life. We are more interested in the fact that the patient has had this disease than in *when* the patient had the disease.)

Exercises

7.1 Decide which of the following sentences are using present perfect to mean continuity until now (write 'A'), which are using it to mean result (write 'B'), and which are using it to mean experience (write 'C').

1) [ ] The People's Party has won 4 elections in the country's history.

2) [ ] The computer has automatically deleted the infected files.

3) [ ] The computer system has been down for an hour now.

4) [ ] The Progressive Party have won the election.

5) [ ] She has written two books.

6) [ ] We have been working on this project since 1996.

7) [ ] The economy has generally improved in recent times.

8) [ ] The stock market has crashed a number of times in the last century.

9) [ ] People have been unwilling to invest in the stock market since the crash last year.

7.2 Read the following sentences and decide which aspect is being used in each. Use the numbers 1-5 below:

    (1) Location in time
    (2) Showing order of events
    (3) Showing that one event continues until another
    (4) Showing a connection between a past event and a present event
    (5) Showing that an experience has happened

1) Rising levels of carbon dioxide **are causing** global temperatures to rise. [ ]

2) The burning of fossil fuels **has resulted** in more than 25% more carbon dioxide in the atmosphere since records **began**. [ ] [ ]

3) Global warming **will create** terrible disasters for humans such as rising sea levels, which **might flood** cities and towns around the world. [ ] [ ]

Chapter 5

4) Global warming **has been causing** sea levels to rise, and this **has led** to the disappearance of some Pacific islands. [   ] [   ]

5) Studies **have shown** that snowfall in the Antarctic **keeps** a balance with melting glaciers there. [   ] [   ]

6) But at the time of these studies, warming in Greenland and the arctic **was causing** ice to melt faster than fresh snow could fall. [   ]

7) The melting ice in the Arctic Ocean **will not contribute** to rising sea levels because when ice floating in water melts, it **displaces** the water that it **has been floating** in. [   ] [   ] [   ]

8) Thermal expansion **happens** when an object is heated; the object **becomes** larger. [   ] [   ]

9) By the year 2050, thermal expansion **will probably have caused** seas levels to rise 50 centimetres. [   ]

10) When we look back in the year 2050, we **will probably wish** that we **had done** something to prevent global warming at the start of the century. [   ] [   ]

7.3 Read the following passages and change the verbs to the appropriate tense. Use the information in this chapter to help decide which tense to use. Use the information in the first part of this chapter to make sure that you construct the tenses correctly.

So that we _____ (understand) future weather patterns, we _____ (need) to look to the past. For the last few million years, the world _____ (move) in and out of glacial periods. Most people _____ (call) glacial periods ice ages, but actually an ice age _____ (be) a period during which ice _____ (cover) at least a part of the earth. At the moment, ice _____ (cover) parts of the north and south poles; therefore, the earth _____ (be) currently in an ice age. During a glacial period, ice _____ (extend) much further south. During the last ice age, ice sheets _____ (extend) almost as far south as Italy in Europe, and as far south as the great lakes in North America, which that ice age _____ (create).

As we _____ (say) before, the earth _____ (move) in and out of glacial periods for over a million years. Glacial periods usually _____ (last) around 100,000 years; the warm periods in between, which scientists _____ (call) interglacial periods, usually _____ (last) around 10,000 years. The longest that an interglacial period _____ (last) _____ (be) 12,000 years. The current interglacial period _____ (last) 10,000 years. This _____ (mean) that a glacial period _____ (begin) very soon. If this _____ (be) true, in the future, the world _____ (not heat) up, it _____ (cool) down.

Temperatures _____ (not remain) constant during glacial periods. During the last glacial, temperatures sometimes _____ (spike) at temperatures much the same as today's temperatures. These warm periods sometimes _____ (last) for a few years. During the last glacial, primitive humans _____ (spread) out across Europe and Asia. They _____ (hunt) the mammoths that _____ (evolve) for that cold weather. At the same time, Homo Neanderthal, a creature that _____ (be) very similar to humans, _____ (live) successfully throughout Europe. Both the mammoth and Homo Neanderthal _____ (die) out when the last glacial _____ (end) because they _____ (be) unable to cope with an environment which _____ (change) rapidly.

When the next glacial comes, it _____ (be) difficult for humans. The cities that we _____ (build) _____ (depend) heavily on large-scale agriculture. Farms across the world _____ (fail); without food, there _____ (be) no food in shops. Millions of people _____ (starve and die). People who survive _____ (live) in a world in which society _____ (break) down. There _____ (be) no police and no armies, and people _____ (have) to scavenge for food. By the time that the glacial ends, 100,000 years in the future, humans _____ (evolve) again into quite different creatures to what we are today.

Reporting in present tense and back-shifting

We report written work that has been published in present simple. Spoken words can be reported in which ever tense is logical, and works published many years ago (e.g. 1000 years ago) can be reported in past simple, but works that have been published in recent years are always reported in present simple. They are treated as *states* since the words have become permanent.

Examples

Jacobs <u>argues</u> that this is not the case. **Or** Watanabe <u>claims</u> that more needs to be done to further the cause. In his article 'High and Dry', Lee <u>states</u> that people living in low-lying atolls are doomed.

When we do use past simple to report what somebody said or wrote, we sometimes need to change the tense in the noun clause.

Back-shifting in past tense

Consider the following sentence:

> **He said that he is researching this topic in detail.**

In this sentence, the person spoke in the past. At that time, he was researching the topic, but it might not be the case that he is researching it now. If it was true at that time but not now, we change the tense of the verb in the noun clause to past tense. If it is true at the time of writing, we use present tense. *States* are often true at the time or writing, while events have often become untrue.

Examples

At the meeting, Jacobs <u>argued</u> that this <u>is</u> not the case. (It is not the case *now*.)

During the conference, Watanabe <u>pointed out</u> that more <u>needed</u> to be done to further the cause. (This was true during the conference, but is not true now.)

If the verb is already in past tense, we may change it to past perfect. Consider the following sentence:

> **'I didn't believe in God when I was young.'**

This might be reported as:

> **He pointed out that he hadn't believed in God when he had been young.**

This is a third use of past perfect that wasn't listed in the earlier section on tense and aspect.

Back-shifting in future tense

When we are reporting that somebody spoke about the future, we may use the word **would**. This word shows that what the person said was in the future but is now in the past.

Examples

Wednesday – Smith: 'I <u>will</u> be late on Friday.'

Friday – James says that Smith said that he <u>would</u> be late today.

Exercises

8.1 Change the tense if it is needed when you report the following sentences

1) Einstein: 'We only use 10% of our brain in our lifetime.'

   Einstein said that _____

   _____

2) Eisenhower: 'The Russians are developing a nuclear bomb.'

   _____

   _____

3) Al Gore: 'The world has limited resources and we should use those resources wisely.'

   _____

   _____

4) Einstein: 'Anyone who has never made a mistake has never tried anything new.'

   _____

   _____

5) A priest: 'We did not know that child abuse was a crime.'

_____

_____

6) Kennedy: 'Communism has never come to power in a country that was not disrupted by war or corruption, or both.

_____

_____

8.2 Report these sentences using would if needed.

1) Hitler: 'The Third Reich will last 100 years.'

_____

_____

2) Walt Disney: 'Nobody will want to hear people talk in movies.'

_____

_____

3) IPCC: 'The world will run out of oil in 2030.'

_____

_____

4) Matlock: 'The Earth will experience another glacial period (ice age) within the next couple of thousand years.'

_____

_____

5) Kennedy: 'We will commit ourselves to sending a man to the moon.'

_____

_____

Future tense back-shifted in adverbial clauses

The story of English tense becomes even more complicated when we consider future tense in adverbial clauses of time.

Adverbial clauses of **time** and **condition** always follow the patterns in the table on the right:

It doesn't matter what aspect the verb in either

Independent clause	Adverbial clause of time
Past	Past
Present	Present
Future	*Present*

clause is in, it will still follow the above patterns. Of course, the adverbial clause can also come *after* the independent clause, so a future independent clause might *be followed* by a present adverbial clause. Consider the following examples:

Examples

Past: When I had finished my English homework, I began my research project.
       Past perfect   *Past simple*

Present: Whenever I am writing a long essay, I try to remember the advice of my English teacher.
          Present continuous   *Present simple*

Future:

When I finish my English homework, I will begin my research project.
    Present simple   *Future simple*

Future:

I will think about it while I am collecting evidence.
Future simple   *Present continuous*

I will begin to collate the data when I have finished collecting evidence.
Future simple   *Present perfect*

Check your grammar carefully when you have finished writing!
Future simple   *Present perfect*

The most important point here is that future perfect changes to present perfect in adverbial clauses relating to the future. This means that we now have *4 uses of the present perfect*:

    1) To show that a state or repeated event continued until the present

    2) To show that a past event has a result in the present or is somehow connected to the present

    3) To show that a person or other creature has had an experience at some point in their life

    4) Future perfect in adverbial clauses

Notice also that instructions and orders that use the imperative (For example: **sit down! Shut up! Go outside!**) are referring to the future; they are saying '***after now, I want you to do this***'. Thus, when there is an adverbial clause after them, it should move back to present tense. If it is future perfect, it will become present perfect. In the example above: ***check your grammar carefully when you have finished writing***, the speaker is saying that the *when clause* should happen first and then the independent clause.

Remember that past perfect and future perfect show the order of events.

    (1) I will finish the research. (2) I will begin to correlate the data.

This becomes either: '***I will finish the research and then I will begin to correlate the data***' or '***I will begin to correlate the data. I will have finished the research by then.***' The future perfect shows that the research will be finished first. Once we use an adverbial clause, however, it becomes: ***I will begin to correlate the data when I have finished the research*** (***will have finished → have finished***).

Exercises

9.1 Write logical adverbial clauses of time for each of the following sentences, or change it to an adverbial clause and add an independent clause.

    1) I will work for that department. _____

        _____

    2) I will write my essay. _____

        _____

    3) I did a lot of research. _____

        _____

    4) I am working on this aspect of my research paper. _____

        _____

    5) I will think about that research that topic. _____

        _____

    6) I will do a lot of research on the issue. _____

        _____

    7) I will have researched whether there is any basis behind these claims. _____

        _____

    8) I have studied English. _____

9.2 Join together the following sentences using the subordinators given.

    1) The law will be passed / there will be more civil liberty (as soon as)

        _____

    2) The world's oil supplies will be depleted / there will be no more plastic (when)

        _____

    3) The university will have a graduation ceremony / you will complete your degree (once)

        _____

    4) Write your first draft / re-write your essay making sure you find all the errors (after)

        _____

    5) Write your essay / try to include as many references as possible (when)

Tense and Conditionals

Conditional statements affect tense in ways not described in the above sections. Conditionals are a type of adverbial clause. Firstly, it is important to remember that there are two types of conditionals in English:

1) **possible**
2) **unlikely**

Examples

Possible – If you **get** 6.5 in the language test, you **will be** able to university.
Unlikely – If you **were** in the other class, you **would** have studied this.

Notice that the **possible** conditionals use **present tense** in the adverbial clause and **do not** use **would** in the independent clause. **Unlikely** conditionals use **past tense** (see note) in the adverbial clause and **would** in the independent clause.

Note

Actually we do not use past tense in the **unlikely** conditionals; we use something called the **'subjunctive'**. Mostly this looks like the past tense of the verb, but there is one exception; the subjunctive form of the verb **be** is **were**, and it does not change for subject-verb agreement. This means that we say '**if I were rich**' not '**if I was rich**'. However, many native speakers ignore this rule, so it is not particularly important that you follow it. Because the subjunctive looks like the past tense in every other case, you, remembering that **unlikely** conditionals are use the past tense is easier than remembering what the word 'subjunctive' means.

Put simply, these two types of conditionals can be used in different tenses can be used in different tenses in the following ways:

Possible

Conditional clause	Independent clause
Future: present (Follows the rules for adverbial clauses in the previous section – independent clause in future tense / adverbial clause in present tense (see page 86)	*Future*: future
Present: present	*Future*: future *Present*: present *Past*: Past
Past: past	*Future*: future *Present*: present *Past*: past

Examples
Future
If he finishes his homework in time, he can go out. *(present simple/present simple)*
If he has not arrived by 6pm tonight, I will have been waiting for 48 hours. *(present perfect/future prefect continuous)*

Examples
Present
If he is the person who makes the decision, I have already lost the contract. *(present simple/present perfect)*
If he is making the decision now, I will have to wait a bit longer. *(present continuous/future simple)*
If he has already made the decision, I was wrong to be impatient. *(present perfect/past simple)*

> **Examples**
> **Past**
> If he made the decision yesterday, I will not win the contract. *(past simple/future simple)*
> If he was making the decision when I saw him, I am in trouble. *(past simple/present simple)*

'Unlikely' conditionals follow the same patterns except that they use the past tense (actually the 'subjunctive') and the modal **would**.

Unlikely

Conditional clause	Independent clause
Future: future is unusual with 'unlikely' clauses. (See Chapter 6, pages 123-129 on adverbial clauses for more explanation of this.)	
Present: past	**Future**: would + V **Present**: would + V **Past**: unusual
Past: past perfect	**Future**: would + V **Present**: would + V **Past**: would have + PP

> **Examples**
> **Present**
> If I won the lottery, I would not come to work tomorrow.
> If I won the lottery, I would not be standing here right now.

> **Examples**
> **Past**
> If I had won last week's lottery, I would go on holiday next week.
> If I had won last week's lottery, I would not be standing here now.
> If I had won last week's lottery, I would not have come to work yesterday.

A more detailed explanation of conditionals can be found in Chapter 6 on adverbial clauses on page 123.

Exercises

10.1 Put the verbs into the correct tenses in the following statements.

1) If you _____ (add) Omega 3 to a child's diet, it helps the synapses in their brain strengthen.

2) If Hitler _____ (stop) when he invaded Czechoslovakia, World War II would probably not have happened.

3) If I _____ (be) president of the world, I would bring an end to poverty and hunger.

4) If a female _____ (win) the next election in the USA, It will be a great victory for women's rights.

5) If the nuclear bomb _____ (not be invented), there might have been many more intense wars in the latter half of the 20th century.

6) If humans _____ (settle) on the moon, they will need to find a reliable source of water and oxygen.

7) If this movie _____ (be made), we would be able to make a lot of money.

8) If children _____ (be exposed) to more than one language as an infant, they are often slow to learn to speak.

9) If you _____ (do) all of the readings, you would have known that this issue has been researched at length.

Chapter 5

Some other issues with tense

There are a number of other considerations that need to be made when selecting tense. The following are some common considerations.

Options with future tense

We have a number of options with future simple for complete events. *Will* or other modals such as *might*, *may*, or *could*, are used to show that the event has been decided at the time of speaking.

> **Examples**
>
> Have you decided what you want to do? I think I will ask the questions; can you write down the responses?

We can use *be going to* to show that the event has been planned or already decided.

> **Examples**
>
> What are you going to do for the research project? I am going to research the effects of AIDS on small villages in Zambia.

We can use **present continuous** with much the same meaning as *be going to*, but it should be noted that present continuous refers to the near future.

> **Examples**
>
> What are you doing next? I'm doing the most interesting part.

We use **present simple** when we want to show that the future events are in a schedule or a timetable.

> **Examples**
>
> When do you leave for New York? The conference is tomorrow, so we leave this afternoon.

Waxing and waning

Present continuous is sometimes used with **comparatives** (V ~er / more V) to show that a **state** is waxing and waning. This means that it is **growing** or **becoming less**. It suggests change. Consider the following examples:

In the first example, the state *become* is used in present continuous with the comparative '**warmer**' to show that the world is changing. *Become* is frequently used in this way. In the second case, *look* is used in the same way.

> **Examples**
>
> The world is becoming warm**er**.
> The Atlantic Ocean is looking **more** like a sewer everyday.

Temporary states

Actually, there are **two types of states**: **strong** and **weak**. *Weak states can be used in the continuous form to show that they are* **temporarily true**. Strong states, on the other hand, are never used like this.

An example of a weak state is *be*. For example: *She is being stupid*. (This does not mean that she is a stupid person; it means that at the moment, the way she is behaving is stupid.)

An example of a strong state is *have*. For example, we would never say: *I am having a car*. Note though, that *have* has several meanings and there are some meanings of *have* which are events, which can be used in the continuous (e.g. *I am having breakfast*).

States that are used in the continuous in this way can be used in past, present, or future *continuous* or in past, present, or future *perfect*

> **Examples**
>
> This project is costing us considerably more than we expected it too.
> These people are being unreasonable with their claims.

continuous. Examples of some strong states include: *have*, *belong*, *contain*, *matter*, and *own*.

Repeated events can sometimes be used in this way. For example, we might say: *the lab frog population is eating a kind of mould at the moment.* This does not mean that they are eating mould as we speak (though it may have this meaning if the context was right); it means that they are always doing this, but that this situation is temporary. (source: *Cambridge Grammar of English Language 2002*, p168)

Other uses of present continuous and past simple

It is also important to note that a lot of people use present simple and present continuous to describe past events. This is an irritating habit that has become popular in modern times. There is little difference in meaning, but the intended feeling is that the listener feels like they are involved in a past event or story.

> **Examples**
> As the Russians close in on Berlin, Hitler is starting to get nervous. His face gradually becomes more haggard and creased. His behaviour is becoming more erratic, and his hair is greyer than ever.

Exercises

11.1 Write sentences using the following prompts

1) (Will for future) _____

_____

2) (Be going to for future) _____

_____

3) (Present continuous for future) _____

_____

4) (Present simple for future) _____

_____

5) (Present continuous to show waxing and waning) _____

_____

6) (Present continuous for temporary state) _____

_____

7) (Present tense for past story) _____

_____

Complete summary of present perfect	
Present perfect to show that a state continued from the past to the present. Used with for/since	*Climate change has been an issue since the 1980s*
Present perfect to show a connection between a past event and the present or to show a result in the present.	*Allegations of climate change have led to a greater environmental awareness.*
Present perfect to show a past experience.	*The world has experienced several major climatic changes throughout its history.*
Present perfect instead of future perfect in adverbial clauses.	*When the world has run out of petrol, climate change will be less of a worry.*
Present perfect used to show simple past tense in non-finite clauses (see Chapter 6, pages 93-94 for more).	*Climate change is thought to have been the cause of the death of Homo-Neanderthal around 10,000 BC.*

Complete summary of past perfect	
Past perfect to show that one event happened before another.	*Once the combustion engine **had been invented**, oil suddenly became very valuable.*
Past perfect to show that one past state continued until another.	*People **had believed** that oil had interesting properties for many years before the combustion engine was invented.*
Past perfect used in back-shifted reported speech	*In 1879, Karl Benz stated that he **had invented** and produced the first automatic carriage; it ran on oil using a combustion engine.*
Past perfect used in 'unlikely' conditional adverbial clauses	*If the Romans **had** not **been invaded** by barbarians, they may have invented the combustion engine too.*

Non–finite tense

Infinitive, gerund, and participial tenses

It is important to understand how tense is formed with non-finite clauses as well as with finite clauses, partly because you need to know this to construct non-finite clauses, and partly because these tense formations are also used with modals.

Tense and aspect can also be shown in non-finite clauses. A full range of tenses cannot be shown, but past, present, and future can be expressed. Active and passive voice can also be shown, as can the continuous, perfect, and perfect continuous aspects.

There are two important points to remember about tense in non-finite verbs. Firstly, modals cannot be used (so future tense can only be expressed through the phrase **be going to**. Secondly, past tense can only be expressed using the structure **have to**. This means that it is hard to tell the difference between the past simple and the present perfect.

Infinitive Tense

Infinitive clauses frequently show tense. This occurs in a range of different uses of infinitives. For more information on infinitives, their uses, and their construction, see Chapter 2, page 25, and Chapter 3, pages 38-44. In the following table, V = base form of verb, PP = past participle

Infinitive tense		Past	Present	Future
Simple	Active	*To have PP**	To V	To be going to V
	Passive	*To have been PP**	To be PP	To be going to be PP
Continuous	Active	*To have been V~ing*	To be V~ing	To be going to be V~ing
	Passive	*To have been being PP*	To be being PP	To be going to be being PP
Perfect	Active	*To have PP**	*To have PP**	To be going to have PP
	Passive	*To have been PP**	*To have been PP**	To be going to have been PP
Perfect Continuous	Active	*To have been V~ing*	To have been V~ing	To be going to have been V~ing
	Passive	*To have been being PP*	To have been being PP	To be going to have been being PP

*Note that the forms for the **present perfect**, **past perfect**, and **past simple** are <u>the same</u>.

Following are some examples of some of the different aspects that can be created in infinitive clauses.

Examples

Present simple
She has asked him ***to re-write*** his paper.

Present passive simple
She has asked for his paper ***to be re-written***.

Past simple
He is reported ***to have presented*** this idea back in 1984. (Note that this must be past simple since the time word is given. Remember that present perfect is only used with the time words *since* and *for*.)

Present perfect
He is known ***to have invented*** a new mechanism that doubles production time. (Note that since no time word is used, we can presume that this is present perfect.)

Future simple
He is thought ***to be going to present*** an explanation of this at the up-coming seminar.

Present continuous
He is said ***to be working*** on a new theory relating to this.

Gerund Tense

Gerunds show tense and aspect in gerund clauses but not when they act as nouns. An example might be: ***Due to his <u>not having conducted</u> thorough research, the results of his paper have been largely discredited.*** (A gerund noun, however, might be: ***<u>the conducting</u> of thorough research has not happened in this case***.)

Gerund tense works in much the same way as infinitive tense, but notice that there is no difference between **active present simple** and **active present continuous**. (For information about construction of gerunds see Chapters 2, page 19 & Chapter 3, pages 35; for information about when to use gerunds see Chapter 3, page 35, and Chapter 11, page 191.)

Gerund tense		Past	Present	Future
Simple	Active	*Having PP**	*V~ing***	*Being going to V***
	Passive	*Having been PP**	*Being PP***	*Being going to be PP***
Continuous	Active	*Having been V~ing*	*V~ing***	*Being going to V***
	Passive	*Havig been being PP*	*Being PP***	*Being going to be PP***
Perfect	Active	*Having PP**	*Having PP**	Being going to have PP
	Passive	*Having been PP**	*Having been PP**	Being going to have been PP
Perfect Continuous	Active	*Having been V~ing*	Having been V~ing	Being going to have been V~ing
	Passive	*Having been being PP*	Having been being PP	Being going to have been being PP

*Note that the forms for the **present perfect**, **past perfect**, and **past simple** are <u>the same</u>.
Note that the forms for the **present simple, and **present continuous** are <u>the same</u>.

> ### *Examples*
> **Present simple**
> She anticipated him ***rewriting*** his paper.
>
> **Present passive simple**
> She has anticipated his paper ***being rewritten***.
>
> **Past simple**
> His ***having rewritten*** his paper yesterday caused some surprise.
>
> **Present perfect**
> Her ***having studied*** Swahili for several years was unknown to the researchers.
>
> **Future simple**
> Her ***being going to study*** Farsi was also unknown to the researchers.
>
> **Present continuous**
> Him ***concentrating*** on the road at the time of the accident was interrupted by her screams.

Exercises

1.1 Write the following verbs first as gerunds, then as infinitives in the tense given in brackets.

	(Gerund)	*(Infinitive)*
1) Broaden (present continuous)	_____	_____
2) Enlarge (present perfect)	_____	_____
3) Deteriorate (past simple)	_____	_____
4) Reduce (present perfect continuous)	_____	_____

Chapter 6

5) Modify (future simple) _____ _____

6) Confine (passive present simple) _____ _____

7) Restrict (passive past simple) _____ _____

8) Emphasise (passive present perfect) _____ _____

9) Speculate (passive future simple) _____ _____

10) Generate (passive present perfect continuous) _____ _____

1.2 Decide which tense and form to put into the gaps in the following passage. Use the verbs in brackets. Passives are written in the form be V. Negatives are in the form not V.

It is said _____ (be) ten thousand years since the last ice age. Since then, temperatures _____ (fluctuate) quite significantly. We can see rises and falls in temperature of several degrees. During a warmer period four thousand years ago, humans _____ (begin) to build the first farms and cities, and we _____ (track) temperatures from that time by looking at the price of food crops. Prices _____ (go up) for a significant period in the past _____ (indicate) temperatures _____ (be) colder at that time; with prices _____ (go) down at certain points in the past, temperatures are understood _____ (be) warmer. To map temperatures prior to the onset of these ancient civilisations, we _____ (look) at tree rings and ice cores drilled in the Greenland ice sheet. Tree rings are also known _____ (tell) us a lot about temperatures in ancient times. Rings _____ (be) thicker tells us that temperatures _____ (be) warmer; thin rings resulted from temperatures _____ (be) cooler.

Of course, much more information about temperatures in the last 1000 years _____ (know). Around 1000 years ago, temperatures are known _____ (be) significantly warmer than today. This is thought _____ (allow) the Viking people of Scandinavia _____ (increase) their populations and _____ (spread) out across the world. Historians _____ (believe) the Vikings not only _____ (settle) in Greenland and _____ (farm) land too cold to farm today, but also _____ (settle) in Canada, which they _____ (call) Vinland, or land of vines, even though today Canada _____ (be) too cold to grow vines. This period _____ (refer) to as the Medieval Warm Period. The Medieval Warm Period _____ (be) a time that _____ (enjoy) great prosperity. Crops across Europe and Asia _____ (be) bountiful; cities _____ (expanded), and people _____ (be) wealthy.

Modals

We use modals for five purposes in English. These purposes are:

1. **Politeness**
2. **Permission**
3. **Obligation / advice**
4. **Certainty / probability / hedging**
5. **Ability**

Forming Modals

Modals are *always* followed by the **bare infinitive**. This means that only the base form of a verb is used after a modal.

Remember that the **infinitive** is the **to V** form of the verb, e.g. *to determine, to assess, to radiate*. The **bare infinitive** is the same except that *to* has been deleted, e.g. *determine*, *assess*, *radiate*. This form differs from the finite form of the verb because it **does not change for subject verb agreement** and because it changes for tense and aspect following the patterns outlined above for infinitive tense.

> **Examples**
> **Correct:**   He can speak Spanish.
> **Incorrect:**   He can speaks Spanish. X
>
> **Correct:**   I ought to have gone to Spain.
> **Incorrect:**   I ought to went to Spain. X

Only one modal in a clause

Remember, only *one* modal can be used with each verb.

> **Examples**
> **Correct:**   He might be able to speak Spanish.
> **Incorrect:**   He might can speak Spanish. X

A list of modals and modal-like structures include:

> **Modals and semi-modals:**
>
> | | | | |
> |---|---|---|---|
> | *be able to** | *had better* | *might* | *shall* |
> | *be allowed to** | *have/has got to** | *must* | *should* |
> | *can* | *have to** | *need to** | *will* |
> | *could* | *may* | *ought to* | *would* |

Notice that several of the modal-like structures in this list with a star* are *actually* **verbs**. These verbs function in the same way as modals, so they have been listed here with modals. However, **unlike modals, they must change tense and agree with the subject**.

Notice that **can** has a past tense **could**, but does not have a future tense. To form future tense, you need to either use **be able to** or **be allowed to** depending on the intended meaning.

No modal in non-finite clause

Notice, also, that non-finite clauses cannot contain modals.

> **Examples**
> **Correct:**   The government's policy on climate change will **possibly** cause them **to lose** the election.
> **Incorrect:**   The government's policy on climate change will cause them **to might lose** the election. X

Politeness

Although it is unlikely that you will use modals of politeness in academic writing, it is still important to understand how they differ from other types of modals. These modals are used to soften questions and instructions to make them seem more polite. They have no actual meaning other than to show politeness.

> **The modals used for politeness are:**
>
> | | | | | | |
> |---|---|---|---|---|---|
> | *can* | *could* | *may* | *might* | *should* | *would* |

> **Examples**
> **Can** you help me? (In other words: help me!) **or** **Could** you please finish quickly? (In other words: finish quickly!)

Note that **might** is a slightly old fashioned word, and that **would** is usually used in set phrases such as **would you mind**, and **would you be able to**.

Permission

Sometimes we want to give or deny permission in academic writing. For example, **people cannot continue to mistreat animals the way that the have been**. Here, the writer is saying that she or he does not believe that people should have permission to mistreat animals.

> **The modals used for permission are:**
>
> | | | | |
> |---|---|---|---|
> | *be allowed to* | *can* | *could* | *may* |

Note that **could** is usually used in requests for permission. Notice, too, that **can** and **could** do **not mean ability** in this sense, they show what people are allowed to and are not allowed to do.

Chapter 6

> **Examples**
>
> You **can** say what you like. **Or** They **can** make these claims, but that does not make them right.

Note that the negative of **can** is one word: **cannot**.

Obligation/advice

Modals of obligation and advice are often used in academic writing.

> **The modals used for obligation and advice are:**
>
> | had better | have to | may | need to | ought to | should |
> | --- | --- | --- | --- | --- | --- |

Note that **must** shows personal opinion, while **have to** can either be personal opinion or a **fact**.

> **Examples**
>
> **Personal opinion:** You must visit London if you are in Europe. **Or** You have to visit London if you are in Europe.
>
> **Fact:** You have to get a proper visa if you want to work in England.

Modals of obligation and advice can be grouped into **choice and no choice**.

Thus, **must and have to leave the person with no choice** (in positive sentences) and **ought to and should leave the person with choice**. *Need to* suggests no choice, but is not as strong as *have to* or *must*.

> **Examples**
>
> **No choice:** The government **must** listen to these experts, or they will face serious problems in the future.
>
> **Choice:** We **should** pay attention to this problem.

Negatives

Notice that **have to has a different meaning in the negative**. *Don't have to* means that the person can do it if they want to, but if they don't that is their choice. Notice also that we sometimes use **should not** to mean **must not**. For example, somebody might say *you shouldn't smoke in here* when they mean you must not.

Note that **should** is much stronger that **don't have to**. **Should** means that it is really better if you do it. **Don't have to** means that you really have a choice.

Choice	No Choice
don't have to	have to
had better	must
ought to	must not
ought not	
should	
should not	

> **Examples**
>
> You **have to** do your homework, but you **don't have to** do question 3. (Question 3 is optional.)
>
> You **should** wear formal clothes, but you **don't have** to wear a tie. (A tie is optional.)

Ability

Modals of ability are commonly used in everyday speech and sometimes used in academic writing.

> **The modals used for ability are:**
>
> | be able to | can | could |
> | --- | --- | --- |

These modals show that a person has the capability to do something.

> **Examples**
>
> We **can** all understand the theory of evolution much better thanks to Leakey's work.
>
> Scientists were better **able to** understand the physics of motion once Einstein's work had been published.

Could tends to be used with states and repeated verbs; **be able to** tends to be used with complete events. *I could walk to work* tends to mean that I had the ability do it **regularly**, whereas, *I was able to walk to work* tends to mean that I had the ability to do it **once**.

Probability / Certainty / Future Tense / hedging

These are the most commonly used modals in academic writing. They are used to form **future tense** and to add doubt to present tense or even past tense statements. These modals can be ranked in probability from very certain to very uncertain. **Hedging** is explained in more detail in a future section.

Probability

| 100% will | 75% ought to / should | 35% could / may / might | 0% will not |

Will, *should*, and ***ought to*** are all used for future tense constructions. ***Might, may,*** and ***could*** are all used for **past**, **present**, and **future.**

Examples

Future

Global warming *will* be a serious problem in the future.

The fuss about global warming *should* die out soon.

People *may* forget about global warming in a few years.

Present

Global warming *may* be a serious problem today.

Past

Global warming may have caused the incredible flooding last year.

Sometimes we use ***must*** as a modal of probability in the **present** and **past tense**.

Examples

He *must* be telling the truth. (Surely he is telling the truth.)

He *must* have left already. (The only possible explanation is that he already left.)

Tenses

As we said above, modals are always followed by the bare infinitive, so we can't use a past or future tense after the modal. However, we can still show tense using modals.

For semi (verbal) modals such as ***have to, be allowed to, be able to,*** we change the tense of the first verb.

We say that these verbs are *modal-like*, because they modify verbs in the same way as modals do, but unlike true modals, they can be preceded by a modal and can change tense and subject-verb agreement.

Examples

*I **had to** go to class yesterday.*

*I **will** be allowed to leave early tomorrow.*

Only the modals of obligation/advice really change tense. These modals change tense using the bare in the same way that the infinitive changes tense.

Past tense

Note that past tense is formed by using the **perfect aspect.**

Examples

Present: I should finish this essay by Friday.

Past: I should have finished this essay by last Friday.

Not: I should finished this essay by last Friday. (Incorrect)

Must have vs Should have

Note the difference in meaning between ***must/might/could have*** and ***should have.***

Should have is the direct past tense of ***should***. However, ***must/might/could have*** show **probability**. Thus, to show the past tense of ***must*** when ***must*** means **obligation/advice**, we have to either use ***had to*** or ***should have***. ***Must have*** means that the only possible explanation is that it happened. ***Might/could*** *have* means that it is possible that it happened.

Examples

Obligation Present: You must finish your essay by Friday.

Past: You should have finished your essay by Friday.

Probability Present: He must be telling the truth. (The only possible explanation is that he is telling the truth.)

Past: He must have been telling the truth. (The only possible explanation is that he *was* telling the truth.)

Chapter 6

Problems with future tense

Modals are not usually used with the future tense because mostly they refer to what is about to happen. However, it is possible to use some modals with the future tense construction **be going to**, to give a sense that the event will happen in the very near future.

The following chart shows how to create tense and aspect using true modals.

Simple aspect		
	Active voice	**Passive voice**
Past	Modal + have + PP *Example* He might have claimed this.	Modal + have + been + PP *Example* This might have been claimed
Present	Modal + V *Example* He might claim this.	Modal + be + V *Example* This might be claimed.
Near Future	Modal + be going to + V *Example* He might be going to claim this.	Modal + be going to be + V *Example* This might be going to be claimed.
Continuous aspect		
	Active voice	**Passive voice**
Past	Modal + have + been + AP *Example* He might have been claiming this.	Modal + have + been + being + PP *Example* This might have been being claimed.
Present	Modal + be + AP *Example* He might be claiming this	Modal + be being + PP *Example* This might be being claimed.
Near Future	Modal + be going to + be + AP *Example* He might be going to be claiming this.	Modal + be going to + be + being + PP *Example* This might be going to be being claimed.
Perfect aspect		
	Active voice	**Passive voice**
Past	Modal + have + PP *Example* He might have claimed this.	Modal + have + been + PP *Example* This might have been claimed.
Present	Modal + have + PP *Example* He might have claimed this.	Modal + have been + PP *Example* This might have been claimed.
Perfect continuous aspect		
	Active voice	**Passive voice**
Past	Modal + have + been + AP *Example* He might have been claiming this.	Modal + have + been + PP *Example* This might have been being claimed.
Present	Modal + have + been + AP *Example* He might have been claiming this.	Modal + have + been + PP *Example* This might have been being claimed.

(V = bare infinitive, PP = past participle, AP = active participle)

Exercises

2.1 Rewrite the following sentences using modals. Try to keep the same meaning.

98

1) I want to use your phone. _____

2) Please do any of the first three questions, but not the fourth. _____
_____

3) It is essential that you complete an outline of your essay before Monday. _____
_____

4) It is better if you make a reference list at the end of your essay outline. _____
_____

5) It is impossible to pass this session unless you complete your essay. _____
_____

6) It is impossible to pass if you do not make an outline of your essay first. _____
_____

7) You probably think it is possible to pass without doing an outline, but it is harder than you think. _____
_____

8) As your English speaking ability is not as good as native speakers, the outline of your essay is very important.
_____
_____

2.2 Change the tense of the following modals to the tense given in brackets.

1) Can understand (Active Past simple) _____

2) Could lead to problems (Active future simple) _____

3) May meet with difficulties (Active present continuous) _____

4) Might be at risk (Active present perfect) _____

5) Will require more information (Passive future simple) _____

6) Would like to be consulted (Active past simple) _____

7) Must be their priority (Active past simple) _____

8) Should be jailed (Active past perfect) _____

9) Ought to do better (Active past perfect continuous) _____

2.3 What types of modals are being used in the following sentences? Write 1 for politeness, 2 for permission, 3 for obligation, 4 for certainty, or 5 for ability.

1) Would you like to finish now? [   ]

2) We should try again another time. [   ]

3) You ought to have finished by now. [   ]

4) When I was young I could put my feet behind my head. [   ]

5) Could I have a little more time? [   ]

6) They had to go already. [   ]

7) You can come whenever you want to. [   ]

8) It could happen. [   ]

9) She must have left already. [   ]

10) You must think more carefully before you do things like that. [   ]

11) She will never be the CEO. [   ]

12) She keeps telling me that I can't sing. [   ]

13) My dog is not allowed to sleep on the couch. [   ]

14) It might be a little cooler tomorrow. [   ]

15) I was able to say what I thought at the meeting.
[   ]

2.4 Write sentences of your own using the modals indicated

1) Need to (obligation) _____
_____

2) Be able to (ability) _____
_____

3) Have to (obligation) _____

_____

4) Must (obligation) _____

_____

5) Must (certainty) _____

_____

6) Would (politeness) _____

_____

7) Might (certainty) _____

_____

8) May (certainty) _____

_____

9) Could (politeness) _____

_____

10) Will (certainty) _____

_____

11) Can (permission) _____

_____

Hedging

In Academic writing, 'hedging' is very important. 'Hedging' means not being definite about a statement. An example might be '*it might rain tomorrow*' rather than '*it will rain tomorrow*'. Hedging is important in English academic writing for a number of reasons. It is important to save yourself from being embarrassed by saying that something is definitely true when it is not; it is important because it saves you from embarrassing other writers by showing them as being completely wrong, and it is important because it helps your writing be accepted by the academic community.

Hedging can be done in a number of ways. It can be done by using modals of probability, by using adverbs of probability, by using adjectives such as '***slight***', '***definite***', and '***remote***'. It can be done by distancing yourself from the claim. It can be done by generalising, and it can be done by choosing stronger and weaker verbs.

The following are some words that we might use to 'hedge' sentences in academic writing.

Modals of probability				
could	may	might	ought to	should

Adverbs of probability				
admittedly	for the large part	maybe	possibly	tentatively
apparently	generally	mainly	presumably	to a certain extent
clearly	largely	obviously	probably	
conceivably	likely	perhaps	seemingly	

Adjectives				
admitted	certain	obvious	probable	uncertain
apparent	clear	possible	unclear	unlikely

Distancing verbs			
appear	look	seem	tend

Choice of reporting verbs						
assume	believe	estimate	imply	indicate	suggest	think

Nouns			
admission	*assumption*	*possibility*	*suggestion*
appearance	*likelihood*	*probability*	*uncertainty*

Another strategy is to use a dummy subject and passive voice, for example: ***it could be said that....***

Of course, native speakers often use a combination of these words to increase or decrease the amount of hedging.

> ### *Examples*
> African leaders say that colonialism is to blame for their problems. However, ***it appears that*** they are wrong.
>
> We ***must assume that*** the early colonial governments cared little for native populations.
>
> The actions of the Soviets ***gave the appearance that*** they did not want to go to war with the US.
>
> ***It has been suggested*** by some that the US government ***might possibly be*** in communication with alien life forms.

In each of the above examples, we do not want to say that they are definitely true, because there is a very real possibility that our interpretation of the evidence might not agree with what actually happened or is happening.

Exercises

3.1 Which of the following sentences do you think might need hedging? What hedge words would you suggest?

1) The human evolved on a meat eating diet.
2) The Sudan government says that it is not responsible for the war in Darfur.
3) The Sudan government is responsible for the war in Darfur.
4) Humans will go crazy travelling the vast distance from Earth to Mars.
5) Robots have a number of essential components.
6) Robots will soon be developed that will be able to do housework.
7) The university is trying to increase its staffing in the robotics department.
8) A microprocessor acts as the brain of a computer.
9) A meteorite that crashed into the earth killed all the dinosaurs.
10) Life once existed on Mars.
11) There are other life-supporting planets in the universe.
12) Women are smarter than men.
13) Driving in South Korea is more dangerous than driving in Canada.
14) If a country changes the side of the road that people drive on, it will cause lots of accidents.
15) If a superstore opens in this town, the small shops will go broke.
16) English is a very complex language.
17) English is more complex than Korean.
18) The Australian government does not care about refugees.
19) Singapore Airline staff are very polite.
20) The dollar will remain stable for the foreseeable future.
21) Not all manufacturing plants generate pollution.
22) Aliens came to Earth before humans developed towns and farms.
23) African leaders say that colonialism is to blame for their problems. However, they are wrong.

Chapter 7 — Adverbial Clauses

Revision

Remember that there are two major divisions between clauses: embedded clauses and extra information clauses. Embedded clauses form part of the independent clause; extra information clauses provide extra information about something in the independent clause. Embedded clauses are mostly noun clauses. Extra information clauses can either describe the verb in the clause and its complement, a noun in the clause, or the whole clause. Adverbial clauses are extra information clauses. They describe the verb in a clause and its complement.

Adverbial clauses

Adverbial clauses describe the verb in an independent clause and its complement; however, this is not always obvious.

In the example here, the reason clause (**because they have funny long necks**) describes the verb *are interested*. It tells the reason why children are interested in giraffes.

> **Example**
> Children are interested in giraffes because they have funny long necks.

Eleven types of adverbial clauses

Adverbial clauses can be divided into twelve types. Following is a list of the twelve types with an example for each type:

1. **Time:** *After children come home from school,* they must do homework.
2. **Place:** Children can study *anywhere it is comfortable.*
3. **Manner:** That man acts *as if he is a king.*
4. **Distance:** Every morning I run *as far as I can.*
5. **Frequency:** I do exercises *as often as it is possible for me to.*
6. **Result:** Maki was *so* kind and beautiful *that I married her.*
7. **Purpose:** I studied hard *so that I would do well in my test on adverbial clauses.*
8. **Reason:** *Because I studied hard,* I did well in my test on adverbial clauses.
9. **Concession:** *Although my family is from Scotland,* I do not speak with a Scottish accent.
10. **Contrast:** Japan is very technologically advanced, *whereas Mexico is quite technologically backwards.*
11. **Conditional:** Spain would be a great place to live *if housing wasn't so expensive.*
12. **Comparative:** It costs more to buy a house in Durban *than it costs to by a house in most parts of Europe.*

Punctuation

Generally, we **don't** put a comma before an adverbial clause if it comes **after** the independent clause, but we **do** put a comma if the adverbial clause comes **before** the independent clause.

> **Examples**
>
> **Independent clause first**
> I did well in my test **because** I studied hard.
>
> **Adverbial clause first**
> **Because** I studied hard, I did well in my test.

There are some exceptions to this rule:

1. *While* and *whereas* have a comma before them. (Note: *while* has a comma before it when it means contrast, but not when it means time.)
2. Many people put a comma before *although*. A comma is not necessary, but it is not wrong to put one.
3. Many people also put a comma before *since* and *as* when they mean reason (but not when they mean time). This helps distinguish between the two meanings of the words. Again, a comma is not necessary, but it is not wrong.
4. Some people put a comma before *because*. A comma before *because* is really not needed, but it is not wrong.

> **Note**
> Placement of commas is really a matter of style. There is no ruling body that decides where commas should go, so different publishing companies have slightly different rules about them. Interestingly, commas were originally inserted to show actors where to pause for a breath when they were reading lines out loud.

> **Note**
> Not all adverbial clauses can come before the independent clause. *Comparative, result,* and *manner* clauses cannot come before the independent clause.

Time

Adverbial clauses of time tell when the event in a clause happened. The adverbial subordinators of time include are listed below.

> **Adverbial subordinators of time:**
>
> | | | | | |
> |---|---|---|---|---|
> | *after* | *as soon as* | *ever since* | *once* | *when* |
> | *after which* | *at which point* | *every time* | *since* | *whenever* |
> | *as* | *before* | *no sooner...than...* | *upon which* | *whereupon* |
> | *as long as* | *by which time* | *now that* | *until* | *while* |

> **Note**
> *By* and *during* are not adverbial subordinators, they are **prepositions**. They cannot be followed by finite clauses; they must be followed by gerund clauses.

Multiple functions

Some students become confused by the fact that some words that can be used as adverbial subordinators of time can have other functions. For example, they can be prepositions or even adverbs. It is important to remember which meaning you are intending when you are writing.

After, before, and *since* can also be used as **prepositions**.

After, before, and *ever since* are also **adverbs**.

> **Examples**
>
> | **Adverbial clause** | **Adverb** | **Preposition** |
> |---|---|---|
> | He did it **before** I got angry. | I've done it **before**. | I'll do it **before** 3.00. |

Multiple meanings

Students also often get confused about the fact that some adverbial subordinators can have more than one meaning.

As, since, and *while* are confusing because they have more than one meaning.
Since can be used as a **time** and a **reason** subordinator.

> **Examples**
>
> | **Time** | **Reason** |
> |---|---|
> | The baby has been screaming **since** 9.30. | The baby is screaming **since** it wants its mother. |

While can be used as a **time** and a **contrast** subordinator.

> **Examples**
>
> | **Time** | **Contrast** |
> |---|---|
> | I saw her **while** I riding the train to work. | The train is fast, **while** the bus is slow. |

As can be used as a *time*, a **reason**, and a **manner** subordinator. Note that *as* actually has two separate meanings for time.

> **Examples**
>
> | Time | Reason | Manner |
> | --- | --- | --- |
> | I talked to her **as** *I bought a ticket.* | I bought a ticket **as** *I wanted to ride the train.* | I assembled the chair **as** *the instruction booklet advised.* |

When, While, As, & During

These three words can sometimes have the same meaning, but often there are subtle differences in meaning. The differences in meaning depend on whether the verb is a state or an event and whether it is complete or incomplete at the time being discussed. (This section talks about **state, events, and repeated events**, if you do not understand these terms, see Chapter 5, pages 72-80.)

Consider the following 8 sentences. Think about which subordinators can be used in each one; some can have more than one option. Write **when, while,** or **as**.

1. _____ I was driving to work, I saw the president of the company.

2. I was driving to work _____ I saw the president of the company.

3. I was surprised _____ the pencil broke.

4. _____ I had my last car, I always worried that it would break down.

5. I was cooking _____ my wife was feeding the baby.

6. I cooked _____ my wife fed the baby.

7. I did my degree _____ I lived in Birmingham.

8. I will be happy _____ I am retired.

9. _____ he became more angry, I became more scared.

Sentences 1 & 2: *when, while*, or *as* of interrupting and interrupted events

The difference between these two sentences is that in the **first** sentence the time **subordinator** introduces the **interrupted** event, and in the **second** sentence the time **subordinator** introduces the **interrupting** event. When you are introducing an **interrupted** event, you can use **when, while, or as.** However, when you are introducing the **interrupting** event, only use **when.**

> **Example**
>
> **Subordinator introduces *interrupted* event: *When/while/as* I <u>was driving</u> to work, I <u>saw</u> George.**
> **Subordinator introduces *interrupting* event: I <u>was driving</u> to work *when* I <u>saw</u> George.**

Sentence 3: *as* for events with no duration

In this case the verb that is used is an **event with no duration**. Some events cannot have duration, or do not *usually* have duration. **Recognise** is an example of a verb which does not usually have duration. Because recognition is instant (one second you don't recognise, the next second you do), it is unusual to talk about something that happened during the time that a person is recognising something. This means that we do **not** use *while* or *as* with these types of verbs. We can only use *when.*

> **Example**
>
> I was surprised **when** *the pencil* <u>broke</u>. (**Break** does not usually have duration although it can in some situations; in this situation we can imagine it happening very quickly.)

Sentence 4: *When* or *while* for stative verbs (states)

In this sentence, the verb in the adverbial clause is a **stative verb**. Stative verbs include verbs like: *love, hate, know, have,* and *be.* These types of verbs **cannot** be used with the subordinator *as.* Instead, we must use *when* or *while.* Even if we use a stative verb in a continuous aspect to show that it is temporarily true, we still **cannot** use *as.*

> **Example**
> **When/While** I **had** my last car, I always worried that it would break down. (**have** is a stative verb.)
> I was wondering what she was wrong with her **when/while** she **was being** silly. (Stative verb **be** used in continuous to show that she was only being silly temporarily; she isn't a silly person.)

Sentences 5, 6, and 7: *While* or *as* to show that two events happened for the same amount of time.

In these two sentences, the same aspect is used in both the dependent and the independent clause. The first sentence uses present continuous in both clauses; the second one uses present simple. In both cases, **while** or **as** would show that the two events happened at the same time for the same length of time. We do not use **when** in this situation.

> **Example**
> I <u>was cooking</u> **while/as** my wife <u>was feeding</u> the baby. **Or** I <u>cooked</u> **while/as** my wife <u>fed</u> the baby.

Notice though, that if the verb in the dependent clause is a state, then the rule from sentence 3 applies: we **cannot** use **as**. Thus, we can only use **while** to show that two states lasted for the same duration.

> **Example**
> I <u>did</u> my degree in Brimingham **while** I <u>lived</u> in Birmingham. (**Live** is a state, so we cannot use **as**.)

Sentence 8: *When* to show the time that something happened.

This is probably the most obvious use of a time subordinator; it simply tells the reader or listener what time the event happened. We use **when** in this situation. The adverbial clause could be replaced with an actual time, for example: *I was in high school <u>when the Chernobyl disaster happened</u>* → *I was in high school <u>in 1986</u>*. (*1986* was when the disaster happened.)

> **Example**
> I will be happy **when** I am retired. (**When** I am retired = in the years that I am retired. I can't name them exactly, because I don't know when they will start or end).

Sentence 9: *As* to show that two things change at the same time

As can also be used to show that two things **change at the same time**. In these situations, we usually use past **simple** tense in both the dependent and the independent clause.

> **Example**
> **As** the cloud **grew** bigger, the weather **got** worse.

> **Notes**
> **While** is more common than **as**, which sounds a little formal. **While** is more common because **as** has many meanings (time, reason, and manner), and these meanings can easily be confused.
> **Whilst** means the same as **while**, but it is more formal.

> **Note**
> Time clauses can come after adverbs of time or prepositional time phrases.
>
> > **Example**
> > The accident that caused the trauma occurred <u>at 6.30pm</u> **after** the traffic had started to subside.

During is a preposition only; it cannot be used as an adverbial subordinator. It can only be complemented by a noun.

Chapter 7

> **Examples**
>
> **During** *the Gulf War*, a lot of soldiers reported symptoms of trauma.
> **During** ~~the soldiers were fighting in the gulf war~~, they reported symptoms of trauma. (*Wrong!*)

Since, Until, Before, After, & By

Students often confuse **since**, **until**, **before**, **after**, and **by**.

Remember is that **by** is a preposition, not a subordinator. It can only be complemented by a noun when it refers to time. Notice that **by** is often used with past perfect or future perfect. (In adverbial clauses, this means that sometimes **by** will be used with present perfect – see page 107 for more on tense.)

> **Examples**
>
> **By** *the end of the Gulf War*, a lot of soldiers had reported symptoms of trauma.
> **By** ~~the soldiers had finished fighting in the gulf war~~, they had reported symptoms of trauma. (*Wrong!*)

Before means that the event in the independent clause happens earlier in time than the event in the dependent clause.

> **Examples**
>
> Colonizing countries must find a way to generate water on the moon *before they can build a colony*.
> (event 1)   (event 2)
> **Before** *colonizing countries can build a colony*, they must find a way to generate water on the moon.
> (event 2)   (event 1)

Before can also indicate that it took a long time until something happened. In this example, **before** means that we arrived in Timbuktu several days *later*.

> **Example**
>
> It was days **before** *we arrived in Timbuktu*.

After means that the event in the independent clause happened later in time than the event in the dependent clause. In this example, the future perfect is back-shifted to present perfect in the adverbial clauses. Adverbial clauses of time that refer to the future always use present tense (see pages 107-108 for more). Actually, **future perfect is not needed** here since **past and future perfect have the same meaning as the adverbial time subordinator** *after*. **When** can also be used in this situation **with past or future perfect** to give the **same meaning**.

> **Examples**
>
> America will claim the eastern half of the moon *after the next lunar module **has been deployed***.
> (event 2)   (event 1)
> **After** *the next lunar module **has been deployed***, America will claim the eastern half of the moon.
> (event 1)   (event 2)
> **After** *the next lunar module **is deployed***, America will claim the eastern half of the moon.
> (event 1)   (event 2)
> **When** *the next lunar module **has been deployed***, America will claim the eastern half of the moon.
> (event 1)   (event 2)

Both **before** and **after** can be preceded by **the amount of time before or after the event**.

> **Examples**
>
> <u>Long</u> **before** *the first American probe landed on the moon*, people had been speculating about future moon colonies.
> <u>Two minutes</u> **after** *the first American probe landed on the moon*, the entire nation was standing still, watching their televisions in awe.

Until is used to say when an event ends, and **since** is used to say when it started. **Until** means that the event in the independent clause continued up to time stated in the dependent clause or in the prepositional phrase. Sometimes we also use **til**, but this is more spoken English than written.

> **Example**
>
> Scientists and technicians in Houston worked around the clock **until** *the probe had returned to earth*.

Until can also mean that the action continued to time that a **result** was reached.

> **Example**
> NASA will continue sending probes to the moon *until they have gathered all of the data that they need.*

Since has two **time** meanings (remember that *since* can also be used to mean *because* and that it can also be a subordinator (or preposition) of time):

(1) *Since* can mean '**continuing from that time until now**'. In other words, it means from when the event started until now. **The dependent and the independent clause** are used with the **present perfect or present perfect continuous**. Use present perfect for states (such as know or love) and for repeated events and present perfect continuous for events. Notice that events with no duration (for example, recognise) are not used with present perfect continuous. Sometimes we also use *ever since* with little difference in meaning.

> **Example**
> *Since the robot **has been** on Mars,* scientists have been able to discover many new and fascinating facts about the planet. (The robot has continued to be on Mars until now, and the scientists have continued to discover new facts until now.)

(2) *Since* can also mean '**from the time that an event was complete until now**'. In this case, the **dependent clause** is mostly in **past simple** and the independent clause is used with the **present perfect or present perfect continuous**. Use present perfect for states (such as *know* or *love*) and for repeated events and present perfect continuous for events.

> **Example**
> *Since the probe **landed** on Mars,* scientists have been able to discover many new and fascinating facts about the planet. (from the time that the landing of the probe was complete until now, scientists have continued to discover new facts.)

Once, Now that, As soon as, & As long as

Students also find the following words confusing: *once, now that, as soon as,* and *as long as*

As soon as and *once* mean that the event in the independent clause happened immediately after the event in the dependent clause:

> **Example**
> *As soon as the probe landed on Mars,* scientists began to investigate the terrain.
> *Once the probe landed on Mars,* scientists began to investigate the terrain.

Now that means *after*, or *as soon as*, but it can only be used in the present. That is, the event must have just finished a short while ago. With **events**, *now that* is **used with the present perfect in the dependent clause and future tense in the independent clause**. With **states**, *now that* is **used with the present simple in the dependent clause and future tense in the independent clause**.

> **Examples**
> *Now that NASA **have landed** a probe on Mars,* they **will attempt** to send one to Venus too.
> *Now that NASA **know** that there is water on the moon,* they **will work** on ways to harvest it.

Compare *now that* with *just as*. *Just as* means at that exact time, or shortly afterwards. It is used to describe past events.

> **Example**
> *Just as the Space Shuttle began to lift off,* there was an enormous clap of thunder.

As long as means that the event in the independent clause is true only for the time that the event in the dependent clause is true. *As long as* **is really a conditional subordinator** like *if*.

> **Example**
> *As long as NASA is well funded,* they will continue to attempt to explore the universe.

Chapter 7

In the example above, NASA will continue attempting to explore the universe during the time that they are well funded, but when they are not well funded, they will stop attempting to explore the universe.

Tense

Tense in adverbial clauses is quite difficult and strange. Consider the following table:

Independent clause	Adverbial clause of time
Past	Past
Present	Present
Future	*Present*

When the independent clause is in past tense, the adverbial clause is in past tense; when the independent clause is in present tense, the adverbial clause is in present tense; however, when the independent clause is in **future** tense, the adverbial clause is in **present** tense. It does not matter what aspect is used (simple, perfect, continuous).

> ### Examples
>
> **Past:** People **listened** in rapture *while* Neil Armstrong **was saying** his first words on the moon.
> (Independent clause)   (dependent adverbial clause of time)
>
> **Present:** The imagination of the public **is** always **captured** *when* a trip to space **is launched**.
> (Independent clause)   (dependent adverbial clause of time)
>
> **Future:** The team in Houston **will be relieved** *when* the spacecraft finally **returns** to Earth.
> (Independent clause)   (dependent adverbial clause of time)

Future perfect becomes present perfect

Following the rules above, when using **future perfect** in an **adverbial clause**, we use **present perfect**, not **future perfect tense**.

> ### Example
>
> **Event 1:** Astronauts **will have built** a space station on Mars.
> (Future perfect: this event will happen before the next event.)
>
> **Event 2:** People **will start to visit** as tourists and settlers. (Future simple: this event will happen second)
>
> → *When* Astronauts **have built** a space station on Mars, People **will start to visit** as tourists and settlers.
>   (future perfect becomes present perfect in adverbial clause)   (Future simple)

Exercises

1.1 Join the following simple sentences to make adverbial clauses of time using the subordinator given.

1) Write a plan of your essay. Check to make sure that your writing is logical. (As)

_____

_____

2) Begin to make a first draft. Write a plan of your essay. (When)

_____

_____

3) Do not begin your final draft. Get somebody to check over your first draft for you. (Until)

_____

_____

4) Finish your final draft. Use a grammar checklist to make sure that your writing is as grammatically accurate as possible. (After)

_____

_____

5) Submit your essay to your lecturer. Check one more time for any grammar mistakes. (Before)

_____

_____

1.2 Write sentences about your life using the following subordinators.

1) (When) _____

   _____

2) (Whenever) _____

   _____

3) (As) _____

   _____

4) (While) _____

   _____

5) (As soon as) _____

   _____

6) (Now that) _____

   _____

7) (After) _____

   _____

8) (Since) _____

   _____

9) (Until) _____

   _____

10) (Before) _____

   _____

11) (As long as) _____

   _____

1.3 Select which subordinators are okay from the following choices (when/while/as).

1) The president was waiting **when/while/as** we arrived.

2) **When/while/as** I was a new employee at the company, I never got to take important trips like this.

3) **While/when/as** I was sitting in the aeroplane, I thought about the speech I would give.

4) It will be a relief **when/while/as** the speech is over.

5) The president was watching me **when/while/as** I was giving the speech.

6) I was worried that people would notice **when/while/as** an sms message arrived on my phone during the speech.

7) **When/while/as** the speech came to an end, I realised that it had been a success.

8) It was great **when/while/as** I was the star of the conference, but of course my stardom soon faded.

Place

Adverbial clauses can also describe place. These clauses use the following subordinators:

Adverbial subordinators of place:			
anywhere	*everywhere*	*where*	*wherever*

Where has a very similar meaning in an adverbial clause and a relative clause.

Notice that the first sentence is **adverbial** because it describes the **verb** *shop*. The second sentence is **relative** because it describes the **noun** *stores*.

Chapter 7

Example

Adverbial clause

Fashion conscious people shop *where they sell Ralph Loren.*

Relative clause

Fashion conscious people shop in stores *where they sell Ralph Loren.*

Students find *anywhere, everywhere,* and *wherever* confusing. Although sometimes they can mean the same thing, they are actually slightly different. Notice also that their meanings change considerably in the negative.

Everywhere means all places.

Anywhere means that it doesn't matter which place.

Take the following two examples: 1) *Paint the wall everywhere.* 2) *Paint the wall anywhere.*

The **first example** means that I want you to **paint the whole wall**. The **second example** means that I want you to **paint only a section of the wall, but you can choose** where.

On the other hand, if I say 1) *You can buy a phone card everywhere*, and 2) *You can buy a phone card anywhere*, then it has much the same meaning because 1) means that *all* shops sell phone cards, and 2) means that **whichever shop you go to**, you can buy a phone card.

Wherever means the same thing as *anywhere*, but notice that we *don't use wherever in negative sentences.*

Example

Positive

In Australia, tourists can see sheep *wherever they go.* ✓

Negative

It is very unusual to say: In Australia, tourists *can't see* sheep *wherever* they go. X

Negatives

Notice that the meanings of *anywhere* and *everywhere* swap around in negative sentences

1) *Don't paint the wall everywhere means that you can paint some of the wall, but not all of it.*

On the other hand, 2) *Don't pain the wall anywhere means that you can't pain the wall at all.*

Similarly, 1) *you can't buy a phone card everywhere* means that **some shops sell phone cards, but some shops do not.**

While 2) *you can't buy a phone card anywhere* means that **no shops sell phone cards.**

Example

Ride your bike everywhere ←*opposite*→ Don't ride your bike anywhere.

Ride your bike anywhere ←*opposite*→ Don't ride your bike everywhere.

Exercises

2.1 Join the following sentences together to make sentences with adverbial clauses of place.

1) You can't buy burdock. You go in England. _____

_____

2) You can find Asian supermarkets almost. You go in English cities. _____

_____

3) A big Asian community is living. There are many Asian shops and restaurants. _____

_____

4) You can buy Asian groceries in most parts of England, but you can't buy them. You go. _____

_____

2.2 Write sentences about your country using the following subordinators

1) (Where)_____

_____

2) (Wherever) _____

3) (Everywhere) _____

_____

4) (Anywhere) _____

_____

5) (Not) (Anywhere) _____

_____

6) (Not) (Everywhere) _____

_____

Manner

Adverbial clauses of manner can be very confusing. Note that both **as** and **as...as...** can also be **prepositions**. Adverbial clauses using these constructions of course need a subject, verb, and perhaps an object.

> **Example**
> **Preposition**   **Adverbial clause**
> Cornish interprets this as well **as** well **as** *Szalavicz.*   Cornish interprets this as well **as** well **as** *Szalavicz*
> .

We can divide adverbial clauses of manner can be divided into three groups:

> **Adverbial subordinators of place:**
> *as*   *as if / as though*   *as adverb as …*

Pro-verbs

Notice the use of the *'pro-verbs'* **do, be,** and **have**. **'Pro-verbs'** like **pronouns** are substituted for verbs to stop them from being repeated. **We use them in some, but not all <u>adverbial</u> clauses.** We use **be** as a proverb for **be** or for a verb in **continuous aspect** or **passive voice**; we use **have** for **has** or for verbs in **present perfect**; we use **do** for all other verbs and we can also use it for **have**.

> **Example**
> **Pronoun**: *The president* has made an announcement; *he* has stated that he will resign.
> **Pro-verb**: The vice president **works** as hard as the president **does**.
>   The vice president **has** as many jobs to do as the president **has/does**.
>   The vice president **is** not as famous as the president *is*.

As if / as though

These two words have exactly the same meaning.

> **Note**
> *As if* and *as though* have the same meaning, but *even if* and *even though* have quite different meanings.

As if and **as though** mean that the action *seems like* some other action.

> **Example**
> He walks *as if* his leg is broken.

In this example, the way he walks makes it *look like* his leg is broken. We don't know if his leg really is broken or not, but there is a tendency to think that it is not broken.

As *adverb* as....

This construction means that the verbs in both the dependent clause and the independent clause can equally be described by the adverb.

The example here means that he and I both walk at the same speed.

> **Example**
> He walks *as quickly as I do.*

Pro-verbs

Chapter 7

Notice that we often don't repeat the verb in the independent clause, but instead use the verbs **do, be,** or **have** or just repeat the modal. This is what we call a **pro-verb**. We use **be** if the verb in the independent clause is *be*, *do* for any other verb, and we use just the modal if the verb has a modal in it. In this case **do** has a similar function to a pronoun. This point is explained above with adverbs of manner as well.

> **Examples**
>
> **Is**
> She *is* singing as well as I *am*.
>
> **Do**
> She *sings* as well as I *do*.
>
> **Modal**
> She *can sing* as well as I *can*.

As

As is the most difficult subordinator to understand. Firstly, it should be noted that **as** has **three different meanings**, but that the meaning intended is not always clear. For this reason, there are usually clearer ways of saying the same thing.

As can mean:

Time - in this meaning, there is little difference between **while** and **as** other than that **while** is used for short or long time periods, and **as** is used only for shorter time periods. Not that we never use commas with this meaning of **as**.

> **Example**
> I drank a coffee **as** *I worked on my assignment.*
> **But** I studied English **while** *I was doing my masters degree.*

Reason – in this meaning, **as** means **because** or **since**. There is no difference in meaning between these words.

> **Example**
> Miami has warmer weather(,) **as** *it is closer to the equator* than New York.

Some people like to put a comma before **as** when it means **because** to help distinguish it from its time meaning.

Manner – this is the hardest meaning to understand. Here **as** means **the way that**. Sometimes it is really not clear from the sentence whether the writer means **because** or **the way that**, for example: *I did my homework* <u>as</u> *my teacher told me to*. Does this mean I did it **because** she told me to or that I **followed her instructions**? In this situation, the comma can be useful. We **don't** use a comma for manner. However, it is probably better to just use a difference word.

> **Example**
> You built the doghouse **as** *the instruction booklet guided you to do it.* (You built the doghouse **the way that** the instruction booklet guided you to do it.)

Note that in this example, you did not build the doghouse **because** the instructions told you to; you **read and followed** the instructions

Exercises

3.1 Use the sentences in the box to make sentences using the subordinator <u>as</u> **(meaning** <u>the way that</u>**)**

A model walks.	She had been advised to in such a situation.	
Her mother made pasta.	I had taught him to.	The instructions tell you to.

1) The dog raised his paw. _____

2) She did CPR on the child. _____

3) Do these exercises. _____

4) She walks. _____

5) She makes pasta. _____

3.2 Decide whether 'as' means *time*, *reason*, or *manner* **in the following sentences. Write *T*, *R*, or *M* in the brackets.**

1) The plane was late as you predicted it would be. [   ]

2) The plane was late, as the pilot was late leaving. [   ]

3) The plane for Manila arrived as the plane for Bangkok departed. [   ]

4) I do not have a car, as I do not need one. [   ]

5) They no longer make cars as they used to make them. [   ]

6) As I looked at the cars in the car shop, a sales person approached me. [   ]

7) I filled in the form as the police officer waited for me. [   ]

8) I filled in the form as the instructions in the box indicated that it should be filled in. [   ]

9) I filled in the form, as I needed to get a refund. [   ]

3.3 Use the sentences in the box to make sentences using the subordinators *as if* or *as though*.

You are not scared.	**He is our boss.**	**You have the road to yourself.**
He did not want to come.	**He is a pirate.**	

1) He looks. _____

2) He talks. _____

3) You should act. _____

4) He sounded. _____

5) You drive. _____

3.4 Join these sentences using the structure as...as...

1) The roads were not busy today. They usually are. _____

_____

2) The palace is ten times bigger. My house. _____

_____

3) I did not do well in the test on adverbial clauses. I had thought I would. _____

_____

4) The student answered the questions quickly. She could. _____

_____

5) Try to finish these exercises quickly. You can. _____

_____

3.5 Write sentences of your own about behaviour using the following subordinators

1) (As) _____

_____

2) (As if) _____

_____

3) (As though) _____

_____

4) (As *adverb* as) _____

_____

Distance and frequency

Adverbial clauses of distance and frequency work in much the same way as adverbial clauses of manner that have the structure *as adverb as* .... The subordinators for distance are: *as far as* and *as distant as*.

As long as is not a subordinator of distance, it is a subordinator of time and condition. See page 107 on time clauses for more details about *as long as*. The subordinators Frequency are: *as often as* and *as frequently as*.

Chapter 7

Examples

Distance	Frequency
I walked as far as I could (walk).	She goes fishing as often as she can.
I walked as far as my friend did (walk).	She goes fishing as often as she has time to.
I always walk as far as my legs allow me to (walk).	She goes fishing as often as my friend does.

Note that *as far as* can also be used as a preposition.

A common expression is *as far as I know*; this means *I have not been told anything different*. Although adverbial clauses of manner, distance, and frequency usually come after the independent clause, this expression can be used before the independent clause.

Example

I drove *as* far *as the bookstore*.

Example

As far as I know, George is a good teacher.

Note that only a limited number of verbs can be used in distance or frequency adverbial clauses.

Exercises

4.1 Join the following sentences together to make adverbial clauses of distance and frequency

1) I carried the box. I could. _____

   _____

2) Everyone should have fun. They possibly can. _____

   _____

3) Buses in this city don't run. They should. _____

   _____

4) I walked. I felt able to walk. _____

   _____

5) She uses a taxi. She has the money to. _____

   _____

4.2 Write three sentences of your own using the distance subordinator *as far as* and three sentences using the frequency subordinator *as often as*.

1) _____

   _____

2) _____

   _____

3) _____

   _____

4) _____

   _____

5) _____

   _____

Result

Adverbial clauses of result show the result of a situation. These clauses use the subordinators *so... that...* or *such ... that....* These subordinators **should not be confused** with the subordinator of purpose *so that*. Consider the following two sentences:

1. *Website creators should use longer URLs <u>so that</u> there is less uncertainty for users.*
2. *There are <u>so many problems</u> <u>that</u> many users are becoming unwilling to navigate to this site.*

In the first sentence, **so that** shows the **reason** why they should use longer URLs. It shows that **there is a plan** or a **purpose**. In the second sentence, **so... that...** shows the **result** of the problems. This section will focus on result clauses, the next section will focus on purpose clauses.

The example on the right means that <u>**as a result of**</u> her being beautiful, I fell in love with her instantly.

> **Example**
>
> She was *so* beautiful *that I fell in love with her instantly*.

We can use these clauses with **adjectives**, **adverbs**, or **nouns**. We use <u>***so***</u> with **adjectives**, and **adverbs,** and we use <u>***such***</u> with **nouns**.

> **Example**
>
> **Adjective**   **Adverb**
> She was *so* clever *that* I felt stupid.   She talked *so* intelligently *that* I had trouble understanding her.
>
> **Noun**
> She was *such* a genius *that* I was in awe of her.

We can put an **adjective** <u>before</u> the **noun**, but we still use <u>***such***</u>.

> **Example**
>
> She was *such* an intelligent girl *that* she passed all of her exams with high distinctions.

We can also put a quantifier (***many, few, a lot of, some***) <u>before</u> a **noun**, but then we use <u>***so***</u> instead of ***such***.

> **Example**
>
> There were *so* <u>many</u> stupid people there *that* I felt clever.
>
> There were *so* <u>few</u> buses running between the two cities *that* I had to wait for several hours.

Exercises

5.1 Join the following clauses to make adverbial clauses of result.

1) Taipei 101 is strong. It can withstand strong typhoons and earthquakes. _____

    _____

2) Nobody knows how many floors it will have. Burj Dubai has been built secretively. _____

    _____

3) Burj Dubai will be a tall building. It will be more than twice the height of Taipei 101. _____

    _____

4) The world's longest suspension bridge, the Akashi Kaikyo bridge, has a strong structure. It can withstand an earthquake of 8.5 on the Richter scale. _____

    _____

5) A major earthquake catastrophe is inevitable. Tokyo, the world's largest city, is built on many earthquake fault lines. _____

    _____

6) Much of it still remains unexplored. The world's largest country, Russia, has much unused land.

    _____

    _____

5.2 Write sentences about the country that you are studying in using the following result subordinators

1) (So + adjective + that) _____

    _____

2) (So + adverb + that) _____

    _____

3) (Such + noun group + that) _____

    _____

4) (So much + noun group + that) _____

_____

5) (So many + noun group + that) _____

_____

6) (So little + noun group + that) _____

_____

7) (So few + noun group + that) _____

_____

Purpose

At the start of the last section, you saw two example sentences:

1. **Website creators should use longer URLs <u>so that</u> there is less uncertainty for users.**
2. **There are <u>so many problems</u> <u>that</u> many users are becoming unwilling to navigate to this site.**

In the first sentence, *so that* shows the **reason** why they should use longer URLs. It shows that **there is a plan** or a **purpose**. In the second sentence, *so... that...* shows the **result** of the problems. This section will focus on purpose clauses.

> **Example**
>
> He is investigating human appreciation of aesthetics *so that* *we have a better understanding of how the mind reacts to beauty.*

Purpose clauses are **similar to reason clauses**; they give the reason for an intended action. Adverbial clauses of purpose use the subordinators *so that* and *in order that*. These subordinators are similar to the coordinator *so*, but are not the same. *So* shows the reason for doing something; *so that* and *in order that* show your reason for doing something that you **planned** to do. In other words, they show that you intended to do the action. Note that *so* can also be used in this situation, but *so that* cannot be used when the event is not planned.

> **Examples**
>
> **So:** I had a cold, *so* I couldn't come to class. (*So that* and *in order that* **cannot** be used in this situation because I didn't *plan* on having a cold.)
>
> **So that / in order that:** I got up early *so that* I wouldn't be late to class. (*So* can also be used in this situation)

There is no difference between *so that* and *in order that*.

If the **subject** in the independent clause and the **subject** in the adverbial clause is the **same**, we can use **an infinitive clause, using <u>in order to</u>**.

> **Examples**
>
> **In order that**   **In order to**
> I got up early *in order that* I wouldn't be late to class.   I got up early *in order to not* be late to class.

Note that in this case the **subject is the same in both the dependent clause and independent clause**. If the subject were **different**, it would **not** be possible to use *in order to*. For example, if we say *I bought a car in order that my wife could use it,* we cannot use *in order to*.

Exercises

6.1 Decide if the following clauses should be combined using *so* or *so that*; then rewrite them as one sentence.

1) People use slang. Outsiders will not understand them. _____

_____

2) Slang allows people to create and reinforce identity. We can say that slang reflects the speaker's experiences, viewpoints, and principles. _____

_____

3) Slang is not understood by everybody. People don't tend to use it outside of their social group. _____

_____

4) People use slang. They appear knowledgeable. _____

_____

5) Historically, slang was originally used by gangsters. Nobody would understand their secret code. _____

_____

6) Similarly, people tend to use swear words. They fit into a group. _____

_____

7) Swear words have changed over time. The words that our parents thought were swear words are no longer swear words.

_____

_____

_____

6.2 Rewrite the following clauses using _in order to_ if possible.

1) The Vervet monkey gives a special call in order that other vervet monkeys know that an eagle is coming.

_____

_____

2) Monkeys know how to hide food from other monkeys so that they can eat it themselves.

_____

_____

3) People have taught some chimpanzees sign language in order that they can communicate simple requests to the monkeys.

_____

_____

4) Some chimpanzees that can use sign language have been given baby chimpanzees to live with so that researchers can observe whether they teach the baby chimpanzees sign language or not.

_____

_____

6.3 Write sentences including adverbial clauses of purpose

1) _____

_____

2) _____

_____

3) _____

_____

4) _____

_____

5) _____

_____

6) _____

_____

Reason

The three main subordinators of reason are: _as, since_, and _because_. These subordinators have exactly the same meaning.

Some people put a comma before these subordinators, particularly with _as_ and _since_ to distinguish them from the other meanings of

Examples

It is hard to believe her **because** she is a liar.

Since she lies so often, people tend to doubt what she says.

As she is stupid, she doesn't realise this.

these subordinators. However, it is not necessary to put a comma.

Exercises

7.1 Join these sentences using subordinators of reason.

1) Attempts to teach chimpanzees to speak in the past have failed. Chimpanzees physically cannot speak.

   _____

   _____

2) They do not have a pharynx. Chimpanzees cannot speak. _____

   _____

3) Researchers have had much more success through teaching chimpanzees to use sign language. The chimpanzees do not need to speak. _____

   _____

4) Chimpanzees that have learned sign language have managed to teach that sign language to their babies. Researchers have been impressed. _____

   _____

5) Chimpanzees have been able to communicate using sign language. Researchers have had to re-evaluate just how intelligent these creatures are. _____

   _____

7.2 Write sentences using the subordinators in the brackets.

1) (as) _____

   _____

2) (since)_____

   _____

3) (because) _____

   _____

Concession

Adverbial clauses of concession are used to contrast two situations. They differ from the direct opposite contrast subordinators in the next section (**while** and **whereas**), which contrast two directly opposite situations.

Adverbial subordinators of concession:

although	*even if*	*even though*	*though*

Although, **though** and **even though** have exactly the same meanings.

Examples
Although *adverbial clauses are important,* many textbooks ignore them.
Even though *French and English have many similar words,* they are quite different languages.
Though *English spelling is very difficult,* it is easier than Chinese writing.

Even if has a somewhat different meaning, however. Compare the following two sentences.

Even though *I study German,* **I can't speak it.**   **Even if** *I study German,* **I won't be able to speak it.**

In the first sentence I studied German, but I can't speak it. In the second sentence, maybe I will study German, or maybe I won't; however, it won't make any difference.

> *Examples*
> **Even though**
> Even though you don't understand adverbial clauses, you should still try to use them. (You don't understand but should use them.)
> **Even if**
> Even if you don't understand adverbial clauses, you should still try to use them. (It doesn't matter if you understand them or not, you should still use them.)

> **Note**
> In past tense clauses, *even if* and *even though* have very little difference in meaning. The difference only really shows up in present and future sentences.

When referring to the future, a clause using the subordinator *even though* can contain a future tense verb. However, a clause using the subordinator *even if* will use present tense to refer to the future (future tense will appear in the independent clause.). This is the same as conditional clauses and adverbial clauses of time.

> *Example*
> **Future**
> *Even though* you **will be** absent, you will still be able to understand the lecture.
> *Even if* you **are** absent, you will still be able to understand the lecture.

Even if can also be used with imaginary conditional clauses. In this situation, we use **past tense** (or *were* for the verb *be*) if the imaginary clause is about now, and **past perfect** for past 'un-real' situations. We use the modal *would* in the independent clause

> *Examples*
> **Imaginary present:** *Even if* I **were** rich, I **would** not **invest** in that sort of scheme.
> **Imaginary past:** *Even if* I **had been** born rich, I **would** not **invest** in that sort of scheme.

Notice the difference between *if*, *even if*, and *even when* in the following examples. In this example, *if* means that I won't give you any money on the condition that I have it, whereas *even if* means I won't give you any money *if I have it or if I don't have it*. In some cases this maybe the same, but *even if* strengthens the fact that it will or won't happen on either condition. In this regard, the difference is similar to *even though*. In the example below, *even though* means that I have a million dollars, but I won't give you any, whereas *even if* means that I might or might not have it, but I won't give it to you.

> *Examples*
> *If* I had a million dollars, I wouldn't give you any.   *Even if* I had a million dollars, I wouldn't give you any.
> *Even when* I have a million dollars, I won't give you any.   *Even though* I have a million dollars, I won't give you any.

Notice that *even when* similarly means *when I have it* or *when I don't have it*.

Exercises

8.1 Decide whether to use *even if* or *even though* (or *both* if either is okay) to join the following clauses.

1) The football manager will loose his job. His team wins. _____

 _____

2) The desalination plant will go ahead. The dams are full. _____

 _____

3) You have been on an aeroplane many times before. You should still keep these points in mind. _____

 _____

4) It was not illegal to use drugs. I still wouldn't use them. _____

 _____

5) Farmers are rejoicing. It is too early to know if it will be a good harvest this year. _____

_____

8.2 Write sentences of your own using the following subordinators.

1) (Although) _____

_____

2) (Even though) _____

_____

3) (Though) _____

_____

4) (Even if) _____

_____

Contrast

The subordinators used to contrast direct opposites are *while, whilst,* and *whereas.*

We can use *while* and *whilst* in adverbial clauses that come **before** the independent clause in the same way as we use although, though, and even though to show concession.

> **Examples**
>
> *While* both my parents are left handed, I am right handed.
>
> *Although* both my parents are left handed, I am right handed. *(No difference in meaning.)*

We can use *while, whilst,* and *whereas* in adverbial clauses that come **after** the independent clause to contrast two direct opposites. Take this sentence, for instance; *although British food is very boring, life in British cities can still be fun*. In this case, we are not comparing to opposite things. British food and British cities are quite different things. On the other hand, if we compare British food and Korean food, we are comparing two opposite things. Usually these types of clauses have subjects that differ only by the way

> **Example**
>
> British food is very boring, *while Korean food is quite delicious.*

they are classified (e.g. **British** food / **Korean** food) or they have two comparable items as their subject. The complement is usually an opposite (e.g. **boring** vs. **delicious** / **tall** vs. **short**).

> **Note**
>
> Direct opposite contrast adverbial clauses have different punctuation from other adverbial clauses, they use a comma whether they come before or after the independent clause.

> **Examples**
>
> America is a great superpower, *whereas Liechtenstein is a tiny country.*
>
> *Whereas Liechtenstein is a tiny country,* America is a great superpower.

While, whilst and *whereas* are *not* used to contrast the event in the adverbial clause with an **unexpected result**.

Exercises

9.1 Decide if the following sentences can be combined using contrast (*while, whilst, whereas*) subordinators or whether they must be combined using concession subordinators (*though, although, even though*). If they can be combined using contrast subordinators, should the subordinate clause come first, or second?

1) He hated the president. He decided to vote for him anyway.

_____

_____

2) Bill Gates has a lot of money. I have only a little money.

_____

3) The official death toll stands at only 20,000. There is little doubt that the real figure is closer to 100,000.

4) She was always cheerful. She was very unwell.

5) I have written many books. My sister has written none.

6) Gilling claims that global warming is not a serious problem. Hardy claims that global warming is a serious problem.

7) We went to the beach. It was raining.

8) I didn't get the job. I was the best qualified person.

9) PCs are the best computers to use for programming. Apples are the best computers to use for computer graphics.

10) It is surprising that he passed. There is no proof that he cheated.

9.2 Write four sentences of your own containing contrast clauses.

1)

2)

3)

4)

Conditionals 1

Conditional clauses are also adverbial clauses. Conditional clauses cause students more confusion than any other type of adverbial clause. The following is a list of words that are used as adverbial subordinators of condition.

Adverbial subordinators of condition:		
As long as	*If*	*lest*
except if	*if only*	*unless*

Chapter 7

Except if, *unless* and *lest* have the same meaning. *Lest* is old-fashioned and not used much today.

> **Note**
>
> *As if* is an adverbial subordinator of manner; it shows the way that it seems or looks like a person acts. It is not conditional. See earlier section on adverbial clauses of manner for more.
>
> *Even if* is an adverbial clause of concession. Clauses using *even if* can sometimes be used in a conditional sense and then follow conditional patterns. See section on adverbial clauses on concession for more.

Unless, lest and *except if* have a meaning of *if not*. The following example means that *if* we *don't* reveal our evidence, they won't either. These subordinators are not used with imaginary conditionals (see table below).

> **Example**
>
> They will not reveal the evidence that they have compiled *unless we reveal our evidence too*.

If only expresses a wish. This example means: I *wish* I had done better at school; *as a result*, I could be earning more money.

> **Example**
>
> *If only I had done better at school*, I would earn more money.

> **Note**
>
> Don't confuse *if __conditional__ clauses* with *if __noun__ clauses*, which are quite different.
>
> > **Examples**
> >
> > This research paper would be better *if it contained more empirical research*.
> > This research paper asks *if it is better to drink two glass of wine a day or not*.

The first sentence is conditional and shows the condition on which the research paper would be better. The second sentence is a noun clause. It reports the yes/no question: 'is it better to drink two glass of wine a day or not?' More on if/whether noun clauses can be found in chapter 4.

Types of conditionals

Most textbooks claim that English has three conditionals, but the following table tells a more complex story.

Condition							
Facts			Future Predictions		Imaginary		
Always		Limited	Strong	Weak	Hypothetical		Not True	
States	Repeated Event				Present	Future	Present	Past

Each of the three types of conditional sentence in English has a number of sub-types. The three types are as follows.

1) **Conditionals that *describe facts***

   > **Example**
   >
   > *If water reaches 100 degrees*, it boils.

2) **Conditionals that *predict the future***

   > **Example**
   >
   > *If I the plane doesn't arrive on time*, we will have to delay the beginning of the conference.

3) **Conditionals that *describe imaginary situations***

   > **Example**
   >
   > *If I won the lottery*, I would be very happy.

1) Conditionals that describe facts

Conditionals that describe facts can be divided into two types:

a) **Conditionals that are <u>always</u> true**

This type can also be divided between those that refer to **states** and those that refer to **repeated events**.

> *Examples*
> *State*: **If you <u>*love*</u> someone**, you will always help them with their problems.
> *Repeated event*: **If water <u>*reaches*</u> 100 degrees**, it boils.

We can also use **when** or **whenever** as a subordinator in these situations. These types of conditionals tend to **use present simple** in the conditional clause and **present simple** in the independent clause

Conditionals that are only true <u>for a limited time</u>.

> *Example*
> **If *it is raining***, we will have to delay our experiment for a few hours.

Here the rain is **does not always happen**; it is happening now. These kinds of conditionals can be in **any tense**. They are similar to **results** (e.g. we would say: **It is raining, so we will have to delay our experiment for a few hours.**)

2) Conditionals that predict the future

These conditionals can either be **strong** or **weak**. If they are **strong** we use <u>**will**</u> to show that we think it will definitely happen. If we are less sure, we can use **other modals** like <u>**might, could,**</u> or <u>**should**</u>.

> *Examples*
> *Strong*: **If *it is hot tomorrow***, we <u>**will**</u> begin the experiment.
> *Weak*: **If *it is hot tomorrow***, I <u>**might**</u> begin the experiment.

These conditionals **use present simple** or **present continuous** in the conditional clause. The independent clause will always contain a **modal of probability**.

Note: we do not use future tense in the adverbial clause even though we are referring to the future. This is the same as adverbial clauses of time which follow the patterns in the table on the below.

Independent clause	Adverbial clause of time
Past	Past
Present	Present
Future	*Present*

3) Conditionals that describe imaginary situations

These types of conditionals describe situations that are not real. There are **two types**: hypothetical **conditionals** and **conditionals that are not real**.

a) **Hypothetical** conditionals talk about situations that **could be real but could be not real**; this could be because the author **doesn't know**, or it could be because the author is just **imagining** the situation. These conditionals can refer to the <u>**present**</u> or to the <u>**future**</u>.

> *Examples*
> **Present hypothetical: (1) If I <u>*were*</u> rich now, I <u>**would**</u> not work. (2) If he <u>*had*</u> more time, he <u>**would**</u> be able to work on his hobby.**

This sentence is imagining the situation now. It could be that it is not true or it could be that the speaker doesn't know if it is true. We use **past tense** (or the subjunctive 'were') in the **conditional clause** and we use the modal **would** in the **independent clause**.

Chapter 7

> **Examples**
>
> Future hypothetical: *If I* __won__ *the lottery tomorrow,* I **would** not work anymore.

This sentence is imagining a situation about the future. It is **not** predicting the future. We use **past tense** in the **conditional clause** and we use the modal **would** in the **independent clause**. Even though we use past tense, it is actually referring to the future.

b) **Unreal** conditionals are similar but they talk about situations that **can't actually be true**. These conditionals refer to the __past__ or to the __present__.

> **Examples**
>
> Present un-real: *If I* __were__ *a woman,* I **would** be able to have a baby.

The conditional clause is in past tense, but it refers to now (except the subjunctive **were**); the independent clause uses the modal **would** to show that this is a hypothetical sentence. **Would** is an indicator that the sentence is imaginary, but it does have a couple of other meanings (see Chapter 5 on tense and Chapter 6 on modals.)

> **Examples**
>
> Past un-real: *If I* __had won__ *the lottery last week,* I **would** not be at work today.

To show that the conditional clause is in the past, we use **past perfect** in the conditional clause (see also chapter 5 on tense). The independent clause again uses **would** to show that this is an imaginary situation.

Exercises

10.1 Join the following sentences together to make conditional adverbial clauses. You may need to change the tense and add modals for the sentences to make sense.

1) European domination of the world was inevitable; we could start world history over again from the start. However, the Europeans will still win.

2) However, this has nothing to do with the genetic make up of Europeans; they are not somehow better people; we could put Africans or Indians or Chinese or Incans in Europe 10,000 years ago, yet the people in Europe will still win.

3) This is because of the flora and fauna of the continent; a tribe of people wanting to settle down and build cities, needs plants and animals that can be domesticated.

4) Africa has plants that can be domesticated, but it doesn't have animals that can be domesticated; for instance, the Zebra can be domesticated. An Africa with domestic animals could have dominated the world.

5) North America has one plant (maize) that can be domesticated and one animal (the turkey); perhaps the North American Indians might have conquered the whole world, but North America had no horses, or it had no cows.

6) South America has one plant and two animals that can be domesticated (the llama and the guinea pig); farming cannot progress. However, a country that has horses or cows can progress.

7) Australia has neither plants nor animals that can be domesticated, so it did not develop farming.

8) In a world in which the emu could be domesticated, it could be used to pull ploughs. _____

9) Eurasia had plenty of plants that could be domesticated (wheat and rice) and it had plenty of animals that could be domesticated (pigs, cows, sheep, horses, chickens); a continent that does not have these plants and animals will not develop farms and cities. _____

10) Farming of these animals and plants easily spread east and west from the Middle East into Europe, India, and China; it is easy for farming methods to spread to other countries. The countries are on roughly the same latitude.

11) It is very hard for farming to spread in a continent that has a north south axis, like the Americas.

12) All of these facts are true, so why was it Europe, not the Middle East, China or India that conquered the whole world?

13) The answer is geography; many small kingdoms can exist to compete with each other over technology and exploration when a continent is mountainous like Europe.

14) It is easy for one kingdom to conquer the whole continent in the situation where a continent has vast flat areas, like China and India.

10.2 Decide whether the following sentences need to be made into hypothetical conditional statements using past tense or past perfect and the words 'would' or would have.

1) If it rains tomorrow, I'll have to cancel my appointment.

2) If sea levels rise, most cities in the eastern region will be under water.

3) If aliens come to Earth, we will be ready to great them.

4) If aliens came to Earth 4000 years ago, we do not know if they came or not.

5) If the people of 1938 knew what we know now, they knew to stop Hitler before his evil atrocities really started.

6) The sea level in the Atlantic might start to rise. In this case the flow of warm water from the Pacific to the Atlantic will stop. This will cause Europe to become cooler than now.

7) If Canada invades the USA, they will not win.

8) The Republicans may win the next election. Should this happen, they will try to stop stem cell research.

9) If a monkey wins the next election, it will be a better president.

10) If I work in Antarctica, I go skiing everyday.

Chapter 7

10.3 Write sentences using the following types of conditionals.

1) Fact always true (state)

_____

_____

2) Fact always true (repeated event)

_____

_____

3) Fact true for a limited time

_____

_____

4) Strong future prediction

_____

_____

5) Weak future prediction

_____

_____

6) Hypothetical present tense statement

_____

_____

7) Hypothetical future tense statement

_____

_____

8) Untrue present tense statement

_____

_____

9) Untrue past tense statement

_____

_____

Conditionals 2

Conditionals can also be created in some other ways. One way is using **inverted word order**; another is using **participial conditional clauses**.

Inverted word order

One way of creating a conditional clause is to change the word order instead of using the word *if*. We use 'question word order'. This can **only be done with <u>past</u> tense imaginary conditionals or <u>present</u> tense imaginary conditionals using '<u>were</u>'.**

> ***Examples***
>
> 1) If I were rich now, I would not work → ***Were*** *I rich now*, I **would** not work.
>
> 2) If he had more time, he would be able to work on his hobby.
> → ***Had*** *he more time*, he **would** be able to work on his hobby.
>
> 3) If I were a woman, I would be able to have a baby. → ***Were*** *I a woman,* I **would** be able to have a baby.
>
> 4) If I had won the lottery last week, I would not be at work today.
> → ***Had I won*** *the lottery last week,* I **would** not be at work today.

Should and inverted word order

We can also use inverted word order with **should** to create real future conditionals or impossible past tense conditionals. See the following examples.

> **Examples**
>
> 1) If he is late, I will be angry → **Should he be late**, I **will** be angry.
>
> 2) If I had won the lottery last week, I would not be at work today.
> → **Should I have won** the lottery last week, I **would** not be at work today.

Reduced conditionals

Conditional clauses can be reduced to participial clauses in the same way that relative clauses can be reduced. More on this can be found in Chapter 10, page 173. This can only be done with conditionals that are combined with **advice** and where **if** describes a **timeless fact** (see **Conditionals 1**, pages 121-126 for more on this). To do this, the conditional clause and the independent clause must share the same subject.

To make a reduced conditional, change the verb to the active or past participle. Use the **active** participle for **active** voice sentences and use the **past** participle for **passive** voice.

> **Example**
>
> If you take South Road, makes sure you don't get caught in traffic every morning. → **If taking** South Road, make sure you don't caught in traffic every morning.

> **Note**
>
> The participle is the **adjective** form of the verb. The verb has **four forms**: the **finite** (verb form), the **gerund** (noun form), the **infinitive**, and the **participle** (adjective form). The adjective form has two forms: active and passive. The active form looks like the gerund (V~ing); the passive form is the past participle (E.g. go, went, **gone**). You can commonly see these forms in some verbs like interest and bore which have the participle forms **interesting** and **interested** and **bored** and **boring**.

Other conditional words

Notice that there are a number of other words that also trigger conditionals. There words are listed in the following box.

> **Other words triggering conditional tenses:**
>
> | | | | | | |
> |---|---|---|---|---|---|
> | assuming | but for | in that case | on condition | so long as | supposing |
> | barring any | in case | in the event | provided | | |

Exercises

11.1 Re write the following conditionals using inverted word order if possible.

1) If I were more careful when I write in English, I would get higher marks.

_____

2) If he had taken more time to investigate the side-effects, this problem would not be occurring.

_____

3) If they had taken the time to read other research on the same topic, this problem would not have arisen.

_____

4) If they were more careful when they do their research, this sort of problem wouldn't arise.

_____

Chapter 7

5) If she considered essay questions more carefully, she would be able to write more involved answers.

_____

_____

11.2 Write inverted conditional sentences of your own.

1) _____

_____

2) _____

_____

3) _____

_____

4) _____

_____

11.3 Re write the following conditionals using *should* if possible.

1) If you see my George, tell him that him that I want to speak to him.

_____

_____

2) Can you tell me if you find an article on 'work ethic' while you're looking.

_____

_____

3) If they had been late, they would have been excluded from the study.

_____

_____

4) If water reaches zero degrees, it freezes.

_____

_____

5) If the professor is busy, his secretary is available.

_____

_____

11.4 Write conditionals of your own using should.

1) _____

_____

2) _____

_____

3) _____

_____

4) _____

_____

12.5 Reduce the following conditionals to participial clauses if possible.

1) If you take this medicine daily, make sure you should make sure you drink plenty of water too.

_____

_____

2) If you study English, you will need to buy this grammar book.

_____

3) Take two copies of each of these documents if you are studying nursing.

4) You won't be able to do this exercise if you haven't read the explanation above.

5) Try to improve the coherence in your writing if you are trying to pass the IELTS test.

Comparison

These clauses compare two nouns. In these clauses we use either the subordinator *than* or the subordinator *as... as...*, or the *same [noun] as...*. *Than* shows how the adjective or adverb in one clause compares to the same adjective or adverb in another clause. We always use a comparative (*more* or *...er*) with *than*.

> ### Examples
> Richard is **_more_** intelligent *than* George is.   Heather drove furth**er** this summer *than Sarah did last summer*.

Note that we could reduce these clauses to just a noun or a noun and a prepositional phrase if we wanted to.

> ### Examples
> Richard is smart**er** *than* George.   Heather drove furth**er** this summer *than Sarah last summer*.

We can also add a quantifier (a word like 'much' or 'a little') to these types of clauses.

> ### Example
> Richard is **considerably** smart**er** *than* George is.

As...as... shows that the adjective or adverb in both clauses are equal.

> ### Example
> My dog is **as** <u>smart</u> **as** George is.

Note that we do not use **as** on its own, so we do not, for instance, say: *My dog is <u>smart</u> as George is.* (X) Similarly, we cannot use **same** in these clauses. You cannot, for instance, say *my dog is <u>as same as</u> George is.* (X) To use **same**, you have to say *my dog is <u>the</u> same as George*. However, this is not an adverbial clause. However, *the same + noun group as...* can be a subordinator.

> ### Example
> The Queen of England has **the same** amount of money in the bank *as Bill Gates does*.

Exercises

12.1 Choose the appropriate subordinator (*as...as, the same ...as, than*) to join these clauses together.

1) I am happier now. I have never been so happy before. _____

2) I am young. My sister is several years younger. _____

3) She is 35 Years old. I am 35 years old._____

4) Richard has an IQ of 150. Albert Einstein had an IQ of 150. _____

5) He wears Oakley sunglasses. I wear Oakley sunglasses. _____

_____

6) PCs are good computers. Apple computers are better. _____

_____

7) Portsmouth is not an interesting a place to live. London is more interesting. _____

_____

8) I don't find adverbial clauses easy to understand. I find relative clauses easy to understand. _____

_____

12.2 Write two sentences of your own containing the subordinator *than*, two containing *as...as*, and two containing *the same...as*.

1) _____

_____

2) _____

_____

3) _____

_____

4) _____

_____

5) _____

_____

6) _____

_____

Chapter 8   Language Patterns

Cause and effect language

It is important to be able to use a variety of different cause and effect words to understand and write about various processes in academic essays. However, because there are a variety of different word forms used in cause and effect language and because small changes in prepositions can change the meaning completely, it is language that needs to be studied in detail.

The following is a list of some cause and effect words:

affect	due to	the purpose of
the effect of... is...	ensue	the reason for... is...
have an effect on	for	since
the aim of	generate	so
arise from	give rise to	so that
arise out of	hence	spark (off)
as	motivate	stem from
because	the outcome of	therefore
because of	owing to	thus
cause	prompt	the upshot of
the cause of ... is...	provoke	
consequently	result from	
as a consequence	result in	
as a consequence of	as a result	
the consequence of ... is ...	as a result of	

Note

Notice the spelling difference between the noun **effect** and the verb **affect**.

For is a coordinator in this case and should not be confused with the preposition **for**, which has a different meaning.

Cause and effect patterns

It is important to know whether the cause comes first or whether the affect comes first. The cause and effect words listed above use the following patterns (**take note of the punctuation** as you read the list). C = cause / E = effect

Cause and effect patterns:

the affect of C is E.	C; as a result, E.	the purpose of C is E.
C affects (V) E.	as a result of C, E.	the reason for E is C.
C has (V) an effect on E.	E results from (V) C.	since C, E. (**or** E, since C.)
the aim of C is E.	C results in (V) E.	C, so E.
E arises from (V) C.	due to C, E.	C so that E.
E arises out of (V) C.	E ensues (V).	C sparked (off) (V) E.
as C, E. (**or** E, as C.)	E, for E.	E stems from C.
because C, E. (**or** E because C.)	C generates (V) E.	C; therefore, E.
because of C, E. C gives rise to (V) E.	the upshot of C is E.	C; thus, E.
C causes (V) E.	C; hence, E.	
the cause of E is C.	C motivates (V) E.	
C; consequently, E.	the outcome of C is E.	
C; as a consequence, E.	owing to C, E. (**Or** E owing to C.)	
as a consequence of C, E.	C prompted (V) E.	
the consequence of C is E.	C provoked (V) E.	

Chapter 8

Exercises

1.1 Decide whether the following fragments are causes or effects and attach them to the cause and effect words given in brackets with appropriate punctuation. Remember to change the form or tense of verbs

1) strokes / blockages in arteries (to cause) _____

2) blocked arteries / blood not getting to part of the brain (to arise from) _____
   _____

3) most strokes / blood clots in the arteries supplying blood to the brain (the consequence of) _____
   _____

4) arteries that are narrowed by a long-term build up of cholesterol and other fats in the artery wall / blood clots (to result in)
   _____
   _____

5) a heart attack if it occurs in the arteries supplying the heart / the same process (to give rise to) _____
   _____

6) rupture of an artery in the brain / a haemorrhagic stroke happens (due to) _____
   _____

7) rupture of an artery in the brain / there is bleeding and squashing of the surrounding tissue (because of)
   _____
   _____

8) rainforest destruction / agriculture and in drier areas, fuelwood collection (the causes of) _____
   _____

9) forest degradation / logging (to result in) _____

10) rainforests / mining, industrial development and large dams also (to affect) _____
    _____

11) a larger threat to the forests / tourism (to generate) _____

12) the timber industry's method of 'selective' logging / natural forest regrowth (the outcome of) _____
    _____

13) autism / it is still unclear what (to give rise to) _____

14) a child with a genetic problems being exposed to one or more problems / recent research suggests that Autism (to result from) _____
    _____

15) these problems / a series of poor interactions between Genes and Nutrients (to result from) _____
    _____

1.2 Join the two parts of these sentences together

1) The aim of [   ]

2) The purpose of [   ]

3) The effect of [   ]

4) The Second World War affected [   ]

5) The popularity of English as an international language has generated [   ]

6) English becoming an international language has given rise to [   ]

7) Worries about 'linguistic imperialism' have motivated [   ]

8) The outcome of [   ]

9) Efforts by the Germans to promote their language as an international language in the early 20th century prompted [   ]

10) The British and American governments poured money into the English language teaching industry so that [   ]

11) The success of English stems from [   ]

12) The upshot of [   ] the importance of English.

a) questions about 'linguistic imperialism'

b) the British and Americans to pour money into the English language teaching industry.

c) English would become the international language.

d) the rise in power of Britain and the United States over the last 200 years has been the rise in influence of English.

e) many countries to reconsider the amount of influence English should be having.

f) English becoming an in international language has been a loss in popularity of French and German.

g) this paper is to discuss what the causes of the increasing popularity of English are.

h) all of the above points is that people all over the world are now learning English whether they want to or not.

i) a whole new industry of teaching English.

j) good timing; English was the most popular language when an international language was needed.

k) an International language is to make it easier for international communities to communicate with each other.

Grammar of cause and effect language

We also need to consider the different grammar structures with the different cause and affect words.

We can divide cause and effect language into the following categories:

> **Types of cause and effect structures:**
>
> **Coordinators**: *for, so*
>
> **Subordinators**: *because, since, as, so that*
>
> **Conjunctive adverbs**: *therefore, consequently, as a result, as a consequence, hence, thus*
>
> **Prepositions**: *due to, because of, as a result of, as a consequence of, owing to*
>
> **Nouns + preposition**: *The effect of, the consequence of, the cause of, the reason for, the aim of, the outcome of, the purpose of, the upshot of*
>
> **Verbs**: *cause, affect, have an affect on, result from, result in, arise from, arise out of, ensue, generate, give rise to, motivate, prompt, provoke, spark off, stem from*

Revision

It is important to understand how these different parts of speech can be used to make meaning. Before understanding how to use these words, we need to review some vocabulary for talking about language.

Independent clause: A clause that can stand alone. Every sentence in academic writing must have an independent clause.

Noun clause: A dependent clause that acts as a noun, often the object of a reporting verb, but also the object or subject of the verb **be** or related verbs such as **become, appear,** and **seem.** The only way you can use a noun clause in cause and effect language is if it is the object or subject of the verb **be** or a related verb, or if you are reporting the cause or effect.

Relative clause: A dependent clause that describes a noun or a clause.

Adverbial clause: A dependent clause that describes the process (verb) in the sentence. Adverbial clauses can show result, reason, or purpose. All of these types of clauses show cause and effect. The subordinators **as,**

since, and *because* all begin adverbial clauses of reason. The subordinator ***so that*** begins adverbial clauses of purpose.

Participial clause: Adverbial clauses and relative clauses can be reduced to participial clauses to shorten them if the dependent clause and independent clause have the same subject.

Gerund Clause: Gerund clauses are non-finite clauses that have the verb in gerund form. They often do not have a subject.

> **Examples**
>
> *Not having a job* is the cause of me being poor.
>
> *George not liking me* has little consequence to me.

Noun Phrase: Noun phrases are nouns along with the adjectives, articles, and other words that help modify the meaning of the noun phrase. Remember the word order for noun phrases: determiner, quantifier, intensifier, adjective, classifier, noun.

> **Example**
>
> The two very ugly school boys.
>
> *Determiner quantifier intensifier adjective classifier noun*

Prepositional phrase: A prepositional phrase begins with a preposition and is followed by a noun phrase or a gerund clause. A prepositional phrase cannot contain a finite verb; it can, however, contain a dependent clause, which can contain a verb.

> **Example**
>
> I gave it **to** *the two very ugly school boys sitting on the bench which is under the tree.*

Infinitive clause: An infinitive clause is a non-finite clause that contains the infinitive form of a verb instead of the finite form. Remember, some verbs are followed by gerund clauses, others by infinitive clauses.

> **Example**
>
> This caused *them to be very happy.*

Forming cause and effect sentences

Having now reviewed these different parts of speech, we can now look at how to form sentences using the different cause and effect words listed above. **Note the punctuation carefully**.

> **Forming cause and effect sentences**
>
> Coordinators are used in the following way:
> *Independent clause*, **coordinator** *Independent clause*.
>
> Subordinators are used in the following way:
> *Independent clause* **subordinator** *dependent clause*. Or **Subordinator** *dep clause*, *Indep clause*.
>
> Conjunctive adverbs are used in the following way:
> *Indep clause*; **conjunctive adverb**, *Indep clause*. Or *Indep clause*. **Conjunctive adverb**, *Indep clause*.
>
> Prepositions are used in the following way:
> *Independent clause* **preposition** *gerund clause*. Or **Preposition** *gerund clause*, *Independent clause*
>
> Noun + preposition structures are used in the following ways:
> ***Noun* preposition** *gerund clause* **is/are/was/were** *gerund clause.*
> Or *gerund clause* **is/are/was/were** *noun* **preposition** *gerund clause.*
>
> Verbs are used in the following ways
> *gerund clause* **verb** *gerund clause*. Sometimes we also have the construction: *gerund clause* **verb** **infinitive clause**. (The verb *to cause* is always used in this pattern.)

Verb complements

Remember that *ensue* cannot have an object. It is **intransitive**.

The following verbs can only be followed by noun phrases and gerund clauses: ***affect, have an affect on, result from, result in, arise from, arise out of, generate, give rise to, provoke, spark off, stem from***

The following verbs can only be followed by noun phrases or infinitive clauses: ***cause, motivate, prompt***

> **Examples**
>
> **Coordinator**
>
> Kress does not approve of increased migration, **for** he has limited understanding of its positives.
>
> **Subordinator**
>
> Kress does not approve of increased migration **because** he has limited understanding of its positives.
>
> **Because** he has limited understanding of its positives, Kress does not approve of increased migration.

> *More Examples*
> **Conjunctive adverb**
> Kress has limited understanding of the positives of increased migration; **therefore,** he does not approve of it.
> Kress has limited understanding of the positives of increased migration. **Therefore,** he does not approve of it.
> **Preposition**
> **Because of** <u>having</u> a limited understanding of the positives of increased migration, Kress does not approve of it.
> Kress does not approve of increased migration **because of** <u>having</u> a limited understanding of its positives.
> **Noun + preposition**
> **The affect of** <u>having</u> a limited understanding of the positives of increased migration, **is** Kress not <u>approving</u> of it.
> **Verb**
> Kress <u>having</u> a limited understanding of the positives of increased migration **results in** him not <u>approving</u> of it.
> Kress <u>having</u> a limited understanding of the positives of increased migration **causes** him not <u>to approve</u> of it.

Exercises

2.1 Identify the parts of speech used in the following cause and effect structures (noun phrase, noun group…etc…). The first one has been done for you.

  1) <u>Bushfires</u> **are** <u>the consequence</u> <u>of both natural causes and human activity</u>.
     (noun)   (verb)   (noun phrase)   (prepositional phrase)

  2) Lightning strikes are the cause of almost all natural bushfires

  3) On January 7, 2003 over 120 bushfires started as a consequence of lightning from thunderstorms in south-eastern Australia.

  4) In late November 1997 over 100 fires in East Gippsland were caused by lightning within a 24-hour period.

  5) All other bushfires on public land are started as a result of human activity.

  6) The reason for approximately 74% of all bushfires on public land is human activity.

  7) On average, approximately 10% of the bushfires that start on public land are due to campfires.

  8) Fires on public land can arise from farmers burning vegetation.

  9) Any equipment or machinery that generates heat or sparks is a potential cause of bushfires.

  10) Other bushfires result from deliberately lit fires, often by children who are playing with matches.

  (Source: http://www.dse.vic.gov.au/dse/nrenfoe.nsf/FID/-90A4796345F5395F4A25679300155A40?OpenDocument)

2.2 Decide which is the cause and which is the effect and then join these sentences using the cause and effect word in brackets

  1) **(Since)**
     _____ People earn more money.
     _____ Prices for goods and services increase because people have more money to spend.

     _____

     _____

  2) **(Because of)**
     _____ Everybody likes pop music.
     _____ The regular beat of pop music sounds very similar to the heartbeat in the womb.

     _____

     _____

  3) **(Due to)**
     _____ People do not understand the clothing, manners, and customs of new migrant groups.
     _____ People always dislike new migrant communities.

     _____

     _____

Chapter 8

4) **(As a consequence of)**

_____ More and more people are opting for plastic surgery to improve their looks.

_____ Magazines and television make people increasingly more aware of their self-image these days.

_____

_____

5) **(To give rise to)**

_____ During the past 100 years, many Pacific island people saw foreigners from Europe, Japan, and America come to their islands. A short while after the foreigners arrived, aeroplanes would come with cargo for the foreigners. The Pacific Islanders thought that this cargo came from gods.

_____ The Pacific islanders started to worship these cargo gods, hoping that the cargo gods would send them cargo too.

_____

_____

_____

6) **(To result in)**

_____Some people go crazy and start to murder people.

_____These days there are increasing problems with overpopulation. Humans only recently evolved from being scavengers, hunters and gatherers. Many humans are not able to adjust to this new environment.

_____

_____

_____

7) **(As a consequence / So)**

_____ Today there are many fewer wars.

_____ In the past countries wanted to show off how strong they were.

_____ Countries had wars. However, today, countries can show off how strong they are at international sporting events such as the Olympics and the World Cup.

_____

_____

_____

8) **(The cause of)**

_____ People have inadequate cooling off or rest periods at work.

_____ People do not consume enough water at work.

_____ Heat-related health problems happen at work.

_____

_____

9) **(The effect of / Therefore)**

_____ People who play computer games too much sometimes do crazy things like killing people.

_____ They think that they can turn off life and start it again.

_____ People play computer games too much.

_____

_____

10) **(The upshot of / Thus)**

_____ Human minds have evolved to understand how things are created.

_____ People tend to believe that the universe must have a creator.

_____ People tend to believe that everything must have a creator.

_____

_____

11) **(To give rise to / hence)**

136

_____ They began to make grunting noises to each other. After time, these grunting noises became words, and the first languages had begun.

_____ Human-like apes long ago needed to make tools.

_____ The need to exchange information about making tools.

_____

_____

_____

12) **(To cause)**

_____ Since the 1950s, the number of women working has increased dramatically.

_____ The unemployment rate has not gone up during that time.

_____

_____

2.3 Write cause and effect sentences of your own using the following words

1) (To have an effect on) _____

2) (To affect) _____

3) (To arise out of) _____

4) (As) _____

5) (As a result) _____

6) (The consequence of … is …) _____

7) (To ensue) _____

8) (For) _____

9) (To generate) _____

10) (To motivate) _____

Chapter 8

Compare & Contrast Language

It is also important to be able to use a variety of different compare and contrast words to understand and write about various processes in academic essays.

The following is a list of some compare & contrast words:

alike	*even though*	*on the contrary*
although	*however*	*the same as*
as...as...	*in contrast*	*the same*
both...and...	*in comparison*	*similar*
but	*in spite of*	*similar to*
by comparison	*just as*	*similarly*
compared to	*just like*	*though*
compared with	*like*	*too*
despite	*likewise*	*unlike*
differ from	*neither...nor...*	*whereas*
differ to	*not only...but also...*	*while*
dissimilar	*on the other hand*	*yet*

Notes

Differ is a verb.

As is not used for comparison apart from in combination with other words. For example, '***he is as a policeman***' does not make sense. You must say '***he is like a policeman***'.

Grammar of compare and contrast language.

We can divide compare and contrast language into the following categories:

Types of compare & contrast structures:

Coordinators: *but, yet, both...and.., neither...nor,*

Subordinators: *although, as...as...., even though, just as, just like, like, though, unlike, whereas, while*

Conjunctive adverbs: *however, by comparison, in comparison, likewise, on the other hand, on the contrary, similarly*

Prepositions: *as...as, despite, just like, like, in spite of, unlike*

Adjectives: *dissimilar, similar, similar to, the same*

Verbs: *differ from, differ to,*

Adverbs: *too*

Participial: *compared to, compared with*

An explanation of how we use coordinators, subordinators, conjunctive adverbs, prepositions and verbs is given on page 133; refer to this explanation as you do the exercises in the next section. Also, notice how the adverbs and participial phrases are used.

Forming cause and effect sentences

Adverbs are used in the following ways:
<u>Gerund clause</u> **adverb** *verb* <u>gerund clause</u>.
Or <u>Gerund clause</u> *verb* <u>gerund clause</u> **adverb.**

Participles are used in the following ways:
<u>Noun phrase</u> **participial phrase** *verb complement.*

Or **participial phrase,** <u>Noun phrase</u> *verb complement.* Or <u>gerund clause</u> *verb* <u>Noun phrase</u> **participial phrase**

> **Subordinators and Punctuation**
>
> Generally, we **put a comma** after a dependent adverbial clause if it comes **before** the independent clause and **no comma** if it comes **after** the independent clause, except:
>
> **1) We usually put a comma before** while and whereas.
>
> **2) Many people put a comma before** although, though, and even though.
>
> **3) Do not put a comma before** as...as... **or** like.

Examples

Adverb
Carlson makes a good point and Johnson does too.

Adjective
Their arguments are dissimilar.

Preposition
Despite having opposing opinions, both authors make valuable contributions.

Verb
Carlson's argument differs from Johnson's argument in three areas.

Participial phrase
Both authors offer excellent solutions to the problem compared to previous authors.
Compared to previous authors, both authors offer excellent solutions.

Exercises

4.1 Rewrite the following sentences using the words in brackets.

1) Many people claim that French is difficult to learn. English is difficult to learn too. **(as...as...)** _____

   _____

2) The English language is like the French language. **(are similar)** _____

   _____

3) There are many differences in English and French pronunciation, but there are also some similarities.
   (although) _____

   _____

4) Several sounds in the English language are like sounds only found in French. **(similar to)** _____

   _____

5) French has many accented letters. English does not have many accented letters. **(whereas)** _____

   _____

6) English has many irregular verbs; French has many irregular verbs. **(just like)** _____

   _____

7) French writing and English writing look similar. **(looks like)** _____

   _____

8) The meanings of many French words are no different to the meanings of many English words. **(the same
   as)** _____

   _____

9) For example, the meaning of the word *ballet* is no different in either language. **(is the same)** _____

   _____

10) Hotel means a place to stay in English; it means a place to stay in French too. **(Just as)** _____

   _____

11) Often the nuance of the vocabulary in English can be unlike its French meaning. **(differ from)** _____

   _____

12) On the other hand, some similar words have actually come into both English and French from one foreign
    language. For example, 'pajama' does not differ in either language because it actually comes from the
    Hindi language of India. **(however, alike, the same)**

_____

_____

_____

13) Nevertheless, even though there is similarity in vocabulary between the two languages, grammatical structures are often quite different. **(On the other hand, despite)** _____

_____

_____

As and Like

These two words cause students a lot of confusion. *Like* is usually used for examples; *as* has a variety of meanings in combination with other words, but used on its own it only has three main meanings: *in the way that*, *because*, and *while*.

Notice the difference between the following uses of *as*:

1. *As* (reason)

As is an adverbial subordinator of reason. It has the same meaning as *because*.

2. *As* (time 1)

As is also an adverbial subordinator of time. There is little difference of meaning with *while*.

3. *As* (time 2)

As has a second meaning as a subordinator of time. Here, *as* means *at the same time as*.

4. *As* (manner)

As has a fourth meaning as an adverbial subordinator of manner. Here it means *the way that*.

It is also often used in the reporting structure '*As Smith points out...*' to show that you as a writer agree with Smith.

> **Examples**
> They repaired the spaceship *as they had promised to.*
> *As Brock suggests*, this will be a major problem in the future.

> **Note**
> These adverbial clauses can be reduced to participial clauses.

> **Example**
> They repaired the spaceship *as promised.*

5. *Subject Verb* **as** adjective / adverb / quantifier **as object**

The adjective, adverb, or quantifier used to describe the subject is equal to the adjective, adverb, or quantifier used to describe the object.

> **Note**
> *as...as...* can be both a preposition and a subordinator.

> **Examples**
> O'Conner's arguments are as interesting as Johnson's.
> O'Conner writes as interestingly as Johnson.
> O'Conner has written as much as Johnson on the topic.

6. *Subject Linking verb* **the same as** *Object*

The word *same* is an adjective, but it follows a different pattern to other adjectives used in the *as...as...* structure. We <u>always</u> use *same* in the pattern ...*is* <u>the</u> *same as*... (although we can change *is* to *seems to be* or *appears*). Remember to put *the* instead of *as*.

> **Example**
> O'Conner's argument is the same as Johnson's argument.

7. *So as to*

So as to is the same as *so that* or *in order to*, and it shows purpose or intention. It is followed by the infinitive form of the verb.

> **Example**
> Carlsson constructed his article *so as* <u>to make</u> it easy to understand and follow his arguments.

8. *As often as*

As often as is a preposition **or** an adverbial subordinator showing manner. This subordinator means that verb in both the independent and dependent clause happen with the same frequency.

> **Example**
> She has been to the source of the disturbance to investigate it as often as she can.

9. *As soon as*

As soon as is an adverbial subordinator of time showing that the event in the independent clause will happen immediately after the event in the adverbial clause.

> **Example**
> She will submit her thesis as soon as she completes it.

10. *As long as*

As long as is a conditional adverbial subordinator that is closely related to time. It has a meaning that the event in the independent clause is (or will be) true for the duration of the time that the event in the adverbial clause is true.

> **Example**
> She will continue studying in Florida as long as she has enough money to. (In other words, she will stop studying if she doesn't have enough money.)

11. *As far as*

As far as is a preposition or an adverbial subordinator showing manner. This subordinator means that the verb in both the independent and dependent clause will last for the same distance.

> **Example**
> When doing their research, they travelled as far as the previous researchers had.

> **Note**
> **As far as** can also be used to mean *this is the best I can do*. We often use it in the expressions *as far as I know*, or *as far as I can see*.

> **Example**
> We have done a lot of research on the topic, and as far as we know, this is the only study that has tested these specific issues.

12. *As well as*

As well as has two meanings. One meaning is *also*. **As well as** should be used between two nouns or between two noun phrases.

> **Examples**
> The researchers studied volcanos as well as earthquakes.
> The researchers investigated volcanos growing in size as well as volcanos shrinking in size.

As well as can also be used to show that a subject and an object do a verb equally well.

13. *As well*

As well means *too*; it comes at the end of a clause.

> **Example**
> The have researched the causes of earthquakes as well.

14. *As is*

As is means *so is* or *also*.

> **Examples**
> Tazieff was a great vulcanologist, as was Krafft.
> You'd better clean that one before using it, but the other one you can use as is.

As is is also used at the end of clauses, especially in spoken English, to mean *without being changed*. This is a fixed expression and does not change for tense.

Chapter 8

15. *Even as*

Even as is an adverbial subordinator of time. It has the same meaning that **as** has, but shows surprise or that it is unexpected.

> ### *Example*
> Even as I write this paper, farmers and villagers in the Darfur area are being tortured.

16. *Just as*

Just as is also an adverbial subordinator of time. It has a meaning that the event in the dependent clause happened either at the exact moment of the event in the independent clause, or that the event in the dependent clause happened at the last minute.

17. *Such as*

Such as means **for example**, but <u>must</u> be used after the noun it describes. It cannot describe **a whole clause, a verb, an adjective, or a pronoun.**

> ### *Examples*
> Many countries have different kinds of minerals which are used for making products, **such as** China. **X** *(This is wrong because China is not a type od product)*
> The immune system is stimulated by an event **such as** an infection causing inflammation, including a burn or injury. *(This is okay because infections and burns are types of events)*

18. *As if / As though*

These two words have the same meaning. They are adverbial subordinators and must be followed by a *clause*. Their meaning is '**in a way that makes it look like...**'

> ### *Example*
> He walks as if he has a broken leg. (From the way he walks, it looks like he has a broken leg.)

19. *As for*

As for is a preposition meaning '**with regard to**' or '**concerning**'. It usually comes at the start of a sentence and is used to reintroduce a topic which was not fully discussed before.

> ### *Example*
> As for Cullen, she can research deep-sea volcanos.

20. *As yet*

As yet means **still**. This adverb usually comes inside the noun group.

> ### *Example*
> She will study the as yet unknown cause of these types of eruptions.

21. Fixed expressions

There are a number of fixed expressions using as, including:

As I was saying, as a rule, as it stands, adjective as it seems, not so adjective as ..., as far as I'm concerned, as it were

22. Idioms:

There are also a number of idioms using as:

as old as the hills, as safe as houses, as distinct from

23. Verbs followed by *as*:

Several verbs can be followed by the preposition **as**: **view as, regard as, treat as, know as, consider as**

Notice the difference between *as* and *like*

People **like** him are never successful. ←→ People <u>**such as**</u> him are never successful.

He walks **as if / as though** he has a broken leg. ←→ He walks **like** he has a broken leg.

He has a car **like** mine. (**<u>not</u> as**)

Exercises

5.1 Put the correct usage of *as* from the list above into the gaps below.

UFOs are an _____ unexplained phenomenon; in recent times there has been a massive proliferation in the number of alleged sightings and abductions. However, it is not _____ UFOs are an entirely new phenomenon. A UFO was reportedly sighted _____ago ____ 1878, when 'a black disk flying at incredible speed' was seen. Most sightings, nevertheless, have been post world war two. However, _____ is often pointed out, many have been sightings of US and Russian test planes and experiments. _____ being man made objects, some have been hoaxes, and some psychological phenomena; however, there has been some unexplainable evidence. Sightings by notable persons such as former US presidents and NASA astronauts _____ mass sightings in which whole towns or cities have seen objects that can't be explained remain mysteries, _____ photographic and video footage do.

Sceptics have pointed out that there are several reasons to doubt these sightings. Firstly, why would aliens travel across the universe _____ Earth to observe us for just a few moments and then leave without contacting us? And secondly, modern physics deems long distance space travel near impossible. For instance, _____ the maximum speed that an object can travel at is slightly below the speed of light, if a spacecraft were to travel at the speed of light, it would take 8.6 years to travel _____ the nearest star and back again; it would take 30,000 years to travel to the centre of the Milky Way, and it would take 2,000,000 years to travel to the nearest galaxy. Thus, _____ modern physics is right, it seems unlikely that aliens would ever be able to travel between universes.

Still, UFOlogists have pointed to other evidence _____ signs of aliens having come to earth in ancient times. One popular idea is that the ancient ideas of gods visiting earth is based on UFOs visiting earth. More compelling, however, is evidence _____ the Piri Reis Map, a map whose depiction of the earth is _____ modern maps, but which was drawn before mankind mapped the earth.

On the other hand, _____ UFOlogists or sceptics debate, with the recent proliferation of mobile phones with video recording functions, very hard to explain video footage of UFOs is being uploaded to the internet. Once such piece of footage is a 28 minute video from Turkey in 2008, in which a security guard videoed a UFO hovering above the earth on two consecutive nights. This evidence does not appear to be a hoax and cannot easily be explained.

5.2 If possible, change the following sentences from *like* to *such as* or *as if*. If it is not possible, write not possible.

1) Statements *like* that always upset people. _____

2) He describes UFOs *like* he has seen one. _____

3) Johnsons's beliefs are *like* Carter's. _____

4) Nobody believes hysterical claims *like* Gibson's. _____

5) *Like* Erickson, James does not subscribe to this view. _____

6) James talks about UFOs *like* he is an expert. _____

7) Most people describing Carter write about him *like* he is insane. _____

Argument and refutation language

Sometimes you will be expected to create an argument. Here, **argument** means stating your position and trying to convince others that your position is correct. Arguments are formed by using cause and effect language and compare and contrast language. However, in English argument, we often use *refutation*. This means mentioning opposing points of views and explaining why they are incorrect; you must also use reported speech noun clauses, and modals and adverbs of probability to do this. This is difficult because you not only need to make it clear

143

which writer has the view that you are taking and whether or not you agree with this view as well as the degree to which you agree.

Refutation

Often we begin by finding reasons why somebody might disagree with our view. For example, we might believe that *being a supermodel would be a great job*. However, other people might think that being a supermodel would be bad because a supermodel has no privacy and is hounded by the paparazzi all the time.

We begin by making a statement such as:

> '*<u>Some people</u> <u>believe</u> that being a supermodel would be bad because a supermodel has no privacy and is hounded by the paparazzi all the time*'.

Within this statement, we can alter '*some people*' to a particular author or expert (it is important to make it clear who has this view), and we can change '*believe*' to another reporting verb. It is important that we do not use the phrase '*as.... points out...*' because this shows that we agree with this view. The objective in this exercise is to disagree.

Appropriate verbs include: *claim, maintain, believe, insist,* and *argue*. *Claim* and *maintain* show that the writer (you) does not agree with the person that they are citing.

Next, we use a strong contrast word such as *however, nevertheless,* or *nonetheless,* and introduce our counter argument.

> ### Example
>
> Some people believe that being a supermodel would be bad because a supermodel has no privacy and is hounded by the paparazzi all the time; however, the fantastic wealth and opportunity to travel would more than outweigh these problems.

In the above example, '*the fantastic wealth and opportunity to travel would more than outweigh these problems*' is the topic sentence for the paragraph; we would expect to see the ideas of wealth and travel for supermodels discussed in this paragraph.

We don't need to say that the opposing view is completely wrong. We can also say that it is based on misguided information, or that it is true, but not important. It is important to use 'hedge' words in this situation. 'Hedge' words can include modals such as *might* or *could*; they can include adverbs such as *probably* or *possibly*, and they can include other structures that distance you from the statement such as *it would seem that...* or *it appears that...*. (More on hedge words can be found on page 100.)

> ### Examples
>
> 1) Some people believe that being a supermodel would be bad because a supermodel has no privacy and is hounded by the paparazzi all the time; however, in actual fact supermodel's have a lot of privacy and are rarely hounded by the paparazzi.
>
> 2) Some people believe that being a supermodel would be bad because a supermodel has no privacy and is hounded by the paparazzi all the time; however, while this maybe true, it is completely overshadowed by the fact that these people make an incredible amount of money for very little effort.

Parallel Structures

Remember also, to pay attention to parallel structures - that is, to repeat the subordinator if needed to show that the next clause is also the view of the author that you are reporting. Consider the following situation:

Some people <u>believe that being a supermodel would be bad</u>. Being a supermodel causes serious psychological problems for young girls later in life, including drug addiction and emotional problems. However, this view is wrong because it is completely overshadowed by the fact that these people make an incredible amount of money for very little effort.

Does the author agree or disagree with the sentence '*Being a supermodel causes serious psychological problems for young girls later in life, including drug addiction and emotional problems*'? If they agree, the argument doesn't flow very well. The author seems to agree with the opposing side and yet go on to refute it. In this situation, we need to repeat the subordinator to make it clear that this statement is also the 'some people's' opinion and not the author's.

> ### Example
>
> Some people <u>believe **that** being a supermodel would be bad **and** **that** being a supermodel causes serious psychological problems for young girls later in life, including drug addiction and emotional problems</u>. However, this view is wrong because it is completely overshadowed by the fact that these people make an incredible amount of money for very little effort.

Exercises

6.1 Think of 2 or 3 refutations of these arguments

1) **Smoking should be illegal**

_____

_____

_____

2) **Marijuana should be legal**

_____

_____

_____

3) **Cheating helps students**

_____

_____

_____

4) **Polygamy is good**

_____

_____

_____

6.2 think of reasons supporting these arguments

1) **Smoking should be illegal**

_____

_____

_____

2) **Marijuana should be legal**

_____

_____

_____

3) **Cheating helps students**

_____

_____

_____

4) **Polygamy is good**

_____

_____

_____

6.3 write refutation sentences for these ideas

1) **Smoking should be illegal**

_____

_____

_____

_____

_____

Chapter 8

2) **Marijuana should be legal**

_____

_____

_____

_____

_____

3) **Cheating helps students**

_____

_____

_____

_____

_____

4) **Polygamy is good**

_____

_____

_____

_____

_____

6.4 write 4 refutation statements of your own.

1) _____

_____

_____

_____

2) _____

_____

_____

_____

3) _____

_____

_____

_____

4) _____

_____

_____

_____

Relative Clauses

Revision

What is a clause?

A clause is a building block of a sentence. It must contain a subject and an event (a finite verb). Very often it contains a complement (often an object).

What is a finite dependent clause?

A finite dependent clause is a clause that begins with a subordinator. It cannot stand alone and must be attached to an independent clause. It must contain a finite verb.

What are the three types of dependent clauses?

There are three types of finite dependent clauses.

These three types of clause have different functions.

> *Three types of dependent clause:*
> 1) Noun clause
> 2) Adverbial clause
> 3) Relative clause

What does a noun clause do?

A noun clause acts like a noun. It functions as the subject of a verb. It can either be the subject of the verb *be* or it can be the object of these verbs or of many (but not all) reporting verbs.

> *Example*
> He proposed *that we change the research process.*

What does an adverbial clause do?

An adverbial clause describes the verb in the independent clause (though this is not always obvious). Unlike a noun clause, an adverbial clause gives *extra information* about the verb in the clause.

> *Example*
> After you have finished your draft, you should begin your research essay.

What does a relative clause do?

A relative clause describes either a noun in the independent clause, or it describes the whole clause. Like an adverbial clause, a relative clause gives extra information about a noun. Sometimes this information is essential (restrictive); sometimes it is not (non-restrictive).

> *Example*
> People who break the law will be prosecuted.

> **Note**
> *Relative clause = adjective clause.* These two words have exactly the same meaning.

> **What are the relative subordinators?**
>
> | | | | |
> |---|---|---|---|
> | *that* | *when* | *whence (old fashioned)* | *where* |
> | *whereby* | *wherefrom* | *whereof* | *whereon* |
> | *whereto* | *whereupon* | *which* | *while (rare)* |
> | *who* | *whom* | *whose* | *why* |
>
> > **Note**
> > *What* is also sometimes used as a relative subordinator in a special form of reduced relative clause. *What* means *the thing that*.
> >
> > > **Example**
> > > This is the thing. The thing irritates him the most. → This is <u>the thing that</u> irritates him the most.
> > > → This is *what* irritates him most.

Chapter 9

> **Note**
>
> It is important to note that some of the subordinators used for relative clauses are also used for other types of clauses. For example, *that* is used for both noun clauses and relative clauses and *when* is used in noun clauses, adverbial clauses, *and* relative clauses.

Three types of relative clause

There are three types of relative clause.

Notice that these types of relative clauses are not different because they are describing the subject or object of an independent clause, they are different because of the grammar of the clause.

> **Three types of relative clause:**
> 1. Subject Relative clause
> 2. Object Relative clause
> 3. Object of a preposition Relative clause

Following are some examples of each type of relative clause.

In **Object Relative Clauses,** the object of a relative clause describes a noun in the independent clause (or the clause itself). In **Subject Relative Clauses**, the subject of the relative clause describes a noun in the independent clause.

> *Example*
> **Object Relative Clause**
> Independent clause: *Richard is a great teacher.*
> Describing clause: *I like ~~Richard~~.*
>   *(whom)*
>
> → *Richard, **whom I like**, is a great teacher.*

> *Example*
> **Subject Relative Clause**
> Independent clause: *Richard is a great teacher.*
> Describing clause: *~~Richard~~ is a genius.*
>   *(who)*
>
> → *Richard, **who is a genius**, is a great teacher.*

> *Example*
> **Object of Preposition Relative Clause**
> Independent clause: *I like **Richard***
> Describing clause: *I gave it to **Richard**.*
>   *~~(whom)~~*
>
> → *I like Richard, **to whom I gave it**.*

> **Note**
> *Subject relative clauses* **do not contain subjects** (the subject is the relative subordinator.
> *Object relative clauses* **do not contain objects**.
> *Object of a preposition* relative clauses **contain subjects and can contain objects**.

> **Notes**
> When **subject or object** relative clauses are restrictive, the subordinator can be left out. The subordinator is never left out of **object of a preposition** relative clauses.

Telling the difference between noun clauses, adverbial clauses, and relative clauses.

Noun clauses can look a lot like *Object* relative clauses, but they are not. Firstly, a noun clause is the object of a verb; a relative clause describes a noun or, perhaps, a clause. Secondly, a noun clause follows a different pattern:

> Noun Clause: **Subordinator subject verb object**
> Relative clause *(Object):* **Subordinator subject verb**
> Relative clause *(Subject):* **Subordinator verb object**
>
> Noun Clause: He said **that he drove the car**
> Relative clause *(Object):* This is the car **that he drove**
> Relative clause *(Subject):* This is the person **that drove the car**

Adverbial clauses can also look like object and object of a preposition relative clauses, but adverbial clauses describe the verb, not the noun.

> Adverbial clause: *I <u>live</u> **where I can see the sea**.*
> Relative clause *(Object of a prep)*: I live in <u>a house</u> **where I can see the sea**.

In the first example, the clause is describing the verb (live). It is an adverbial clause.
In the second example, the clause is describing the noun (house). It is a relative clause.

Exercises

1.1 What types of clauses are these? Circle *noun*, *adverbial*, or *relative*.

1) He went to the pub when he had finished his homework. **(noun/adverbial/relative)**

2) She said that she was hungry. **(noun/adverbial/relative)**

3) 1986, when they finished high school, was the year of the Chernobyl nuclear disaster. **(noun/adverbial/relative)**

4) That it was wrong was a serious problem. **(noun/adverbial/relative)**

5) She lived where she could see the sea. **(noun/adverbial/relative)**

6) Pirates who worked in the Caribbean made lots of money. **(noun/adverbial/relative)**

7) The idea is that students will demonstrate how well they speak English. **(noun/adverbial/relative)**

8) A dictionary is a book that contains meanings. **(noun/adverbial/relative)**

9) Gale Tibble works in a place where she can have fun. **(noun/adverbial/relative)**

10) The fact that Homer Simpson is funny is the main reason why 'the Simpsons' is such a great TV show. **(noun/adverbial/relative)**

1.2 What types of relative clauses are these? Circle *subject, object*, or object of a preposition.

1) Richard, who is a genius, teaches English. **(subject/object/object of a preposition)**

2) George Clayton, whom I have met, is not a genius. **(subject/object/object of a preposition)**

3) She likes my dog, which is a black Pomeranian. **(subject/object/object of a preposition)**

4) Edmonton is a sprawling city that is not very exciting. **(subject/object/object of a preposition)**

5) I used to live in Toronto, which is a very exciting city. **(subject/object/object of a preposition)**

6) I would like to visit New York, about which I have heard a lot. **(subject/object/object of a preposition)**

1.3 Write two *subject* relative clauses of your own and two *object* relative clauses of your own.

1) Subject _____

2) Subject _____

3) Object _____

4) Object _____

Position of relative clause

A relative clause **should be as close as possible to the noun it is describing** unless the noun is followed by a prepositional phrase, in which case it can come either after or before the prepositional phrase.

Sometimes the relative can describe the whole clause. When this happens it is always non-restrictive, and we always use the subordinator *which*.

> **Example**
> Cuba is an **island** *that has a communist government.*
> **With prepositional phrase**
> *Cuba is an **island** in the Caribbean that has a communist government.*
> **Relative clause describing whole clause**
> *The student was from Burkina Faso, **which** was very interesting.*

Exercises

2.1 Circle which of the following sentences has the relative clause in the correct position.

1) Jill, who works at the University of Toronto, has a beautiful black dog. **(correct/incorrect)**

2) Many words are understood by my dog, which I have taught him. **(correct/incorrect)**

3) It is true that my dog can count, which is very clever of him. **(correct/incorrect)**

4) This is my dog, which is a black Pomeranian. **(correct/incorrect)**

5) My dog is black, which I love very much. **(correct/incorrect)**

6) I have another dog in Japan, which is a Yorkshire Terrier. **(correct/incorrect)**

7) The dog in Japan is not so smart, which doesn't know so many words. **(correct/incorrect)**

8) He moved there in 2004, when I came to live in Canada. **(correct/incorrect)**

9) One day I hope to live with both of my dogs, when I can find a way to bring the Yorkshire Terrier to Canada. **(correct/incorrect)**

10) In the mean time, I think about my Yorkshire Terrier often, which I miss. **(correct/incorrect)**

Restrictive/Defining & Non-restrictive Relative clauses

Some relative clauses are 'extra information', others are important for the meaning of the sentence. For example, in the sentence **The Queen of England, who is quite old, worked as a mechanic during the war,** we know who the Queen of England is, so the relative clause is extra information. This is an example of a non-restrictive relative clause. On the other hand, in the sentence **The car that I want is over there**, we need the relative clause to make sense of the sentence. **The car is over there** doesn't make sense because *the car* is a specific car, and we don't know which specific car is being talked about unless the relative clause tells us, or unless the information is given earlier in the text. This is an example of a defining relative clause.

Remember that we use commas with non-restrictive clauses and that we don't use commas with restrictive/defining clauses.

Remember, also, that a non-restrictive clause can indicate that one event happened after another, e.g.: **I told George Bush, who told the Queen of England.**

Non-restrictive

<u>Non-restrictive</u> clauses give extra information about something.

Names of things are always followed by **non-restrictive** clauses even if you don't know the name.

> *Example*
> *The moon, which shines radiantly, is very beautiful.*

Proper nouns are always followed by **non restrictive** clauses.

> *Example*
> *Kangaroos, which are native to Australia, are delicious.* **Or** *Ouagadougou, which is a city in Africa, is the capital of Burkina Faso.*

> *Example*
> *John, who is a good teacher, can explain relative clauses.*

Nouns with a possessive pronoun are usually **non-restrictive**.

> *Example*
> *My brother, who lives in the country, is an idiot.*

Dates such as '*1989*' and '*The thirteenth of October*' are always **non-restrictive**.

> *Example*
> *1972, when I was born, was the year that Nixon was elected president.*

Restrictive / Defining

Textbooks often state that *restrictive* and *defining* relative clauses are the same thing; however, this is not really so. In either case, we do not use commas, but there are some small differences. Understanding the differences can help to understand the punctuation. **Restrictive** relative clauses **restrict or limit the range of plurals;** defining relative clauses **give us needed detail about a noun.**

Defining

Often **an independent clause doesn't make sense without a <u>Defining</u> clause.** Take the following two passages for example.

1) There is a need to improve services in this area. The need is greatest in the western part of the area.

2) The section that most needs reviewing is part 2.

In the first passage, *need* is introduced first as *a need* and then talked about as a specific need as *the need* in the following sentence. In this case, a relative clause is not needed. We know which need we are talking about from the first sentence.

In the second passage, *section* is talked about as a specific *section* by the use of the word *the* to make it specific. However, we do not know which specific *section* we are talking about, so a relative clause is needed to **define** the noun – to tell us which specific *section* we are talking about.

> **Example**
>
> *This is the person whom I met.*
> (*This is the person* doesn't make sense as a sentence since as it is about a specific person, but we don't know which one.)

Thus, a clause using '*the*' before a *noun when the noun hasn't been identified before is often **defining**, as the **defining** clause is needed to identify the specific noun.

However, a **defining** clause can **also** be used after the articles *a* or *an*. *A* and *an* show that we are talking about one noun out of many (*a car* means one car out of all the cars in the world). A defining relative clause might be used to tell us more specifically **which one noun out of many**.

> **Example**
>
> *David is a teacher who works at University College.*

Note that when you have the construction *.... is a ....,* it is always followed by a restrictive clause (but not when it is *... is the...*)

Similarly, the construction '*one of the ....*' is always followed by a restrictive clause.

> **Example**
>
> *One of the teachers who works at University College is David.*

Restrictive

Restrictive relative clauses don't define nouns, they limit the range of plural nouns. Take the following two sentences for example:

> **1) Pirates should go to jail.**
> **2) Pirates who kill people should go to jail.**

In the first sentence, all pirates should go to jail because the plural *pirates* refers to *all pirates*. In the second sentence, this is limited to just pirates who kill people because the relative clause **limits the range of the plural**.

Sometimes, then, whether a relative clause should be restrictive or non-restrictive depends a lot on the meaning of the writer or speaker. Take the following two sentences for example.

> **1) Pirates who kill people should go to jail.**
> **2) Pirates, who kill people, should go to jail.**

In the first example, '*pirates*' is limited to just those who kill people by the restrictive relative clause. This sentence means that *only* pirates who kill people will go to jail.

In the second example, killing people is extra information about pirates. This implies that *all* pirates kill people and *all* pirates should go to jail.

> **Note**
>
> *That* cannot be used in a non-restrictive clause. Thus, you can**not** say: *New York, that is a great city, is very safe.* X

Exercises

3.1 Write D (defining), R (restrictive), or NR (non-restrictive) in the space next to the sentence and punctuate them if needed.

1) Ronald Reagan who was president of the United States in the 1980s suffered from Alzheimer's. [   ]

2) George Bush Senior was the president who succeeded Ronald Reagan. [   ]

3) Being president of the United States was a position that the next president who was named William Jefferson Clinton did not take seriously. [   ] [   ]

4) One of the presidents in the 1970s who was considered weak by many due to his failure to handle the Iran Contra Scandal properly was Jimmy Carter. [   ]

5) Presidents that are involved in corruption should resign and that is what happened to Richard Nixon who was forced to admit involvement in Watergate. [   ] [   ]

6) The president that came between Nixon and Carter was President Gerald Ford. [   ]

7) Prior to Nixon, the United States' presidency which is a very powerful position was held by Lyndon Baines Johnson who was also known as LBJ in the years after Kennedy's murder which is thought by many to have been a conspiracy. [   ] [   ] [   ]

Describing *things*

To describe things we use *which* or *that* or we **omit the subordinator**. *That* is only used in restrictive clauses. **The subordinator can only be omitted in** <u>restrictive/defining **OBJECT**</u> **relative clauses**.

To make a relative clause, we delete the noun that we will describe in the independent clause from the relative clause. We replace this noun with a relative subordinator, and move the subordinator to the front of the clause. Remember that the relative clause *must* follow the noun it describes.

> ### *Examples*
> **Non-restrictive - Subject**
>
> Sony is stocked in every department store in the world. ~~Sony~~ is considered the best electronics brand in the world.
>
> → *Sony, <u>which is considered the best electronics brand in the world</u>, is stocked in every department store.*
>
> **Non-restrictive - Object**
>
> My television is a Sony. I bought ~~my television~~ from Daimaru.
>
> → *My television, <u>which I bought from Daimaru</u>, is a Sony.*
>
> | **Restrictive/defining – Subject** | **Restrictive/defining - Object** |
> |---|---|
> | Sony is a company. ~~The company~~ is based in Japan. | Myer is a shop. I often visit ~~a shop~~. |
> | Option 1: *Sony is a company <u>which is based in Japan</u>.*
Option 2: *Sony is a company <u>that is based in Japan</u>.* | Option 1: *Daimaru is a shop <u>which I often visit</u>.*
Option 2: *Daimaru is a shop <u>that I often visit</u>.*
Option 3: *Daimaru is a shop <u>I often visit</u>.* |

Exercises

4.1 Join the following clauses together to make a sentence with a relative clause (note that the first sentence is the independent clause). Remember to use the correct punctuation.

1) South Korea has several large companies. Large South Korean companies are called *Chaebol*.

   _____

2) LG produces electronic and petrochemical goods. LG is a large South Korean Company.

   _____

3) Goldstar began in 1947. The company was originally just called Goldstar.

   _____

4) In 1995, the company changed its name to Lucky Goldstar. The letters LG represent Lucky Goldstar.

   _____

5) Samsung is another *Chaebol*. Samsung means three stars.

   _____

6) Samsung telephones are excellent quality as are the cars. They also make cars.

   _____

7) Samsung is pronounced sʌmsɒŋ. People often mispronounce Samsung as sæmsʌŋ.

   _____

Describing people

To describe people we use **who**, **whom**, or **that** or we *omit the subordinator*. **That** is only used in restrictive clauses. **Whom** is only used is *object* relative clauses. **The subordinator can only be omitted in restrictive/defining object relative clauses**.

Both **who** and **which/that** can be used as relative pronouns for animals; however, using **who** gives the animal a personality. Thus, **who** is preferred more for pets and for children's stories in which animals can talk.

Examples

Non-restrictive - Subject
James Dean, **who** died in a horrific car accident, was a teenage heartthrob.

Restrictive/defining - Subject
Option 1: James Dean was a person **who** was a teenage heartthrob.
Option 2: James Dean was a person that was a teenage heartthrob.

Non-restrictive - Object
James Dean, **whom** many people admired, died in a car accident.

Restrictive/defining - Object
Option 1: James Dean was a person **whom** many people admired.
Option 2: James Dean was a person that many people admired.
Option 3: James Dean was a person many people admired.

Notice that we prefer **that** after superlatives such as **the best**, **the most beautiful**, or **the prettiest**.

Note
Whom sounds very formal and many people use **who** instead of **whom**.

Example
He is **the best** person **that** I have ever met.

Exercises

5.1 Join the following clauses together to make a sentence with a relative clause (note that the first sentence is the independent clause). Remember to use the correct punctuation.

1) Sir Isaac Newton was a mathematician and a physicist. He wrote *Philosophiæ Naturalis Principia Mathematica*.

   _____

2) Sir Isaac Newton was a physicist. Many modern scientists idolise him.

   _____

3) Physicists are scientists. Scientists investigate the laws that govern the physical world.

   _____

4) Albert Einstein was also a physicist. Many people believe him to have been a genius.

   _____

5) Chemists are another kind of scientist. History is also full of famous chemists.

   _____

6) Michael Farraday was a chemist. Michael Farraday was famous for his work on magnetic fields.

   _____

5.2 Now write 4 sentences of your own using *who* or *whom*.

1) _____
2) _____
3) _____
4) _____

Chapter 9

Whose

Whose shows possession. Although **whose** is usually used for people, there is no possessive relative pronoun for objects, so if absolutely necessary, one should use **whose**. However, this should be avoided if possible.

It is perfectly okay to use **whose** when describing companies or organizations.

Whose can used in *subject* and *object* relative clauses. **Whose cannot** be omitted.

Subject relative clauses using **whose** are easy. Delete the word that possesses the relative clause (this word will probably have **'s** on the end); replace this word with **whose**, then locate the relative clause next to the noun being described.

> **Examples**
> **Subject Relative Clause**
> This is the school. ~~The school~~'s <u>students are naughty</u>. *(whose)*
> This is the school **whose** <u>student's are naughty</u>.

Object relative clauses using **whose** are more complicated and students often find them confusing. First, find the word that is possessive (with **'s** on the end), delete it and replace it with **whose**. Then move **whose** and the word that it possesses to the front of the clause. The rest of the clause keeps the same word order.

> **Examples**
> **Object Relative Clause**
> This is the school. <u>I met</u> the ~~school~~'s <u>principal</u> <u>on Monday</u>.
> (This is the school. <u>I met</u> **whose** <u>principal</u> <u>on Monday</u>.)
>
> → This is the school **whose _principal_** <u>I met</u> <u>on Monday</u>.

In this example, **school's** has been deleted and replaced with **whose**. **Whose principal** then moves to the front of the clause. **I met** and **on Monday** join up to make the rest of the clause. These clauses are quite unusual because the object comes *before* the subject.

The correct word order for *object* relative clauses is 1) whose, 2) object of possessive noun, 3) subject, 4) verb, 5) adverbials and prepositional phrases.

Exercises

6.1 Join the following clauses together to make a sentence with a relative clause (note that the first sentence is the independent clause). Remember to use the correct punctuation.

1) Apple is a computer company. The computer company's logo is recognised by everyone.

   _____

2) Apple make products such as the i-pod and i-phone. Apple's products have immense popularity.

   _____

3) Customer loyalty is important to Apple. Millions of people across the world use Apple's products.

   _____

4) My great grandfather started a company called Holden & Frost with a man named Holden. My great grandfather's name was Frost.

   _____

5) Frost later sold his share in the company. People now know the company's name as Holden.

   _____

6) Holden is a company. The company's cars are owned by almost a quarter of the Australian population.

   _____

7) Holden is now owned by General Motors. Holden's cars are exported to many countries.

   _____

8) The Commodore is a car. People can see the car's shape all over the world from South Korea to Saudi Arabia.

   _____

9) The company is trying to build more fuel-efficient cars to cope with changing demand. The people of Adelaide depend on the company's success.

   _____

6.2 Now write 4 sentences of your own using the word 'whose'

1) _____
   _____
   _____

2) _____
   _____
   _____

3) _____
   _____
   _____

4) _____
   _____
   _____

That & which as objects of prepositions (in which / which...to / that...to)

Relative clauses are often the **object of prepositions**. These relative clauses are different from the *subject* and *object* relative clauses that we have studied above. They must have a subject and an object.

The preposition can be any preposition depending on the verb or noun involved.

Compare the following types of relative clause. In each case **Steven is a genius** is the independent clause.

Subject – ~~Steven~~ is a teacher. → Steven, <u>who is a teacher</u>, is a genius.
     (s) (v) (o)   (v)   (o)

Object – I like ~~Steven~~. → Steven, <u>whom I like</u>, is a genius.
     (s) (v) (o)   (s) (v)

Object of a preposition – I gave the pen to ~~Steven~~. → Steven, <u>to whom I gave the pen</u>, is a genius.
     (s) (v) (o)   (s) (v)   (o)

        Or   Steven, <u>**whom** I gave the pen to</u>, is a genius.

Note

If the verb in the relative clause is a **phrasal verb** that ends with a preposition, the preposition must come at the **end** of the clause.

Example

These are problems. I will not *put up* with the problems. → These are problems *with which* I will not *put up*.

To which is formal. ***Which...to*** and ***that...to*** are informal. If you are describing people, you *must* use ***whom***.

The subordinator **can be omitted in informal restrictive/defining** relative clauses.

Examples

This is the food. I put sugar on the food.

formal	This is the food *on which* I put sugar.
informal **(which)**	This is the food *which* I put sugar *on*.
informal **(that)**	This is the food *that* I put sugar *on*.
informal **(___)**	This is the food I put sugar *on*.

Exercises

7.1 Join the following clauses together to make a sentence with a relative clause (note that the first sentence is the independent clause). Remember to use the correct punctuation.

1) Finding a language school can be a challenge these days with so many to choose from. You can satisfy your learning needs at the school.

   _____
   _____

2) English schools are rare. Good Language programmes are run at these schools.

_____

_____

3) Programmes before going on to university are common. All students must pass through these programmes.

_____

_____

4) Schools are rare. All students graduate with satisfaction from these schools.

_____

_____

5) Schools are even less common. Textbooks are not routinely used in these schools.

_____

_____

6) Students need to choose schools carefully. They will study at these schools.

_____

_____

7) Many students prefer schools. Students from many different countries go to these schools.

_____

_____

8) Other students choose schools based on the location of the school within the city. They will prepare for university at these schools.

_____

_____

7.2 Now write five sentences of your own with relative clauses as objects of prepositions.

1) _____

_____

_____

2) _____

_____

_____

3) _____

_____

_____

4) _____

_____

_____

5) _____

_____

_____

Describing places (Where)

Students are often confused about how to use **where** and **when**. Teachers often tell students that **where** is used to describe place and that **when** is used to describe time. However, this is not really true. We also use **which** and **that** to describe place and time. **Where** and **when** are **object of a preposition** relative clauses.

Note

Object of a preposition relative clauses have **subject**, **verb**, **and object**, while the subject clause has no subject, and the object clause has no object.

Note

Relative clauses using the subordinator *where* always have a subject.

Compare the following relative clauses. In each case *I have been to New York* is the independent clause.

Subject - ~~New York~~ is big. → I have been to New York, **which** is big.
(s)   (v) (c)   (v) (c)

Object - I like ~~New York~~. → I have been to New York, **which** I like.
(s) (v)   (o)   (s) (v)

Object of a preposition - You have a flat in ~~New York~~.
(s)   (v)   (o)

→ I have been to New York, **in which** you have a flat.
(s)   (v)   (o)

Or (using *where*) → I have been to New York, **where** you have a flat.
(s)   (v)   (o)

In which can be replaced with *where*. *Where* can be used in a restrictive or a non-restrictive clause.

Thus, we can use *where* or *in which* (or *at which* or *to which*) to describe a noun that is the object of a preposition.

Exercises

8.1 Join the following clauses together to make a sentence with a relative clause (note that the first sentence is the independent clause). Remember to use the correct punctuation.

1) Britain is the place. The English language originated in this place.

_____

_____

2) English later spread to many countries including the United States. Two major accents of English are spoken there.

_____

3) The southern United States is the home of one major accent. The southern United States has a proud history.

_____

4) The northern United States is where the other major accent is spoken. The northern United States is the home of the 'Yankies'.

_____

5) Canada is home to another regional dialect of English. An accent blending British and United States pronunciations is spoken in Canada.

_____

6) Then, there is India. India is regarded as having the most marked accent.

_____

_____

7) Lastly, there is Australia. People speak with a mixture of different accents in Australia.

_____

_____

Chapter 9

8.2 Now complete these four sentences with relative clauses using the subordinators *where*, *in which*, or *at which*.

1) My hometown _____

_____

_____

2) _____ Africa _____

_____

_____

3) _____ is a place _____

_____

_____

4) I like to go to cities _____

_____

_____

Describing *time* (When)

The rules for using *when* are exactly the same as the rules described above in *where*.

Remember that *when* is used only for object of a preposition relative clause. Remember that *when* is always followed by a subject.

> **Examples**
>
> **Subject** - I remember the day. The day was fun. → I remember the day <u>that was fun</u>.
>
> **Object**: - I remember the day. You enjoyed the day. → I the day <u>that you enjoyed</u>.
> Or → I remember the day <u>you enjoyed</u>.
>
> **Object of preposition** - I remember the day.
> He was born *on the day*. → I remember the day ***when*** <u>he was born</u>.
> Or I remember the day ***on which*** <u>he was born</u>.
> Or I remember the day ***which*** <u>he was born</u> ***on***.
> Or I remember the day ***that*** <u>he was born</u> ***on***.
> Or I remember the day <u>he was born</u> ***on***.

Exercises

9.1 Join the following clauses together to make a sentence with a relative clause (note that the first sentence is the independent clause). Remember to use the correct punctuation.

1) In 2002 the World Cup was held in Japan and South Korea. Brazil won the World Cup in 2002.

_____

_____

_____

2) 2008 was the year. Spain won the European Cup for the first time in 44 years in 2008.

_____

_____

_____

3) The year was 1966. 1966 had the most exciting World Cup. _____

_____

_____

4) 1966 was the year that the cup was held in England. England beat Germany to take the World Cup in 1966.

_____

_____

_____

5) South Africa hosted the World Cup in 2010. 2010 was the first time an African nation has hosted it.

_____

_____

_____

6) The year will be the beginning of a new era. Asian or African nation wins the World Cup in the year.

_____

_____

_____

8.2 Now write four sentences of your own with relative clauses using the subordinator *when*.

1) _____

_____

_____

2) _____

_____

_____

3) _____

_____

_____

4) _____

_____

_____

Describing quality or quantity

These clauses are used when you want to describe a section of a group. They use subordinators like ***most of whom, many of which, the best of whom, the worst of which***.

> ### Example
> There are some *girls* in the cafeteria. Not all of the *girls* are pretty; ***most of them*** are pretty.
>
> **Relative clause → There are some *girls* in the cafeteria, *most of whom* are pretty.**

Quantity

Relative clauses describing quantity use ***most/many/some/all/two of whom/which*** (any quantifier can be used). We do not use ***that*** in this type of relative clause. Clauses of quantity are **always non-restrictive**. The subordinator cannot be omitted. They can be **subject** or **object** relative clauses. Object of a preposition relative clauses of this type are rare though not impossible.

> ### Examples
> **Quantity of people (object)**
> I have ten *friends*. I met ***most of my friends*** last year. → *I have ten **friends, most of whom** I met last year.*
> **Quantity of people (subject)**
> I have ten *friends*. ***Most of my friends*** went to Colombia last year. → *I have ten **friends**, **most of whom** went to Colombia last year.*
> **Quantity of things (object)**
> I have ten *cars*. I bought ***most of my cars*** this year. → *I have ten **cars, most of which** I bought this year.*
> **Quantity of things (Subject)**
> I have ten *cars*. ***Most of my cars*** were made in Germany. → *I have ten **cars, most of which** were made in Germany.*

Chapter 9

Quality

Relative clauses describing quality use the subordinators *the best/worst/most beautiful of whom/which* (any superlative can be used). They follow the same rules as those describing quantity. Clauses of quality are **always non-restrictive**; the subordinator cannot be omitted. They can be subject or object relative clauses.

> ### *Examples*
> **Quantity of people**
> I have ten friends. I met my best friend last year. → *I have ten friends, <u>the best of whom</u> I met last year.*
> **Quantity of things**
> I have ten cars. I bought my favourite car this year. → *I have ten cars, <u>my favourite of which</u> I bought this year.*

Exercises

10.1 Join the following clauses together to make a sentence with a relative clause (note that the first sentence is the independent clause). Remember to use the correct punctuation.

1) Australia has five major cities. Most of Australia's five major cities are located along the east coast.

_____

_____

_____

2) The people of Sydney believe that their city is the best. Australians from the countryside don't always like some of the people of Sydney. _____

_____

_____

3) On the other hand, this is not what the people of Melbourne believe. Many of the people of Melbourne were born overseas. _____

_____

_____

4) Melbourne is the home to many sporting events. The most exciting of these sporting events is the Australian Football League Grand Final. _____

_____

_____

5) The beaches around Brisbane are popular with tourists. People across the world have heard of the most popular of these beaches. _____

_____

_____

6) The smaller cities of Australia vary in size and in the services they provide their populations. A few of these smaller cities are also popular tourist destinations. _____

_____

_____

7) The cities of Australia are all in the top 100 best cities in the world. The fourth most populous of these cities is Perth. _____

_____

_____

8) Unfortunately, these cities are becoming expensive to build a house in. Economists are now also listing the largest of these cities in the top ten most expensive cities in the world. _____

_____

_____

10.2 Now write four sentences of your own, two with quantity relative clauses and two with quality relative clauses.

1) _____

2) _____

3) _____

4) _____

Describing whole clauses

Non-restrictive clauses can also be used to describe whole clauses. Often this gives a feeling of time sequence.

> **Example**
> He gave it to George, **who** gave it to Bill, **who** gave it to Ronald.

However, non-restrictive clauses can also **describe the process or event in the independent clause.**

> **Example**
> *Global warming is causing sea levels to rise*, **which** is a serious problem.

> **Note**
> In this case the relative clause does not describe *rise*, it describes *the fact the sea levels will rise*.

These clauses can be **subject** or **object** relative clauses. They are **always non-restrictive**, and always use the subordinator **which** (or **who, whom, where, when**, but **not that**). They very often use verbs such as **be, mean, indicate, explain** and quite often have other clauses embedded in them.

> **Examples**
> Global warming is causing sea levels to rise.
> The fact that global warming is causing sea levels to rise means that many cities will soon be flooded with water.
> → Global warming is causing levels to rise, **which** *means* that many cities will soon be flooded with water.
> (The relative clause describes *global warming causing sea levels to rise*.)

Exercises

11.1 Join the following clauses together to make a sentence with a relative clause (note that the first sentence is the independent clause). Remember to use the correct punctuation.

1) Cows are left outside in the cold during winter. This fact means that many of them die.

_____

_____

2) Many cows die. This fact is not a serious problem for farmers. _____

_____

3) Chickens live in small cages. This suggests that they do not have enough room to move.

_____

_____

4) The animal rights movement has been upset about this for a while now. This has resulted in some action being taken.

_____

_____

_____

11.2 Now write four sentences of your own describing a whole clause.

1) _____

_____

_____

2) _____

_____

_____

3) _____

_____

_____

4) _____

_____

_____

Infinitival Relatives

These relative clauses are created from **object of a preposition relative clauses**; they use the subordinators *to which* + **Infinitive clause** / *to whom* + **Infinitive clause**.

The subject is never clearly stated (as with participial clauses); the subject is, however, usually understood to be the person being addressed. It is possible to **omit** both the **preposition and the subordinator** (This is called a **bare** infinitive relative). These types of infinitives are either built from clauses that contain **modals of advice or ability**, or from *instructions* or *orders*.

> **Examples**
> **Infinitival Relative**
>
> She is the best person. You *can* give it ~~to her~~. → She is the best person *to whom* <u>to give</u> it.
>   *(modal of ability)*
>
> She is the worst person. *Don't* give it ~~to her~~. → She is the worst person *to whom* <u>to give</u> it.
>   *(instruction)*
>
> **Bare Infinitival Relative**
>
> She is the best person. You can give it ~~to her~~. → She is the best person <u>to give</u> it.

Exercises

12.1 Join the following clauses together to make a sentence with a relative clause (note that the first sentence is the independent clause). Remember to use the correct punctuation.

1) They are the people. Give it to them. _____

_____

_____

2) I am the person. Sing it to me. _____

_____

_____

3) These are the books. You should delve into these books. _____

_____

4) The director is the person. You need to write to the person. _____

_____

_____

5) This is a subject. You could write about this subject. _____

_____

_____

Relative clauses using subjects of noun clauses

Sometimes relative clauses are constructed from clauses that contain noun clauses. When the subject of a clause containing a noun clause describes a noun in another clause, it is no different from an ordinary relative clause.

> ### Example
>
> This was said by **Kirgianos**. **Kirgianos** claims <u>that the result will never be known</u>.
>
> **Relative clause** → This was said by **Kirgianos, who** claims <u>that the result will never be known</u>.

However, we may want the subject or the object of the noun clause to describe a noun in the previous clause. When this happens, some major complications occur.

> **Subject of Noun clause**
> *(Noun clause)*
> This was the **result**. Kirgianos claimed <u>that the **result** would never be known</u>.
> *(subject)*
> Step 1) *replace the subject with which/that*: This was the **result**. Kirgianos claimed <u>that *which* would never be known</u>.
> Step 2) *delete the noun clause subordinator*: This was the **result**. Kirgianos claimed <u>~~that~~ *which* would never be known</u>.
> Step 3) *move the subordinator (**which** or **that**) to the front of the clause*: This was the **result**. *which* Kirgianos claimed <u>would never be known</u>.
>
> → This was the result *which* Kirgianos claimed <u>would never be known</u>.
>
> *Object of a noun clause*
> *(Noun clause)*
> These are the **results**. Kirgianos claimed <u>that he would release the results</u>.
> *(object)*
> Step 1) *replace the object with which/that*: These are the **results**. Kirgianos claimed <u>that he would release *which*</u>.
> Step 2) *move the subordinator (**which** or **that**) to the front of the clause*: These are the **results**. *which* Kirgianos claimed <u>that he would release</u>.
>
> → These are the **results** which Kirgianos claimed <u>that he would release</u>.

> ### Example
>
> Riggs discussed the findings. His undergraduate students had decided that these findings needed further work.
>
> → Riggs discussed the findings ***that his undergraduate students had decided <u>needed further work</u>***.

Exercises

12.1 Join the following clauses together to make a sentence with a relative clause (note that the first sentence is the independent clause). Remember to use the correct punctuation.

1) Johnson raises several new issues in his latest paper. Johnson writes that we need to remain cautious about hasty judgments in these situations. _____

_____

_____

2) The paper mentions phase two. It is thought that phase two might eliminate a lot of the earlier problems.

Chapter 9

3) The Bull Offensive has been studied extensively. Ostapuk mentions that Syahputra planned the Bull Offensive.

4) Much has been written about the causes of this, but little focus has been made on the results. Mifuni believes that the causes of this are of little significance anyway. _____

5) An overpowering need for accompaniment is a natural side effect of situations like this. Joachin states that this need has been witnessed in many different people of all ages and from all cultures.

Transitivity and relative clauses

Transitivity can affect relative clauses in two ways. Transitivity means that relative clauses can appear to have a **subject and** an **object**.

Revision

English has **transitive**, **intransitive**, and **ditransitive** verbs. Transitive verbs have objects; intransitive verbs do not have objects; ditransitive verbs have two objects. (See Chapter 3, pages 28-35 for more on transitivity.)

Intransitive verbs

Intransitive verbs **cannot have objects**. They cannot be used in passive voice. These verbs cannot be used in passive voice because to make passive voice, we take the object and make it into the subject. If there is no object, we cannot make it a subject. Some examples of these verbs include: (See Appendix 6, page 203 for a more complete list)

> **Intransitive verbs:**
>
> | | | | | |
> |---|---|---|---|---|
> | come | emerge | go | last | result |
> | decline | ensue | happen | live | succeed |
> | disappear | fluctuate | occur | remain | wait |

Transitive verbs

This group of verbs **have** an **object**. Examples include *kill, love,* and *do*. These verbs *can* always be used in *passive* voice. Most verbs fall into this category.

Ditransitive verbs

This group of verbs is special. These verbs can have **two objects**. They form passive voice differently from other verbs; they have two passive voice options. Examples of these verbs include *tell, give,* and *write*.

> *Examples*
>
> **Intransitive verb**
> The professor disappeared.
>
> **Transitive verb**
> The professor stopped the discussion.
>
> **Ditransitive verb**
> The professor gave **the students** *a lot of help*.
> Subject   verb   object   object

Intransitive verbs cannot be used to form object relative clauses. Ditransitive verbs can have a subject, verb, and object in relative clauses.

Intransitive verbs

Because intransitive verbs **do not have** objects, it is impossible to make an object relative clause with these types of verbs.

> **Example**
>
> The building *__which__ the professor disappeared* is very large. **X (Incorrect)**

If we change this sentence back into two separate independent clauses, you can see that it doesn't make sense. *Which* means *the building* in this sentence. Since the relative clause is in the form *Subordinator subject verb*, it must be an object relative clause. This means that *the building* is the object in the sentence *the professor disappeared the building*. But since *disappear* cannot have an object, **this sentence doesn't make sense**.

> **Note**
>
> __Subject__ relative clauses **do not contain subjects** (the subject is the relative subordinator.
>
> __Object__ relative clauses **do not contain objects**.

Similarly, a **verb in passive voice cannot have an object, and thus cannot make an object relative clause**.

Ditransitive verbs

At the start of this chapter, we discussed how there are three types of relative clause. The main two types that we are interested in here are **subject** and **object** relative clauses. Remember that subject relative clauses do not have **subject** and object relative clauses do not have **objects**.

> **Examples**
>
> Relative clause *(Object):*   **Subordinator *subject verb***
> Relative clause *(Subject):*   **Subordinator *verb object***
>
> Relative clause *(Object):*   This is the car **that he drove**
> Relative clause *(Subject):*   This is the person **that drove the car**

However, a ditransitive verb (a verb with two objects) can make it look like we have a relative clause with the structure **subordinator subject verb object**.

> **Examples**
>
> There is *__the report__*. (Independent clause)
>
> Which
> **I gave Johnson** *the report*. → there is *__the report__* **that *I gave Johnson***
> Subject verb   object   object   Subject verb   object

Notice that this only works with the direct object (*__the report__*). The indirect object (*__Johnson__*) needs to use the prepositional form *__to whom__* or *__to which__* in this kind of relative clause.

Exercises

13.1 Find the errors in the following sentences

1) Aliens, which they have probably visited the earth, no doubt exist somewhere.

2) The Darfur crisis that the worst violence in Africa happened was genocide.

3) Some scientists that have been found a strong relationship between levels of blood-sugar addiction and addiction to fast food are working to change the taste of the food.

4) Some amino acids such as the essential amino acids that it must be obtained from diet are needed to meet body requirements.

5) The second graph explains that the US uses the largest amount of minerals such as phosphorus, which is used 8322 tonnes in one person's life.

Chapter 9

13.2 Combine the following sentences to construct relative clauses.

1) Several assignments are due next week. The professor has given us several assignments.

   _____

   _____

2) The letter has not arrived yet. We have written Johnson a letter to protest his recent actions.

   _____

   _____

3) Everyone was surprised at the truth. Johnson's behaviour tells us the truth about his beliefs.

   _____

   _____

4) They are waiting for a result. We hope to deliver them a result by the end of the week.

   _____

   _____

5) The ministry is awaiting answers. We do not guarantee them any answers.

   _____

   _____

Chapter 10

Participial Clauses

Absolute Clauses and Appositive Phrases

Revision

Remember that clauses are the building blocks of a language. There are two types of dependent clause: finite and non-finite. Generally, we can say that a finite clause contains a *finite verb* and that a non-finite clause contains a non-finite verb.

A finite clause can contain any of these different functions of verbs, but it **must** include *one finite verb*. In a non-finite clause either the gerund, the infinitive, or the participle will function as the verb in the clause. In this chapter we will look at non-finite clauses containing participles functioning as verbs.

> Verbs can have several functions:
>
> **Noun** (gerund)
> **Complements** (infinitives)
> **Adjective** (participles)
> **Processes** (verbs/events).

> *Examples*
> ***The different functions of verbs***
> **Noun form of verb (gerund)**
> Rotting: When looking after food, it is important to minimise *rotting*.
> **Adjective form of verb (Participle)**
> Rotting: *Rotting* apples need to be thrown out.
> Rotten: If customers find *rotten* apples, they will complain.
> **Infinitive form of verb**
> To rot: Hot weather causes apples *to rot*.
> **finite form of verb**
> Rotted: All of the apples that we harvested last year *rotted* last summer.

> *Examples*
> *Non-finite clauses*
> **Gerund clause**
> She saw me driving a car.
> **Infinitive clause**
> I asked him to drive me home.

Finite Verbs	Non-finite verb forms
sing	*sing* (The bare infinitive, which is not a verb, looks exactly like the verb)
sang	*to sing*
sings	*to be Singing*
will sing	*sung*
is singing	*singing*
was singing	*having sung*
will be singing	*having been sung*
has sung	*being sung*
was sung	
has been sung	
has been being sung	

Participle clauses contain a verb that is in participial form. Note that participial clauses can be recognised two ways. (1) They do not have subjects, and (2) The event/process is always either in ~ing form (the present (active) participle) or the past (passive) participle form. We use the words **present participle** and **past participle**, but really these are **active** and **passive** forms of the adjective.

> *Examples*
> **Active**
> Matthew, having finished his essay, is feeling satisfied and happy.
> **Passive**
> The customer cheated out of his money was angry.

Chapter 10

Exercises

1.1 Decide if the underlined sections are phrases, non-finite clauses, or finite clauses. Write P, NF, or F

1) She reported <u>that there are still many unexploded landmines throughout Cambodia</u>. [   ]

2) The Tasmanian tiger is thought to be extinct <u>although many people claim to have seen one</u> in recent years. [   ]

3) The Prius is a hybrid car Toyota is developing <u>to try to reduce dependence on petrol</u>. [   ]

4) Many people do not like driving electric cars <u>because they don't have a great deal of power</u>. [   ]

5) <u>Because of the problem of landmines in many war torn countries</u>, there has been a movement in recent years to ban them altogether. [   ]

6) Mobile phone use when driving has been banned <u>due to accidents constantly happening</u> as a result of driving while talking on phones. [   ]

7) <u>Wanting to limit the information that people are receiving</u>, various governments have begun censoring the internet. [   ]

8) Internet censorship, <u>not yet happening in western democracies</u>, is an idea being discussed by many activist groups. [   ]

9) The depletion of non-renewable fuel sources has caused <u>many car companies to look to alternative fuel sources for the future</u>. [   ]

10) <u>Whether we donate organs or not</u> is up to the individual. [   ]

11) <u>Whenever two large banks want to merge</u>, there are always fears that the new larger bank will use its new financial power to drain more money from individuals already struggling to meet repayments. [   ]

12) <u>Using mobile phones</u> while you are driving is illegal in some countries. [   ]

13) <u>To understand English</u> is to open gates to future careers. [   ]

14) Internet censorship is becoming a reality in places <u>where governments are eager to control knowledge</u>. [   ]

Participles

The adjective form of a verb is called the participle. Participles can be in active or passive voice.

Active participles

Active participles are formed by adding ~ing to the verb. The active participle looks like the gerund, but it is not. Remember, the active participle describes a noun, the gerund *is* a noun.

That is *amusing singing*. (Here *singing* is a noun (gerund), and *amusing* is an adjective describing *singing*.

Passive participle

The passive participle is the 'PP' form of the verb. For regular verbs this is the same as the past tense. For irregular verbs, you will have memorised this form at lower levels of English. Remember memorising *go-went-gone*, *eat-ate-eaten*? *Gone* and *eaten* are the past participles of these verbs.

Examples

Gerund
I like *walking*.

Participle
The *interesting* teacher has many students.

Verb	Past participle
cause	caused
forbid	forbidden
play	played
understand	understood
write	written

Uses of participles

Active and passive participles have three uses. They can be used to form the different aspects of verbs (perfect, continuous, continuous perfect) and to create passive voice; they can be used as adjectives, and they can be used to make adjectival or adverbial clauses (which we call participial clauses)

Participles used to form verb aspects (tenses) and voice. (For a full explanation of *aspect* see Chapter 6 on tenses.)

We use both the active and passive participles to form different aspects (tenses). It is important to remember that the active or passive participle on its own does not form an aspect or voice (and is in fact not a verb).

We use the verb *be* with the *active participle* to form the *continuous aspect*.

We use the verb *have* with the *past participle* to form the *perfect aspect*.

We use the verb **be** and the *past participle* to form *passive voice*.

> **Example**
> *Continuous:* He *is finishing* his report.   *Perfect aspect:* He *has finished* his report.
> *Passive voice:* His report *is finished*.

Participles used as adjectives

Participles can also be used as adjectives. These adjectives are either in active or passive voice. They are always followed by a noun because all adjectives are followed by nouns (unless they are the complement of the verb **be**).

> **Examples**
> **Active**   **Passive**
> Nobody enjoyed the *boring* teacher's lessons.   The *bored* student was very unhappy.

Participles used in non-finite clauses

Participial clauses are non-finite formed from participles that either describe a noun or a verb. Participial clauses can be seen as shortened versions of relative or adverbial clauses.

> **Note**
> To turn a relative or adverbial clause into a participial clause, you must have the **same subject** in the independent and dependent clause.

> **Examples**
> **Relative clause:** The teacher *who is explaining participial phrases to you* is a genius.
> **Participial clause:** The teacher *explaining participial phrases to you* is a genius.
> **Adverbial clause:** *Because he is a genius*, he attracts many students to his classes.
> **Participial clause:** *Being a genius*, he attracts many students to his classes.

Changing relative clauses into participial clauses

To change a relative clause into a participial clause, you must have same subject in the dependent and independent clauses.

> **Examples**
> **Different subject**
> Pearce, whom many writers criticise, claims that the global economy is about to collapse. (Participial clause not possible)
> **Same subject**
> Pearce, who has many supporters and followers, claims that the global economy is about to collapse.
> (Participial clause possible: Pearce, having many supporters and followers, claims that the global economy is about to collapse.)

To construct the participial clause, you need to know if the finite verb in the relative clause is in active or passive voice. If it is in active voice, delete the relative subordinator and change the verb to the active participle. If it is in passive voice, delete the relative subordinator and change the verb to the past participle.

> **Active**
> **Relative clause:** *Participial clauses, ~~which~~ are easy to learn, can be used to make your writing more concise.* (The verb in this clause is **are**; this is a form of the verb **be**. The active participle for this verb is **being**.)
> **Participial clause:** *Participial clauses, being easy to learn, can be used to make your writing more concise.*
> **Passive**
> **Relative clause:** *Grammar ~~which~~ is learned in this class is useful.* (The verb in this clause is **is learned**; this is a form of the verb **learn**. The passive participle for this verb is **learned**.)
> **Participial clause:** *Grammar learned in this class is useful.*

> **Examples**
> **Relative Clause:** The boy ~~who~~ <u>ate</u> the apple must have been happy.
> **Participial clause:** The boy eating the apple must have been happy.
> **Relative Clause:** The baby ~~that~~ <u>was crying</u> in the next room has now stopped crying.
> **Participial clause:** The baby crying in the next room has now stopped crying.
> **Relative Clause:** The mistake ~~that~~ <u>is made</u> every time is that students forget to delete the relative subordinator.
> **Participial clause:** The mistake made every time is that students forget to delete the relative subordinator.
> **Relative Clause:** Relative clauses, ~~which~~ <u>can</u> also <u>be called</u> adjective clauses, can easily be shortened to participial clauses if they have the same subject as the independent clause.
> **Participial clause:** Relative clauses, also called adjective clauses, can easily be shortened to participial clauses if they have the same subject as the independent clause.

Adverbs

In the above example, it can be seen that the relative clause contains the adverb 'also', and so does the participial clause. We **keep** the adverb in participial clause.

Modals

As can also be seen in the last example, true **modals cannot be used in participial clauses** or, in fact, in any non-finite clause (Modal-like structures that are really verbs can be reduced to participles. See Chapter 7 for more on true modals and modal-like structures.)

Instead of a modal, we must use an adverb or just delete the modal structure.

> **Examples**
> **Relative clause:** Students who can't understand participial clauses often have problems in other areas of grammar too.
> **Participial clause:** Students not understanding participial clauses often have problems in other areas of grammar too.

Negatives

This last example is an example of a negative participial clauses. Notice that if the verb in the relative (or adverbial) clause is negative, then we put **not** before the active or passive participle in the participial clause.

Punctuation

Remember that participial clauses can be restrictive/defining and non-restrictive in the same way that relative clauses can. See Chapter 9, pages 150-151 for more details on restrictive/defining and non-restrictive clauses.

> **Examples**
> **Restrictive:** Christchurch is a city currently being criticised for having a lack of imagination when it comes to development.
> **Non-restrictive:** Christchurch, described by many as 'boring', struggles to attract new migrants.

Before the independent clause

Non-restrictive participial clauses can come before the independent clause. Restrictive/defining participial clauses cannot. Note that this use makes the participial clauses look exactly like an adverbial clause of reason that has been reduced to a participial clauses. Also, note that the participial clause must come before the noun it is describing, not before another noun.

> **Example**
> Described by many as 'boring', Christchurch struggles to attract new migrants.

Exercises

2.1 Reduce the relative clauses in the following sentences to participial clauses

1) Claims for autonomy by many groups in Europe have been hindered by factors that include 'internal colonialism', economic dependence, and world wars.

2) Ethnic minorities that demand autonomy usually have a long history of independence.

_____

_____

3) For this reason, many ethnic minorities in Europe who would prefer autonomy have lagged well behind in their claims.

_____

_____

4) Ethnic minorities that are seen to be economically dependent on the 'parent country' have little hope for independence.

_____

_____

5) On the other hand, some ethnic minorities can be richer than the 'parent country', which can lead to feelings of resentment.

_____

_____

6) A 'brain drain', which happened in many poorer ethnic groups over the last 50 years, meant less effective nationalist leaders in such areas.

_____

_____

7) Scotland, which has experienced a 'brain drain', is an example of a poorer ethnic group.

_____

_____

8) Catalonia, which did not suffer from the same phenomenon, is considerably wealthier than its 'parent country'.

_____

_____

9) In many cases, ethnic groups which were given a considerable degree of autonomy over the past 100 years were less vocal in demands for independence.

_____

_____

10) Independence movements in the United Kingdom, which were affected by the euphoria of victory after World War 2, have progressed less towards autonomy than groups in other countries.

_____

_____

2.2 Write sentences of your own including participial clauses

1) (Active) _____

_____

2) (Active) _____

_____

3) (Active) _____

_____

4) (Passive) _____

_____

5) (Passive) _____

6) (Passive) _____

_____

Continuous Aspect in Participial Clauses

While tense is not usually expressed in participial clauses, aspect can be.

Continuous aspect **can** be expressed in **passive voice** participial clauses, but **not** in **active voice** participial clauses. There is no logical explanation for this, it is just the way English is.

To change a continuous passive voice relative clause to a continuous passive voice participial clause, we delete the relative subordinator, and we replace the finite verb with *being* + *past participle*.

Relative clause: ***Christchurch is a city*** ~~***that***~~ ***is being criticised** for having a lack of imagination*.

Participial clause: ***Christchurch is a city** being criticised **for having a lack of imagination**.*

> ### *Examples*
> **Active continuous**
> *Relative clause:* The guests who were staying at the hotel were unhappy.
> *Participial clause:* The guests staying at the hotel were unhappy.
> **Passive**
> *Relative clause:* The hotel that is being built in the east of the city will have 88 floors.
> *Participial clause:* The hotel being built in the east of the city will have 88 floors.

Perfect Aspect and Participial Clauses

Unlike the continuous aspect, the perfect aspect **can** be shown in **both active and passive voice**.

In active and passive voice, the perfect aspect is constructed by deleting the relative subordinator and changing the auxiliary verb *have* to *having*.

> ### *Examples*
> **Active voice**
> *Relative clause*: Lin, ~~who~~ has tried very hard throughout the semester, has been rewarded for her hard work.
> *Participial clause*: Lin, having tried very hard throughout the semester, has been rewarded for her hard work.
> **Passive voice**
> *Relative clause*: The students ~~who~~ have been given prizes are happy.
> *Participial clause*: The students having been given prizes are happy.

Exercises

3.1 Rewrite the relative clauses in the following sentences as participial clauses.

1) Wales is an example of a region which has been diluted with colonists from the 'parent country'.

_____

_____

2) Western Europe, which is moving closer to becoming a federation of states, has many ethnic minorities which are asserting autonomy without risk of economic isolation.

_____

_____

3) Tibet, which has been demanding autonomy from China, is another ethnic minority.

_____

_____

4) Ethnic minority rights, which are being ignored by the media and government throughout China, are also a concern for the southern Mongol people.

_____

_____

5) The Islamic minority in Western China is another ethnic group which has had trouble with issues of autonomy.

_____

_____

6) Russia is another country which has been struggling with ethnic groups which have been demanding autonomy.

_____

_____

7) Ethnic autonomy, which is even being considered for the Lapp people of Northern Scandinavia, is an issue which affects both rich and poor countries alike.

_____

_____

8) Australia, the United States, Canada, and New Zealand are all examples of countries which have been affected by struggles for recognition by aboriginal ethnic minorities.

_____

_____

3.2 Write sentences of your own using continuous and perfect participial clauses.

1) (Active continuous) _____

_____

2) (Active perfect) _____

_____

3) (Active perfect) _____

_____

4) (Passive continuous) _____

_____

5) (Passive perfect) _____

_____

6) (Passive perfect) _____

_____

Changing adverbial clauses to participial clauses

Adverbial clauses that use the subordinators **before, after, when, while** (time only), **as** (time or reason, but not manner), **since, because**, or **if** can be reduced to participial clauses in the same way that relative clauses can **as long as they share the same subject** as the independent clause.

To change an adverbial clause to a participial clause, delete the subordinator (according to the rules explained below), delete the subject (and change the pronoun in the independent clause to a real subject), and replace finite verb with the active or passive participle.

> **Active**
> _Adverbial clause:_ ~~Because~~ ~~Laura~~ studies hard, She will do well in her exam.
> _Participial clause: Studying_ hard, Laura will do well in her exam.
> **Passive**
> _Adverbial clause:_ ~~Because~~ ~~the lesson~~ was well prepared today, it went well.
> _Participial clause:_ Well prepared today, the lesson went well.

Chapter 10

The difference between reducing relative clauses and reducing adverbial clauses to participial clauses is that in **some** but not all adverbial participial clauses, the subordinator is **not** deleted.

Examples

Because he is crazy, he was put in jail. → Being crazy, he was put in jail.

Before he went to jail, he went to court. → Before going to jail, he went to court.

Note

If the adverbial subordinator is deleted, the participial clause must come *before* the independent clause. If the adverbial subordinator is kept, the participial clause can come before or after the clause it describes.

Examples

Because he is crazy, he was put in jail. → Being crazy, he was put in jail. **Not** He was put in jail being crazy.

Before he went to jail, he went to court. → Before going to jail, he went to court. **Or** He went to court before going to jail.

The rules about deleting or keeping the subordinator are as follows:

Keep	Delete	Optional
before	as (when it means reason or time)	after
if	because	when
since (when it means time)	since (when it means reason)	while

> **Note**
>
> If you keep *since,* it gives a meaning of time; if it is deleted, it means reason.
>
> *As* is *always* deleted in participial phrases.

Examples

Since (time)

Adverbial clause: Police in England have been troubled for the last week since they found a horse on the 12th floor of an apartment building.

Participial clause: Police in England have been troubled for the last week since finding a horse on the 12th floor of an apartment building.

Since (reason)

Adverbial clause: Since their getaway car was too small, two armed robbers in England were forced to leave behind 400,000 pounds.

Participial clause: Their getaway car being too small, two armed robbers in England were forced to leave behind 400,000 pounds.

As

Adverbial clause: As he ate his wife's passport, a Russian man has been arrested.

Participial clause: Having eaten his wife's passport, a Russian man has been arrested.

Examples continued

After

Adverbial clause: A cyclist in Colorado was hit by a train 6 hours after he was hit by a car.

Participial clause: A cyclist in Colorado was hit by a train 6 hours after being hit by car.

Exercises

4.1 Change the following sentences to participial clauses where possible. (Note, it is not possible in every case.)

1) In 1945, a man called Vannevar Bush first dreamed up internet websites when he imagined a desk with screen projecting books and a keyboard to access them which he called a Memex. _____

_____

2) Before they could create the first web page in the early 1970s, they had to connect together all of the computers at the Pentagon, which weighed over 100 tonnes each. _____

_____

3) As this page was successful, we have the internet today. _____

_____

4) Since the internet started with this page in the early 1970s, the internet has come a long way. _____

_____

5) While he was working at CERN in Switzerland in 1989, Tim Berners-Lee invented the first real web page using html.

_____

_____

6) Interestingly, when a website cannot be found today, we get a message saying '404: not found' because when a website could not be found at CERN, the computers redirected the users to room 404, which was the room where the central computer was kept at CERN. _____

_____

_____

7) Before the internet was called 'the internet', it was called APRANET; the name 'internet' was thought up in 1990 to make it sound more exciting. _____

_____

8) After web browsers came into being in 1992, web browsers started receiving the first SPAM messages

_____

9) If instant messaging was not invented in 1996, instant messaging would not have made the internet the interactive chatting device that it is today. _____

_____

10) While we now struggle to cope with e-mail overladen with SPAM, we are also now able to access the internet on our mobile phones. _____

_____

Absolute clauses

Absolute clauses are another type of non-finite clause which uses participles. There are two differences between participial clauses and absolute clauses.

Firstly, unlike a participial clause, an absolute clause contains a subject.

Secondly, an absolute clause is always non-restrictive. They always give extra information although sometimes is can be important extra information: absolute clauses always give extra information about an entire clause.

> **Examples**
>
> *A severe storm appearing on the radar*, the meteorologists raced to the phone to alert the media.
>
> Both expeditions should arrive around the same time, *all things being equal*.

Remember, theses phrases consist of *subject + participle*, and are separated from the independent clause by a comma.

Exercises

5.1 Insert the information in the second sentence into the first sentence as an absolute phrase.

1) The rules about voting have gradually changed over the last century. Women have been demanding more rights since the late 1800s. _____

_____

2) Men hold the best and highest paid jobs, and the vast majority of the positions of power in the world. The western world is a largely patriarchal society. _____

_____

Chapter 10

3) It is clear that it is difficult for women to ascend to the top of patriarchal societies. France, the United States, and Japan have never had a female leader. _____

_____

4) There are several examples throughout history of societies run by females, proving that societies do not *have* to be run by men. The Indian tribes of North America were often run by the females of the tribe.

_____

_____

5) Women have won many rights, including the right to vote over the last 100 years. Many men predicted that the increase in women working throughout the last few decades would lead to greater unemployment; however, this simply has not been so. _____

_____

_____

Appositive Phrases

Non-restrictive subject relative clauses with the verb *be* in them can also be reduced to appositive phrases. This is a simple but useful procedure. Take the following example.

President Obama, who <u>is</u> a great man, is deserving of the Nobel Prize that has been bestowed upon him.

We **delete the subordinator** and the verb *be,* and we have an appositive phrase:

President Obama, a great man, is deserving of the Nobel Prize that has been bestowed upon him.

> ### Example
> John Stewart, ~~who was~~ **the country's longest serving prime minister**, has always been a member of the Conservative Party.
> → John Stewart, **the country's longest serving prime minister**, has always been a member of the Conservative Party.

Exercises

6.1 Reduce the following relative clauses to appositive phrases if possible.

1) Mozart, who was a famous composer, is considered to have been a musical genius by some.

_____

_____

2) Classical music, which differs from pop music in a number of aspects, does not put as much emphasis on the player as on the composer.

_____

_____

3) Pop music, which is the most popular form of music today, tends to be played by groups of musicians that both like to take credit for their work, and shun changes in their line up.

_____

_____

4) Music that is heard regularly on the radio today is often a re-make of previous works.

_____

_____

5) John Coltrane, who is considered one of the greatest jazz musicians of all time, is a musician whose music is often covered by other artists.

_____

_____

Cohesion

Cohesion

Cohesion is an important part of writing; it is considered in all major testing systems such as the IELTS test. Cohesion is the way that ideas link together. It involves pronouns, passive and active voice, transition words, topic sentences, and thesis statements. But perhaps most importantly, it involves the location of new and old information; we will refer to this as **theme**.

Theme

Consider the following passage. Each sentence is written in two different ways. Decide which way you think makes a more logical paragraph.

a. *Banking has been revolutionized by the ATM and Internet banking.*

b. *(1) An ATM is a convenient way to access your account.*
   (2) A convenient way to access your account is an ATM.

c. *(1) Customers can use ATMs twenty-four hours a day, 7 days a week.*
   (2) ATMs allow customers to use them twenty-four hours a day, 7 days a week.

d. *(1) An ATM can be used to withdraw cash and to deposit money.*
   (2) Customers can utilize the ATM to both withdraw cash and to deposit money.

e. *(1) Transfers can be made between accounts and an account summary can be accessed.*
   (2) Customers can make transfers between accounts and can access an account summary.

f. *(1) On the other hand, Internet banking does not require cards or pin numbers.*
   (2) On the other hand, cards or pin numbers are not required with Internet banking.

g. *(1) Internet banking is done in the privacy of personal computers.*
   (2) Personal computers are used for Internet banking.

h. *(1) Doing Internet banking on personal computers is much safer as more complex passwords can be used and the chances of fraud are lower.*
   (2) More complex passwords can be used and the chances of fraud are lower, so doing Internet banking on personal computers is much safer.

i. *(1) However, there is a major draw back compared to ATMs with Internet banking.*
   (2) However, Internet banking has a major draw back compared to ATMs.

j. *(1) The draw back is that it is impossible to withdraw cash.*
   (2) The impossibility to withdraw cash is the drawback.

Now consider the correct passage:

Banking has been revolutionized by the ATM and Internet banking. An ATM is a convenient way to access your account. ATMs allow customers to use them twenty-four hours a day, 7 days a week. Customers can utilize the ATM to both withdraw cash and to deposit money. Customers can make transfers between accounts and can access an account summary. On the other hand, Internet banking does not require cards or pin numbers. Internet banking is done in the privacy of personal computers. Doing Internet banking on personal computers is much safer as more complex passwords can be used and the chances of fraud are lower. However, Internet banking has a major draw back compared to ATMs. The draw back is that it is impossible to withdraw cash.

Notice how **new information** is always introduced in the **complement position**, and **old information** is always located in the **subject position**. As long as we keep the same subject, we are maintaining the same theme. This paragraph has four themes: ***ATM, internet banking, customers***, and ***a drawback***.

Chapter 11

> **Example**
>
> There are a number of problems with *giving food to hungry people*.
> New information (1)
>
> *Giving food to hungry people* depresses *local financial markets*.
> Old information (1)   New information (2)
>
> *Giving food to hungry people* does not provide local farmers with *incentives* to grow more food.
> Old information (1)   New information (3)
>
> *Incentives* have been considered *the key to solving the problem*.
> Old information (3)   New information (4)

You can see that we have two choices when we write a sentence. We can use the same **subject** from the previous sentence, **or** we can use an **object** from the previous sentence as a subject. However, we cannot introduce new information as a subject.

> **Example**
>
> There are a number of problems with *giving food to hungry people*.
> New information (1)
>
> *Incentives* have been considered *the key to solving the problem*. X (This doesn't make sense because the
> New information (2)   New information (3)   subject has no connection to the
>   previous sentence.)

Exercises

1 Choose from sentence (1) and sentence (2) to make a coherent paragraph.

a) (1) A food crisis has been looming over the past couple of years.
    (2) There has been a food crisis looming over the past couple of years.

b) (1) Previous food crises were different from this food crisis.
    (2) This food crisis is different from previous food crises.

c) (1) Previous food crises were caused by drought or war.
    (2) Drought or war cause previous food crises.

d) (1) High food prices are causing this food crisis.
    (2) This food crisis is being caused by high prices.

e) (1) Prices are high because of increased demand from China and India as they become richer and eat more meat.
    (2) Increased demand from China and India as they become richer and eat more meat is driving prices higher.

f) (1) Prices are also high because of the increased demand for bio-fuels pushing up the price of grain.
    (2) The increased demand for bio-fuels, which is pushing up the price of grain, are another cause of prices being high.

g) (1) Less land being used for food crops and a lower supply of food are the results of recent demand for bio-fuels.
    (2) Bio-fuels mean less land being used for food crops and a lower supply of food.

1.2 Find the errors in cohesion in the following text.

1) America has an insatiable appetite for meat. China and India have imported an appetite for meat as they gradually become richer. However, there are a number of problems with this diet. First of all, money is wasted when we eat meat because it takes 7 bowls of cow food to get one bowl of human food (meat) from the cow. Wasting 6 bowls of food is the equivalent of eating a bowl of meat.

2) A second problem with the meat diet is that it is causing incredible damage to the environment. The volume of methane being released is almost double the amount of gas being released by cars. A massive over consumption of water to feed the animals is the result of the meat diet. A massive amount of methane being released into the atmosphere is also a result of the meat diet. Methane is a global warming gas, much stronger than CO_2. The belches and excrement from cows release methane.

1.3 Write a logical next sentence for the following sentences.

1) The computer is a useful invention

_____

_____

2) There have been a number of changes made to the road rules in the last year.

_____

_____

3) Arabic and Western cultures differ in a number of ways.

_____

_____

4) It is good that women have finally earned the right to pay equality in modern society.

_____

_____

5) An interesting fact that has been discovered is that there is not one culture in the world that dislikes chocolate.

_____

_____

Passive voice & Cohesion

The use of passive voice is very closely related to cohesion. English has two 'voices': **active voice** and **passive voice**. **Active voice** is the normal SVO word order that we use in most sentences. **Passive voice** involves moving the object of a clause to subject position and changing the form of the verb.

> **Example**
>
> **Active voice:** The course <u>explores</u> *a number of topics*
> Subject   verb   object
>
> **Passive voice:** *A number of topics* <u>are explored</u> during the course.
> Subject   (verb changes form)

To understand how we use passive voice in cohesion, it is important to understand how we form passive voice. To understand how we form passive voice, we need to be aware of 6 types of verbs,

a) **Linking verbs**
b) **Intransitive verbs**
c) **Transitive verbs**
d) **Ambitransitive verbs**
e) **Ditransitive verbs**
f) **Ergative verbs**

Linking verbs

Linking verbs are verbs like **be, appear,** and **seem**. These verbs are special. They can have objects, but they cannot be used in passive voice.

> **Example**
>
> I **am** a teacher. → A teacher **is being**. X (Linking verbs are not used in passive voice.)

Intransitive verbs

Intransitive verbs are verbs that cannot have objects. **Intransitive verbs cannot be used in passive voice.** These verbs cannot be used in passive voice because to make passive voice, we take the object and make it into the subject. If there is no object, we cannot make it a subject.

> **Examples of these verbs include:**
>
> | | | | | |
> |---|---|---|---|---|
> | come | emerge | go | live | result |
> | decline | ensue | happen | occur | succeed |
> | disappear | fluctuate | last | remain | wait |

Chapter 11

> **Examples**
> **Active voice:** The accident happened. → **Passive voice:** ????? *was happened*. (No object exists to be made subject)
> The results *were disappeared* by the computer. **X** (not possible because *disappear* is intransitive)

Transitive verbs

This group of verbs **must have** an **object**. Examples include *kill, love,* and *do*. These verbs **can** always be used in **passive** voice.

Ambitransitive verbs

This group of verbs includes most verbs. They can be used with or without an object. Examples include *drive, eat,* and *speak.* These verbs **can** be used in **passive** voice when they have an object.

Ditransitive verbs

This group of verbs is special. These verbs can have **two objects**. They form passive voice differently from other verbs; they have two passive voice options. Examples of these verbs include *tell, give,* and *write*.

> **Example**
> **Ditransitive verb with two choices for passive voice**
> **Active voice:** The professor gave the students a lot of help in the assignment.
>   Subject   verb   object   object (the first object is called the indirect object; the second object is
>   called the direct object)
> **Passive voice 1:** We were given a lot of help in the assignment.
>   Subject   verb   object (When we make the indirect object the subject of a passive, we can still have an object
> after the passive. *This is the only case when you can have an object after a passive voice verb.*)
> **Passive voice 2:** A lot of help was given to us in the assignment
>   Subject   verb (When we make the direct object the subject of a passive, we cannot have an object after the
> passive verb. The indirect object changes to the prepositional phrase to us.)

Ergative verbs

This group of verbs is an unusual group of verbs that don't require passive voice when the object moves to subject position. Examples of these verbs include *blow up, cook,* and *bake*.

> **Example**
> The terrorist blew up the police station. → The police station blew up.

> **Note**
> A passive voice verb <u>cannot</u> usually have an object. An *exception* to this is with *ditransitive verbs* such as *give* or *write* (verbs that can have *two objects*). The first example here reconstructs an incorrect passive voice with an object to show how it doesn't make sense. The second example shows how a ditransitive verb might have an object.
>
> > **Example**
> > **Passive voice with an object**
> > The spider <u>was killed</u> knife. **X (Incorrect passive voice)**
> > Subject   verb   object
> >
> > Somebody <u>killed</u> the spider knife. **X (This does not make any sense.)**
> > (We don't know who the subject is.) (**The spider** moves back to the object position.)

Tense & aspect in passive voice

A full list of examples of tense and aspect in both active and passive voice can be found in chapter 5; however, the following table outlines how to construct each aspect in passive voice.

	Past	Present	Future
Active simple	V~ed / irregular past	V/V~s	Modal + V
Passive simple	**Was/were PP**	**Is/am/are PP**	**Modal + be PP**
Active continuous	Was/were ~ing	Is/am/are V~ing	Modal + be V~ing
Passive continuous	**Was/were being PP**	**Is/am/are being PP**	**Modal + be being PP**
Active perfect	Had PP	Have/has PP	Modal + have PP
Passive perfect	**Had been PP**	**Have/has been PP**	**Modal + have been PP**
Active perfect continuous	Had been V~ing	Have/has been V~ing	Modal + have been V~ing
Passive perfect continuous	**Had been being PP**	**Have/has been being PP**	**Modal + have been being PP**

PP = past participle. E.g. *go / went / gone* (**Gone** is the past participle of *go*.)

Cohesion and passive voice

Sometimes we state the person or thing that does the action in a prepositional phrase beginning with **by**, but sometimes we do not.

> ### Example
> It **is claimed (1)** that fish farming might be a solution to the problems of fish depletion.
>
> A person **was murdered (2)** this morning at Brighton Beach; the body **was found (3)** this morning by two tourists out for an early morning walk.

In the first case **(1)**, a **by phrase** is not used because we do not have a specific subject. Here the subject is really **people in general**. For more on passive voice in reported speech, see Chapter 4, page 52. In the second case (2), the newspaper that printed this story may know who the murder was, but cannot say for legal reasons; thus, a **by phrase** is not used. In the third case, a **by phrase is** used. This is because the reason for using passive voice here was related to **cohesion**.

> **Reasons for using passive voice include**
> 1. **We do not know the subject**
> 2. **We do not want to say the subject**
> 3. **Passive voice creates better _cohesion_**

Thus, the reason why we sometimes put the **by phrase** in and sometimes leave it out depends on our reason for using passive voice.

In the previous sections, we saw how we create cohesion in a passage by always placing **old information** in the **subject** position and **new information** in the **object position**.

> ### Example
> There are a number of problems with *giving food to hungry people*.
> <u>New</u> information (1)
>
> *Giving food to hungry people* depresses *local financial markets*.
> <u>Old</u> information (1)   New information (2)
>
> *Giving food to hungry people* does not provide local farmers with *incentives* to grow more food.
> <u>Old</u> information (1)   New information (3)

Often teachers and textbooks will tell you that we use passive voice 'to emphasise the subject'. But, what does this mean? Why would you emphasise the subject? Well the answer is that we are **not** really **emphasising the subject**, we are **using passive voice** to make sure that **old information is in the subject position and new information is in the object position**. Consider the following table sentences.

Chapter 11

<table>
<tr><td>No cohesion</td><td>Good cohesion (using passive voice)</td></tr>
<tr><td>Passive voice is a very useful tool.
We use passive voice to create cohesion in a text.
New   Old</td><td>Passive voice is a very useful tool.
Passive voice is used to create cohesion in a text.
Old</td></tr>
</table>

The sentences on the left introduce new information in the subject position. The sentences on the right have far better cohesion because the subject position is filled with old information. This is achieved by using *passive voice*.

Example

First sentence: Cows are the most widespread type of ungulates.

2nd sentence option 1: Farms **keep** cows for the production of meat and dairy products. **X** (no cohesion)
new   old

2nd sentence option 2: Cows **are kept** on farms for the production of meat and dairy products. ✓ (Passive
old   new   voice creates cohesion.)

Exercises

2.1 Change these verbs to passive voice if possible using the correct tense

1) Investigate _____
2) Is happening _____
3) Is keeping _____
4) Caused _____

5) Have ensued _____
6) Has produced _____
7) Have been using _____

2.2 Change the verbs in bold in these clauses to passive voice if possible

1) Scientists *call* the current of warm, salty water that ocean currents *move* up the African coast to Europe the Great Ocean Conveyor Belt.

_____

_____

2) The Gulf Stream *joins* this flow of water and together they *affect* European temperatures.

_____

_____

3) This flow of warm water *keeps* temperatures in Europe considerably warmer than those of comparable latitudes in Asia, Russia, and North America.

_____

_____

4) Once the warm water reaches Greenland, the cooler weather rapidly *cools* it.

_____

_____

5) Because cold temperatures and high salinity *encourage* the water to sink, it *descends* to the bottom of the ocean once it reaches Greenland and *freezes.*

_____

_____

6) Ocean currents along the bottom of the Atlantic then *carry* the water back out to the Indian and Pacific Oceans along the ocean floor.

_____

_____

7) Sea water around Greenland, which global warming *is making* warmer and less salty, *is* thus *affecting* the flow of the Great Ocean Conveyor Belt.

_____

8) If this flow of water ***stopped***, Europe ***would experience*** significant cooling.

9) Thus, ironically, current climate change trends **could cause** major cooling rather than warming.

2.3 Find the errors in passive voice in these sentences.

1) This is because it was already consumed everything.

2) Prior to 10,000 years ago when almost all parts of the earth was covered by ice, the temperature was slightly fluctuated between -52°F and -50°F.

3) An ice age has been continued from millions of years ago until now.

4) Some scientists have been found a strong relationship between levels of blood-sugar addiction and addiction to fast food.

5) We has been already lived 10,000 years in a warm period called an interglacial.

6) The U.S. uses the largest amount of minerals such as phosphorus, which is used 8322 tonnes in one person's life.

2.4 Fix the _cohesion_ of the following passages by _using passive voice_.

1) Our solar system and galaxy could quite suddenly come to an end without us knowing it due to a gamma ray burst. A gamma ray burst can explode across 8 billion light years of space. Scientists detect about three hundred of these blasts each year. A burst like this would wipe away our galaxy before we even knew what had hit us.
    (Adapted from Charles Flowers 2002, *Instability Rules*, p15)

2) Lord Kelvin, who was born in 1824 in Belfast, was the son of a professor of mathematics. The University of Glasgow admitted him at the age of ten. By the age of 20, he had completed studies in both London and Paris, Cambridge University had elected him a teacher and researcher, and he had written several mathematical papers.
    (Adapted from Bill Bryson 2003, *A Short History of Nearly Everything*, pp76-77)

3) Plague is a disease. Rats carry this disease. Fleas carry it from one rat to another, but human beings can catch it if fleas infest them. In crowded Medieval cities, this happened quite frequently.
    (Adapted from Charles Van Doren 1991, *A history of knowledge*, p151)

Chapter 11

Adverbial clauses & Cohesion

Adverbial clauses can come before or after the independent clause. Our decision about whether to place the adverbial clause before or after the independent clause relates to cohesion.

Remember that there are twelve types of adverbial clause. Following is a list of the twelve types with an example for each type. More information can be found on each of these types of adverbial clause in chapter 6.

1. **Time:** *After* *children come home from school,* they must do homework.
2. **Place:** Children can study *anywhere* *it is comfortable.*
3. **Manner:** That man acts *as if* *he is a king.*
4. **Distance:** Every morning I run *as far as* *I can.*
5. **Frequency:** I do exercises *as often as* *it is possible for me to.*
6. **Result:** Maki was *so* kind and beautiful *that* *I married her.*
7. **Purpose:** I studied hard *so that* *I would do well in my test on adverbial clauses.*
8. **Reason:** *Because* *I studied hard,* I did well in my test on adverbial clauses.
9. **Concession:** *Although* *my family is from Scotland,* I do not speak with a Scottish accent.
10. **Contrast:** Japan is very technologically advanced, *whereas* *Mexico is quite technologically backwards.*
11. **Conditional:** Spain would be a great place to live *if* *housing wasn't so expensive.*
12. **Comparative:** It costs more to buy a house in Durban *than* *it costs to by a house in most parts of Europe.*

Remember that while most adverbial clauses can come before and after the independent clause, not all can (or at least it is not common for some to come before the adverbial clause).

Adverbial clauses that can come **before and after** the independent clause include:

1. **Time:**

> *Example*
>
> **After children come home from school,** they must do homework.
> Children must do homework *after they come home from school*.

2. **Reason:**

> *Example*
>
> **Because I studied hard,** I did well in my test on adverbial clauses.
> I did well in my test on adverbial clauses *because I studied hard*.

3. **Concession:**

> *Example*
>
> **Although my family is from Scotland,** I do not speak with a Scottish accent.
> I do not speak with a Scottish accent *although my family is from Scotland*.

4. **Contrast:**

> *Example*
>
> **Whereas Mexico is quite technologically backwards**, Japan is very technologically advanced.
> Japan is very technologically advanced, *whereas Mexico is quite technologically backwards*.

5. **Conditional:**

> *Example*
>
> **If housing wasn't so expensive,** Italy would be a great place to live.
> Italy would be a great place to live *if housing wasn't so expensive*.

> **Note**
>
> Note the punctuation in the examples above. When the adverbial clause comes before the independent clause, we separate the two clauses with a comma. When the adverbial clause comes after the independent clause, we do not put a comma. The exception is contrast using the subordinators *while* and *whereas*. We always use a comma with these subordinators.

In the previous sections, we saw how we create cohesion in a passage by always placing **old information** in the **subject** position and **new information** in the **object** position.

> **Example**
>
> There are a number of problems with *giving food to hungry people*.
> <u>New</u> information (1)
>
> *Giving food to hungry people* depresses *local financial markets*.
> <u>Old</u> information (1)   New information (2)
>
> *Giving food to hungry people* does not provide local farmers with *incentives* to grow more food.
> <u>Old</u> information (1)   New information (3)

In the same way, if an adverbial clause contains **old information**, we will often place it **before** the independent clause. If it contains **new information**, we will often place it **after** the independent clause.

> **No cohesion**
>
> Rachmaninoff was born into a noble Russian family in 1873.
> His mother began to give him piano lessons *__after__ he **turned four**.
> New   Old
>
> **Good cohesion** (By placing the adverbial clause *before* the independent clause)
>
> Rachmaninoff was born into a noble Russian family in 1873.
> *__After__ he **turned four**,* His mother began to give him piano lessons.
>   Old   New

In the first case, there is little cohesion because the second sentence begins with new information. In the second case, greater cohesion is achieved by placing the adverbial clause *before* the independent clause; that way, the old information is at the start of the second sentence and the new information is later in the sentence.

In the above examples, old information is repeated in the adverbial clause, but sometimes an adverbial clause contains new information. Note in the following example how the adverbial clause comes *after* the independent clause because it only contains **new information**.

> **Example**
>
> Rachmaninoff was born into a noble Russian family in 1873.
> Rachmaninoff was taught by Anna Ornatskaya from 1882 to 1885 *__until__ debt **forced the family home to be sold**
> old   new   new
> and the family* **to move to Moscow**.

Notice that this cohesive rule doesn't just apply to adverbial clauses; it also applies to prepositional phrases, especially those using prepositions such as *due to, in spite of, despite,* and *because of*.

Exercises

3.1 Fix the cohesion of the following passages by moving adverbial clauses

1) Tchaikovsky's family educated him to become a civil servant even though music was his love as a child. Although his family didn't want him to, he ignored this education as an adult and began a musical career at the St. Petersburg Conservatory. As his musical ability developed, Tchaikovsky wrote many different types of music from symphony to opera. Personal crises and emotional trouble followed him throughout his life although he was very successful. Depression was a common problem throughout his life because of this.
   (Adapted from http://en.wikipedia.org/w/index.php?title=Pyotr_Ilyich_Tchaikovsky&oldid=324645182)

   _____

   _____

   _____

   _____

   _____

2) Winston Churchill coined of the term 'iron curtain' to describe Eastern Europe after World War II. The USSR and the West had been allies while World War II had been raging, but the USSR had not forgotten that the Western Allies had tried to bring down the USSR during the Russian Civil War. The USSR remained wary of the Allies and they tried to set up a buffer zone between them and the West because of this. This buffer zone had its beginnings before World War II had really started. In 1939, after negotiations on a military, economic, and political agreement had been finished, the USSR and Germany signed a trade and non-aggression agreement. After this agreement was signed, the Baltic States and Eastern Poland were invaded by the USSR. This was the beginning of the buffer zone. Their friendship had

deteriorated into a bitter war by 1945, while the USSR and Germany were friends at the start of the war. The USSR became even more determined to create a buffer zone around their country because firstly the Allies and then Germany had betrayed them. Thus, after the war, the USSR decided to keep and expand control of Eastern Europe.

(Adapted from http://en.wikipedia.org/w/index.php?title=Iron_Curtain&oldid=324764522)

_____

_____

_____

_____

_____

_____

_____

_____

_____

_____

Transition words and cohesion

We have already seen how we create cohesion in a passage by always placing **old information** in the **subject** position and **new information** in the **object** position.

Example

There are a number of problems with *giving food to hungry people*.
                                    <u>New</u> information (1)

Giving food to hungry people depresses *local financial markets*.
<u>Old</u> information (1)   New information (2)

Giving food to hungry people does not provide local farmers with *incentives* to grow more food.
<u>Old</u> information (1)   New information (3)

Sometimes, however, we need to change the topic within a paragraph. Consider the following paragraph.

Example

Germany's most famous leader was Hitler. He was born in Austria in 1889, **_and_** he joined the German army in 1914. He became a corporal in the Army, **_but_** he was wounded in a gas attack in 1917. After the war, he became a painter in **Vienna**. **Vienna** was home to many painters at the time. *However*, Hitler did not like Vienna and left for Munich in 1920. Munich was home to a revolutionary movement that wanted to overthrow the government in Berlin.

In this paragraph, *Hitler* is the topic of the first theme. This theme continues until the word *Vienna*. After that, a new theme starts with the subject *Vienna*. But then, the author wants to talk about *Hitler* again. *Hitler* is no longer old information from the last sentence. This is where a **transition word** is needed. Here the author has used *however* to show contrast between this sentence and the last. Notice also, that **coordinators** are used to show relationships **within** a theme.

Transition words are often conjunctive adverbs. The following is a table listing coordinators (for use within a theme) and conjunctive adverbs (for use between themes).

	Coordinators (show relationships *within* themes)	**Transition words (Conjunctive adverbs)** (Show relationships *between* themes)
Adding a point	*and, nor, or*	*also, besides, further, furthermore, in addition, moreover*
Unexpected contrast	*but, yet*	*however, nevertheless, nonetheless*
Direct contrast		*in contrast, on the other hand*
Result	*So*	*accordingly, as a consequence, as a result, consequently, hence, therefore, thus*
Sequencing		*at the same time, finally, firstly, lastly, meanwhile, secondly, subsequently, thirdly*
Condition		*anyway, in that case, otherwise*
Adding an Example		*for example, for instance*
Adding a similarity		*likewise, similarly*
Emphasis or restatement		*actually, anyway ,certainly, in fact, indeed, in other words*

A complete list of conjunctive adverbs can be found in the Appendix 5, page 201.

> **Note**
>
> **Besides** means *also* or *moreover*, but it has the extra meaning that the added point is more important than the earlier point. For example: '*I didn't do my homework because I was tired; besides, my mother was sick.*'
> In this example, the implication is that '*my mother was sick*' is a more important point than *my being tired*.

Other uses of transition words

Transition words can also be used **within** a theme to show **result**, **contrast**, or **example**. Notice the difference in punctuation style between the two uses.

a) **Result**

> *Example*
>
> Hitler became a corporal in the army, but he was wounded in a gas attack**; as a result,** he had to leave the front.

b) **Contrast**

> *Example*
>
> Munich was home to a revolutionary movement**; however,** Vienna had been home to pacifists and peace-makers.

c) **Refutation**

> *Example*
>
> Hitler argued that the Jews were responsible for all of Germany's problems**; however,** this view was bigoted, emotive, and not based on any real evidence.

d) **Example**

> *Example*
>
> Hitler made many enemies**; for example,** he upset Mussolini by refusing to shake his hand.

Chapter 11

Punctuation

Conjunctive adverbs

There are two options for punctuation with conjunctive adverbs. They can either begin a sentence, or follow a semicolon. They are **always** followed by a comma. Use a **full stop** and begin a new sentence when you are **changing topic or theme** in a paragraph. Use a **semicolon** when you are showing **result, contrast, or example within a theme**.

> **Examples**
> **Beginning a new sentence**
> It is thought continuing global warming will make the Gulf Stream stop. *Therefore,* we should reconsider our environmental policy
> **Following a semi-colon**
> The author thinks that the Gulf Stream will stop*; therefore,* he thinks that Europe will become much colder than it is today.

Coordinators

Coordinators always have a comma before them.
Try to only use coordinators within themes and keep conjunctive adverbs for use between themes.

> **Example**
> He wrote about global warming*, and* he wrote about global politics.

Exercises

4.1 Insert appropriate coordinators and conjunctive adverbs into the following essay to show changes in theme and to link ideas within themes.

Recently civilization marked the end of another century. In 1900 many predictions were made about the year 2000. Some of these came true, such as the prevalence of cars, electric trains, air conditioners, and refrigerators. Others were way off the mark. An example is floating fortresses above cities. Another example is the extinction of all animals. Another example is the extermination of all insects. Other events and inventions, such as the two world wars, aeroplanes, man walking on the moon, television, and computers, were simply not imagined. This essay will try to make as accurate predictions as possible about the year 2100. It will look at the fields of technology. It will look at the field of transportation.

Firstly, lets look at three aspects of technology: computers, mobile phones, and robots. Computers will of course become smaller and smaller. It is quite possible that advances in nanotechnology will allow computers to become almost invisibly small. There are practical limitations to how small a computer might become. Keyboards need to be a reasonable size for people to use them. Computer screens need to be a reasonable size. It is possible that computers could be voice, or possibly even mind activated and could talk to us. There will still be times when we want to work in silence with our computers. Mobile phones will become smaller. They will be limited in size by issues of practicality. One possibility is that mobile phones will be implanted in our brains. Perhaps computers will be implanted too. Whenever we want to call somebody or take a photo of something, we will be able to do so using a device directly connected to our brains. Robots appear ever more allusive. Many predictors in the 1900s imagined that by 2000, we would have robots helping us with housework. This simply hasn't happened yet. Robots remain bulky, inefficient, and very expensive. There is, however, one exception: robot vacuum cleaners that move around the floor automatically sensing furniture and other objects, cleaning as they go. Robots will probably be no more common in 2100 than they were in 2001.

Secondly, lets imagine what transportation will be like when petrol supplies will have been virtually depleted and electric, ethanol, and hydrogen fuelled cars will prevail. It is certain that by 2100 AD, much of the world's oil supplies will have been depleted. There will still be oil available. It will be produced by an expensive extraction process from peat and from nearly empty oil wells. Public transportation will no longer rely on petrol. Aeroplanes will probably be fuelled either by ethanol, a biofuel produced from plants, or from super-cooled hydrogen. The problem with widespread use of biofuels is that if today all the crops in the world were switched to ethanol production, we still wouldn't have enough fuel for all of our cars. Biofuels will probably be the domain only of aeroplanes. Supercooled hydrogen could also be used for aeroplanes. It could be used for vehicles, probably those needing more energy, such as trucks and tractors. As battery technology improves, it is more and more likely that the future will see an abundance of small electric cars, fitted with an amazing array of electric devices. No doubt they will not have keys. They will instead be started at the press of a button which will recognise the owner's fingerprint. They will be fitted with advanced GPS systems that will know where traffic jams are. The GPS systems will guide the cars around the traffic problems. Cars will also be fitted with sensors that will prevent cars from hitting each other and even other objects. Finally, it is quite possible that these cars will become fully automatic. They will be able to drive themselves to a given destination, and park themselves at the end.

Pronouns & Cohesion

Pronoun use is also related to cohesion; in fact, pronouns can be important for creating cohesion between ideas. Let's look at the paragraph about Hitler from the previous section again.

> ### Example
> Germany's most famous leader was *Hitler*. *He* was born in Austria in 1889, and *he* joined the German army in 1914. *He* became a corporal in the Army, but *he* was wounded in a gas attack in 1917. After the war, *he* became a painter in *Vienna*. *Vienna* was home to many painters at the time. *However, Hitler* did not like *Vienna* and left for *Munich* in 1920. *Munich* was home to a revolutionary movement that wanted to overthrow the government in Berlin.

Pay attention to the following points in this example:

1. Firstly, the first mention of **Hitler**. Does not use a pronoun. After that, throughout the theme, **he** is used for **Hitler**. Notice that the pronoun _generally_ refers to the subject of a theme.
2. Secondly, notice that a pronoun _generally_ does not refer outside of its theme. Thus, after the transition word **however**, which marks a topic change, the noun **Hitler** is used again instead of he. Notice also, that the word **Vienna** is used, not **it**.

Unclear Pronouns

It is important to make it clear what a pronoun represents. Basically, there are three unclear situations that students use pronouns.

1. Referring to something outside of the text.

Some students use a pronoun that refers to something outside of the paragraph without it being clear what the pronoun represents.

> ### Example
> There will be a meeting for them on the next day; it is on the whiteboard in their room. If you would like to add anything to it, please do so.

Who are '**they**' in this example, and what is '**it**'? Students often make this mistake in academic writing in three situations. Firstly, they might refer to an article without first introducing it.

> ### Example
> In this article, the author claims that Chavez is very misguided and arrogant.

The above example is fine as long as we know which article we are talking about; in other words, 'this article' must have already been introduced. Otherwise, the reader does not know which article or which author thinks this.

> ### Example
> The graph shows the rate of investment in Colombia over the last ten years.

Chapter 11

Again, this sentence is fine if the writer has already introduced the graph, but otherwise which graph is the person talking about?

> **Example**
>
> **Question three:** What is the main cause of the conflict between Colombia and Venezuela?
>
> **Student writing:** It is American investment and the build up of the Colombian army.

Here the writer has referred to the essay question. *It* represents **the main cause**. Don't refer to essay or test questions in your writing. A better answer would be: *'**The main cause of the conflict between Colombia and Venezuela is American investment and the build up of the Colombian army**'*.

2. Ambiguous pronouns

Some students write clauses in which there are many nouns that the pronoun could possibly represent. This can make it very hard to understand the writing.

> **Example**
>
> If parents don't take care of how they feed their children, **they** may have health problems later in life.

In this example, who are **they** – the children or the parents? In this case, the student meant the children, but it could be interpreted either way. Remember that pronouns _generally_ refer to the subject of a theme.

3. Wrong pronoun

Some students use *'it'* when they mean *'this'*. *'It'* is used for a pronoun representing the last noun. *'This'* is used for a pronoun representing the last *clause*. This mistake is **very hard** for native speakers to follow.

> **Example**
>
> You should immunize your child against poliovirus at 12 months. **This** is because 12 months is the safest age to infect a baby with **it**.

This refers to *'**immunizing your child against poliovirus at 12 months**'*. If the author had written *it* here, the reader would have presumed that *it* referred to **poliovirus** as it does at the end of the clause.

Notice that *'one'* can also be a pronoun. Consider the following sentence:

> **Example**
>
> There are three problems, the most important **one** is his attitude, but the other **ones** also need consideration.

In this case, the first *'one'* is a pronoun, meaning the first problem; the second *'one'* is a pronoun meaning the other two problems. It is plural because it is a pronoun for two things.

Remember that the pronoun *it* can also be a dummy subject.

> **Example**
>
> It is true that he would make a good employee.   It is really hot today.
>
> It is said that he has extensive experience.   It is three o'clock.

In the first two examples, it is clear that *it* has no meaning, but in the second two examples, it could be argued that *it* means **the weather** or **the time**, but actually again in these cases, *it* has no meaning.

Exercises

5.1 Insert pronouns into the following paragraphs.

Proponents of global warming need better perspective. Firstly, the statistics that the proponents are using are very questionable; secondly, the proponents fail to see the big picture, and thirdly, the proponents are searching for evidence to prove the hypothesis that global warming is correct rather than testing the hypothesis scientifically.

The proponents' statistics are questionable for several reasons. If a scientist wants to determine temperatures from more than a hundred years ago, the scientist must resort to tree rings. Although rings provide a broad picture of what has been happening, rings are nowhere near as accurate as statistical data from satellites and should not be used in the same graph. The inaccuracy of rings is why the statistics used to create the 'hockey stick' graph are so easily discredited; the statistics are not based on hard data. On top of the inaccuracy of rings, the temperatures taken by meteorologists in the first half of the 20th century are questionable because the data was not taken under strict enough conditions. For example, some data were taken in sheds, and some under trees. Moreover, the urban heat island effect also calls this data into question. Many people know that many of the weather stations that were once located in countryside are now located in cities. When a person records temperatures in urban areas and the countryside, there is always a considerable difference. Cities are hotter. Take Orange County for example. Orange County is now located in the Greater Los Angeles urban area, but in 1900 was a small fruit-farming region. Data showing that temperatures have risen in Orange County since 1900 merely show that Orange County has evolved from a farming area to an urban area.

5.2 Find 17 errors with pronouns in the following paragraph:

Proponents of global warming fail to see the big picture because whether you consider it to be warming or cooling really depends on when he starts from. Lets take seven different possible starting points: 100,000,000 years ago, 10,500 years ago, 3000 years ago, 1000 years ago, 150 years ago, 20 years ago, and 10 years ago. 100,000,000 years ago, the dinosaurs still roamed the earth. At that time, the earth was considerably warmer than that is today; there were no polar ice caps; in fact, Antarctica was covered in rain forests. If one makes this point in time a starting point, it is clear that it has undergone a massive cooling. 10,500 years ago, the last ice age was coming to an end. During this time, the earth was considerably cooler than there is today; the polar ice caps spread as far south as the great lakes in North America and northern Italy in Europe. If I take this time as a starting point, it is clear that this has undergone massive warming. 3,000 years ago, global temperatures were somewhat warmer than today. It had just peaked at one of the many high points that we have experienced in the period since the last ice age. During this warm period, the first cities and civilizations began to flourish. If we take this point in time as a starting point, we can see a slight cooling in them. 1000 years ago, the earth was in yet another warm one, somewhat warmer than today. It was during this period that the Vikings were able to settle and farm the now snowy and inhospitable lands of Greenland. Again, taking then as a starting point, we can see a slight cooling in global temperatures. 150 years ago, the world was in a significantly cooler period. That was known as the 'little ice age'. Taking that as a starting point, the world appears to be going through a period of rapid warming. 20 years ago there was about half a degree cooler than today; it has been through it that scientists have observed the so-called global warming effect; however, 10 years ago in 1998, world temperatures peaked at record highs. Since this temperatures have declined. Thus, if we take it as a starting point, we can see a clear trend of global cooling. Therefore, it is easy to argue that whether the world is warming or cooling all depends on your perspective.

Gerund Clauses, Noun Clauses and Cohesion

Gerund clauses are also used to create cohesion in texts. Consider the following sentences.

> **Example**
>
> It is argued that *humans should eat meat*. *This* is because *humans evolved on a meat diet*. *Humans having evolved on a meat diet* has resulted in our relatively small stomachs and huge brains, *but this* alone is not reason enough to claim *that modern humans should eat meat*.

Notice that *this* in the second sentence refers to the gerund clause '*humans should eat meat*'. In the first sentence, the information '*humans should eat meat*' is introduced as *new information* in the *object* position. In the second sentence it becomes **old information** in the **subject** position.

Chapter 11

In the third sentence, the **old information** clause *'humans evolved on a meat diet'* has been made into the **subject** of the clause. This has been done by making the clause into a **gerund clause**. The writer has not used the pronoun *this* because this is a new theme. Remember that every time you start a new theme, you must restate your subject rather than using a pronoun. In the final clause, the pronoun *this* is used to refer to *'humans evolved on a meat diet'* because this is still inside the same theme.

When we make a clause into the subject of a clause, we either use a noun clause or a gerund clause. We use a **noun clause** with the verb **be** and **gerund clauses** with **other** verbs.

To make a noun clause, simply place *that* before the clause, or place a **wh-word** (*who, what, when, where, why, how*), or use *if* or *whether*. For more on noun clauses, see Chapter 4.

To make a gerund clause, simply change the **finite verb** in the clause to a **gerund**. For more on gerund clauses, see Chapters 2, page 19 & Chapter 3, page 35.

> *Example*
>
> *That technology is advancing at such a fast rate* is scary to some people.
>   subject   verb   object
>
> *People fearing new technology* often results in people rejecting it despite its convenience.
>   subject   verb   object

Remember that **gerund clauses cannot contain modals**, so modals need to be replaced by **adverbs**.

> *Example*
>
> People *might fear* this new technology. → People *possibly fearing* this new technology.

Exercises

6.1 Add gerund clauses into the spaces provided based on the information given.

1) Since the beginning of the Swine Flu pandemic, *scientists have been searching for a vaccine*.

   _____ is a good thing because they may succeed a lot quicker than anyone had hoped since it turns out that people have an unexpected degree of immunity to the pandemic.

2) The Swine Flu virus has actually been circulating since 1977, but until now *scientists believed this virus had not created any immunity*.

   _____ had resulted from the current virus spreading faster than would be expected if there were widespread immunity to it.

3) A recent article printed in a popular science magazine stated that *contact lenses may soon be able to contain tiny microchips and tiny screens* that we will be able to read while we are wearing the contact lens.

   _____ would lead to a wide range of new technological possibilities, including instant sub-titles for foreign language speakers in front of our eyes.

6.2 Add noun clauses into the spaces provided based on the information given.

1) According to a recent news article, *the last ice age or glacial period probably began in just a few months, rather than taking decades to start* as had been previously thought.

   _____ is proof that we should not be complacent about how soon another ice age may start.

2) The defendants left the country so that *they could avoid repaying debts*.

   _____ is a common reason for migrants to leave the country.

3) *Submitted sites cannot currently be edited or deleted*.

   _____ is a problem with the programming and not a fault of the website owners.

6.3 Improve the cohesion of the following passage using gerund clauses and noun clauses.

It can be difficult to hear what is being said at noisy parties. But people who are good at music seem to be better at hearing what is being said at noisy parties. Playing an instrument appears to improve how well we can pick up emotional signals when we are talking. Also, musicians use their brains in a way that helps them distinguish between speech and background noise. Scientists did a test. Scientists asked musicians and non-musicians to listen to people talking in quiet and noisy environments while their brain activity was being monitored. If there was background noise, the brain was slower to respond, but it was found that musicians were less slow to respond than non-musicians. It is undoubtedly partly genetic, but the scientists have suggested that musical training will help even the very non-musical. Thus, it could really assist both children with autism and with language difficulties, who often find this quite difficult.

(Adapted from http://www.newscientist.com/article/dn18147-noisy-parties-no-problem-for-musical-brains.html)

Topic sentences

Another key part of cohesion is the topic sentence. The topic sentence is important because it tells the reader what the paragraph is about. Generally the topic sentence is the first or second sentence in the paragraph, but it doesn't have to be. The topic sentence is also important because it creates cohesion in the paragraph. Consider the following paragraph.

> *Prentile and Jebb state that fast food contains many more calories than other meals of the same size, which means that people have more calories even though they eat the same amount of food. In addition, Dr. John Hoebel has done a study on rats, demonstrating that after they stop having fast food, rats have similar symptoms to withdrawal from nicotine or morphine.*

What is the topic of this paragraph? It seems to talk about calories and about withdrawal symptoms. What is the connection? The topic is clearly about fast food, but the number of calories and the withdrawal symptoms don't seem to have any relationship.

A topic sentence gives the paragraph cohesion:

> ***Fast food is unhealthy because of the number of calories and because of its addictive nature.*** *Prentile and Jebb state that fast food contains many more calories than other meals of the same size, which means that people have more calories even though they eat the same amount of food. In addition, Dr. John Hoebel has done a study on rats, demonstrating that after they stop having fast food, rats have similar symptoms to withdrawal from nicotine or morphine.*

Now the relationship between the two ideas is much clearer. Also, the topic of withdrawal symptoms is now old information that can be gathered from the topic sentence.

It is important to remember that the supporting evidence must relate to the topic sentence. Topics unrelated to the topic sentence cannot be introduced. Thus, the following paragraph lacks cohesion:

> ***Fast food is unhealthy because of the number of calories.*** *Prentile and Jebb state that fast food contains many more calories than other meals of the same size, which means that people have more calories even though they eat the same amount of food. In addition, Dr. John Hoebel has done a study on rats, demonstrating that after they stop having fast food, rats have similar symptoms to withdrawal from nicotine or morphine.* X

Despite the addition of a topic sentence, the information about withdrawal symptoms is still not related to the topic sentence.

Exercises

7.1 Add logical topic sentences to these paragraphs.

1) _____

_____

Dogs were first domesticated by humans around 15000 years ago. They were domesticated from wolves who either were friendly to humans, were attracted to the warmth of human fires, or were found as babies by humans. It did not take humans long to realise that these animals were both useful hunters and good companions. Cats, on the other hand, were probably domesticated almost 10,000 years ago. Again, cats were probably attracted to the warmth of human fires or were found as babies. Their usefulness to humans largely centred around their ability to catch mice and rats and other undesirable rodents.

2) _____

_____

In classical music, the emphasis is on the composer of the music, not on the players. In fact, classical music groups frequently change members with few people raising an eyebrow. Popular music places emphasis on the players. Bands frequently become headline news with few people even noting the fact that they are playing an interpretation of another person's work. Perhaps as a result of this, the changing of members of a pop group frequently becomes headline news or leads to the demise of the music group.

3) _____

_____

Theravada, which is the oldest type of Buddhism, is popular in Sri Lanka and Southeast Asia; it is stricter form of the Buddhism, in which adherents attempt to live as pure and honest a life as possible. Mahayana, which is known as the 'lesser path' is popular in East Asia; adherents believe that the path to Nirvana is long and unachievable in one lifetime. Buddhism is not really a religion, but rather, a way of life. One semi-religious aspect of Buddhism is its belief in reincarnation; however, mostly it is a philosophy about life.

Appendix

Appendix 1: Finite tense and aspect

	Active		Passive	
Simple	**Regular**	**Irregular**	**Regular**	**Irregular**
Past	*V~ed / Irregular Past*		*Was/were Past Participle*	
	I stated this.	I told him.	This was stated.	He was told.
Present	*V~s / V~*		*Am/Is/are Past Participle*	
	I state this.	I tell him.	This is stated.	He is told.
Future	*Modal V*		*Modal be Past participle*	
	I will state this.	I will tell him.	This will be stated.	He will be told.
Perfect				
Past	*Had Past Participle*		*Had been Past Participle*	
	I had stated this.	I had told him.	This had been stated.	He had been told.
Present	*Has/have Past Participle*		*Has/have been Past Participle*	
	I have stated this.	I have told him.	This has been stated.	He has been told.
Future	*Modal have Past Participle*		*Modal have been Past Participle*	
	I will have stated this.	I will have told him.	This will have been stated	He will have been told.
Continuous				
Past	*Was/were Active Participle*		*Was/were being Passive Participle*	
	I was stating this	I was telling him.	This was being stated.	He was being told.
Present	*Am/is/are Active Participle*		*Am/is/are being Passive Participle*	
	I am stating this.	I am telling him.	This is being stated.	He is being told.
Future	*Modal be Active Participle*		*Modal be being Passive Participle*	
	I will be stating this.	I will be telling him.	This will be being stated.	He will be being told.
Perfect Continuous				
Past	*Had been Active Participle*		*Had been being Passive participle*	
	I had been stating this.	I had been telling him.	This had been being stated.	He had been being told.
Present	*Have/has been Active Participle*		*Have/has been being Passive Participle*	
	I have been stating this.	I have been telling him.	This has been being stated.	He has been being told.
Future	*Modal have been Active Participle*		*Modal have been being Passive Participle*	
	I will have been stating this.	I will have been telling him.	This will have been being stated.	He will have been being told.

Appendix

Appendix 2: Infinitive and gerund tense and aspect

Infinitive tense and aspect

	Active		Passive	
Simple	**Regular**	**Irregular**	**Regular**	**Irregular**
	V~ed / Irregular Past		*Was/were Past Participle*	
Past	me to have stated this.	me to have told him.	this to have been stated.	him to have been told.
	V~s / V~		*Am/Is/are Past Participle*	
Present	me to state this.	me to tell him.	this to be stated.	him to be told.
	Modal V		*Modal be Past participle*	
Future	me to be going to state this.	me to be going to tell him.	this to be going to be stated.	him to be going to be told.
Perfect				
	Had Past Participle		*Had been Past Participle*	
Past	me to have stated this.	me to have stated this.	this to have been stated.	him to have been told.
	Has/have Past Participle		*Has/have been Past Participle*	
Present	me to have stated this.	me to have stated this.	this to have been stated.	him to have been told.
	Modal have Past Participle		*Modal have been Past Participle*	
Future	me to be going to have stated this.	me to be going to have stated this.	this to be going to have been stated.	him to be going to have been told.
Continuous				
	Was/were Active Participle		*Was/were being Passive Participle*	
Past	me to have been telling him.	me to have been telling him.	me to have been telling him.	This to have been being stated.
	Am/is/are Active Participle		*Am/is/are being Passive Participle*	
Present	me to be telling him.	me to have been telling him.	me to be telling him.	This to be being stated.
	Modal be Active Participle		*Modal be being Passive Participle*	
Future	me to be going to be telling him.	me to be going to be telling him.	me to be going to be telling him.	This to be going to be being stated.
Perfect Continuous				
	Had been Active Participle		*Had been being Passive participle*	
Past	me to have been telling him.	me to have been telling him.	me to have been telling him.	This to have been being stated.
	Have/has been Active Participle		*Have/has been being Passive Participle*	
Present	me to have been telling him.	me to have been telling him.	me to have been telling him.	This to have been being stated.
	Modal have been Active Participle		*Modal have been being Passive Participle*	
Future	me to be going to have been telling him.	me to be going to have been telling him.	me to be going to have been telling him.	This to be going to have been being stated.

(for bare infinitive tenses, delete *to* from all of the above boxes.)

Gerund tense and aspect

	Active		Passive	
Simple	**Regular**	**Irregular**	**Regular**	**Irregular**
Past	*V~ed / Irregular Past*		*Was/were Past Participle*	
	me having stated this.	me having told him.	this having been stated.	him having been told.
Present	*V~s / V~*		*Am/Is/are Past Participle*	
	me stating this.	me telling him.	this being stated.	him being told.
Future	*Modal V*		*Modal be Past participle*	
	me being going to state this.	me being going to tell him.	this being going to be stated.	him being going to be told.
Perfect				
Past	*Had Past Participle*		*Had been Past Participle*	
	me having stated this.	me having stated this.	this having been stated.	him having been told.
Present	*Has/have Past Participle*		*Has/have been Past Participle*	
	me having stated this.	me having stated this.	this having been stated.	him having been told.
Future	*Modal have Past Participle*		*Modal have been Past Participle*	
	me being going to have stated this.	me being going to have stated this.	this being going to have been stated.	him being going to have been told.
Continuous				
Past	*Was/were Active Participle*		*Was/were being Passive Participle*	
	me having been telling him.	me having been telling him.	me having been telling him.	This having been being stated.
Present	*Am/is/are Active Participle*		*Am/is/are being Passive Participle*	
	me telling him.	me having been telling him.	me telling him.	This being stated.
Future	*Modal be Active Participle*		*Modal be being Passive Participle*	
	me being going to be telling him.	me being going to be telling him.	me being going to be telling him.	This being going to be being stated.
Perfect Continuous				
Past	*Had been Active Participle*		*Had been being Passive participle*	
	me having been telling him.	me having been telling him.	me having been telling him.	This having been being stated.
Present	*Have/has been Active Participle*		*Have/has been being Passive Participle*	
	me having been telling him.	me having been telling him.	me having been telling him.	This having been being stated.
Future	*Modal have been Active Participle*		*Modal have been being Passive Participle*	
	me being going to have been telling him.	me being going to have been telling him.	me being going to have been telling him.	This being going to have been being stated.

Appendix

Appendix 3: Types of verbs

Bare infinitive	Infinitive	Gerund	Infinitive or gerund
feel[3]	afford[2]	acknowledge	attempt[1]
hear[3]	agree[2]	advocate	begin[1]
help	allow[3]	anticipate	continue[1]
let[3]	appear[1]	appreciate	forget[1&4]
make[3]	arrange[2]	avoid	go on[1]
see[3]	ask	comprehend	hate[2]
watch[3]	attempt[1]	conceive	intend[2]
	cause[3]	consider[1]	love[2]
	challenge[3]	contemplate	mean[2&4]
	choose	debate	plan[2&4]
	claim[1]	define[1]	prefer[2]
	convince[3]	delay	propose[2]
	dare[3]	deny	regret[1]
	decide[2]	describe	remember[1&4]
	demand[3]	detest	start[1&4]
	deserve[1]	discover	stop[1&4]
	drive[3]	discuss	suggest[2]
	expect	dislike	try[1]
	fail[1]	document	
	force[3]	emphasise[1]	
	grow[1]	endure	
	guarantee[2]	enjoy	
	happen[1]	escape[1]	
	hasten[1]	evaluate[1]	
	help	excuse[3]	
	hope[2]	explain	
	hurry[1]	feel like[1]	
	learn[1]	finish[1]	
	like	give up[1]	
	long[2]	hypothesise	
	manage[1]	ignore	
	neglect[2]	illustrate	
	offer[1]	imagine	
	pay[2]	imply[1]	
	plan[2]	indicate	
	pledge[2]	insist on	
	pretend[1]	interpret	
	promise[1]	investigate	
	refuse[1]	involve	
	resolve[2]	justify	
	say[2]	keep on[1]	
	seek[2]	leave off[1]	
	seem[1]	mention	
	send[2]	mind	
	struggle[2]	miss	
	swear[1]	predict	
	teach[3]	propose	
	tell[3]	postpone	
	tend[1]	practice[1]	
	think[1]	put off[1]	
	threaten[2]	question	
	vow[2]	reject	
	want[2]	resent	
	wish[2]	reveal	
		risk[1]	
		spend time[1]	
		suggest	

Notes on non-finite clauses

1. No subject
2. subject optional using subordinator for
3. Must have subject (no subordinator)
4. Different meaning with gerund and infinitive

Note that for some words (e.g. *happen*) the word has a different meaning from its common meaning when used with an infinitive.

Words with no note can choose to either have a subject or not

Appendix 4: Reporting verbs, indirect objects, and types of complements

	That	Wh-word	If/whether	Infinitive	No indirect object	Indirect object optional using *to*	Indirect object optional using *with*	Indirect object needed	Indirect object optional
accept	✓	✓			☆				
acknowledge	✓	✓	N			☆			
admit	P	N	N			☆			
advocate	S					☆			
affirm	—	—	—	—					
allow	S			✓				☆	
answer	M								☆
anticipate	M	✓			☆				
appreciate	✓	✓			☆				
argue	✓	P	P				☆		
ascertain	✓	✓	N		☆				
ask	S	✓	✓	✓					☆
assume	✓				☆				
assure	✓							☆	
attribute	—	—	—	—					
believe	✓								☆
challenge	✓	✓	✓	✓	☆				
cite	—	—	—	—					
claim	✓				☆				
clarify	✓	✓	N				☆		
comment	✓	P	NP			☆			
comprehend	✓	N	N		☆				
concede	✓					☆			
conceive	✓	N			☆				
confess	✓	P				☆			
confirm	✓	✓	N		☆				
consider	✓	✓	✓		☆				
contemplate		✓	✓		☆				
contend	✓					☆			
contest	—	—	—	—					
contradict		✓			☆				
convince	✓	P		✓				☆	
debate		✓	✓				☆		
decide	✓	✓	✓	✓	☆				
declare	✓					☆			
deduce	✓	✓			☆				
define		✓			☆				
demonstrate	✓	✓				☆			
deny	✓	✓				☆			
describe		✓				☆			
detect	✓	✓	✓		☆				
determine	✓	✓	✓		☆				
disagree		P	P				☆		
disclose	✓	✓	N			☆			
discover	✓	✓			☆				
discuss		✓	✓				☆		
dispute		✓	✓		☆				
divulge	✓	✓	N			☆			
document	✓	✓	N		☆				
emphasise	✓	✓				☆			
ensure	✓				☆				
establish	✓	✓	N		☆				
estimate	✓	✓			☆				
evaluate		✓			☆				

Appendix

	That	Wh-word	If/whether	Infinitive	No indirect object	Indirect object optional using *to*	Indirect object optional using *with*	Indirect object needed	Indirect object optional
examine		✓	✓		★				
explain	✓	✓	✓			★			
feel	✓				★				
forget	✓	✓	✓	✓	★				
foresee	✓	✓			★				
grant	✓				★				
guarantee	✓	✓							★
guess	✓	✓			★				
highlight		✓				★			
hypothesise	✓	✓			★				
identify	✓	✓	✓		★				
ignore	✓	✓			★				
illustrate	✓	✓				★			
imagine	✓	N	N		★				
imply	✓	M				★			
indicate	✓	M	N			★			
infer	✓	M				★			
inquire		✓	✓		★				
insist	✓	P			★				
interpret		✓			★				
investigate		✓	✓		★				
justify		✓				★			
know	✓	✓	N	✓	★				
learn	✓	M		✓	★				
maintain	✓				★				
mention	✓	N	N			★			
object	✓				★				
perceive	✓	N	N		★				
persuade	✓			✓				★	
plead	S					★			
point out	✓	✓	N			★			
posit	✓				★				
predict	✓	✓	N	✓	★				
presume	✓			✓	★				
proclaim	✓				★				
profess	✓	P		✓		★			
propose	✓					★			
prove	✓	✓	N			★			
query		✓	✓		★				
question		✓	✓		★				
quote		✓			★				
realise	✓	M			★				
reason	✓					★			
rebut	✓				★				
recognise	✓	M	N		★				
refute	—	—	—	—					
reject		✓		✓	★				
remember	✓	✓	N	✓	★				
respond	✓	P				★			
retort	✓					★			
reveal	✓	✓	N			★			
revise		✓			★				
say	✓	N	N	✓		★			
see	✓	✓	N		★				
signify	✓	✓		✓		★			

	That	Wh-word	If/whether	Infinitive	No indirect object	Indirect object optional using *to*	Indirect object optional using *with*	Indirect object needed	Indirect object optional
speak		P	P			★			
specify	✓	N	N	✓		★			
state	✓	✓	N	✓		★			
submit	✓			✓		★			
suggest	✓			✓		★			
suppose	✓				★				
survey		✓	✓		★				
take the view	✓				★				
talk		P	P		★				
teach	✓	✓	N						★
tell	✓	✓	N	✓				★	
think	✓	P	P		★				
understand	✓	✓			★				
wonder		✓	✓			★			

M = requires a modal in the noun clause

S = only used in the subjunctive

N = usually used with a negative reporting verb

P = requires a preposition between reporting verb and noun clause

NP = requires a preposition and is usually only used with a negative reporting verb

— = this verb looks like a reporting verb, but is not used to report information

Appendix

Appendix 5: Coordinators, Conjunctive adverbs, and Subordinators

Coordinators

for[1]	and	nor	but	or	yet	so

Conjunctive adverbs

above all	equally	in fact	otherwise
accordingly	finally	in other words	rather
alternatively	for example	instead	similarly
after all	for Instance	likewise	still
afterwards	further	meanwhile	that is to say
also	furthermore	moreover	then
anyway	hence	namely	thereafter
as a consequence	however[5]	nevertheless	therefore
as a result	in addition	next	thus
at any rate	in any case	nonetheless	undoubtedly
besides	incidentally	now	
certainly	in contrast	on the one hand	
consequently	indeed	on the other hand	

Subordinators

Noun Clause	Relative Clause	Adverbial Clause	
how[4]	preposition + which	after[2]	just as
if	preposition + whom	after which	like
that[3]	that[3]	although	no sooner… than…
what[4]	that…. preposition	anywhere	now that
when[4]	what[4]	as[2]	once
where[4]	when[4]	as + adverb + as	since[2]
whether	where[4]	as if	so that
which[4]	whereas	as long as	so + adjective + that
while	whereby	as soon as	so + adverb + that
whilst	which[4]	as though	so much/many/little/few… that
who[4]	which…. preposition	at which point	than
whom[4]	while	because	the moment
whose[4]	whilst	before[2]	though
why[4]	who[4]	by which time	unless
	whom[4]	even if	until
	whom… preposition	even though	upon which
	whose[4]	ever since	what[4]
	why[4]	every time	whatever
		everywhere	when[4]
		except if	whenever
		except that	where[4]
		how[4]	wherever
		however[5]	whereupon
		if	while
		in case	whilst
		in order for	
		in order that	

Note

1) *For* can also be a preposition. It has a different meaning as a preposition. As a coordinator, it means *because*.

2) *After, as, before,* and *since* are also prepositions. *After, before,* and *since* have the same meaning as prepositions. *As* has a variety of different meanings in different contexts. Even as a subordinator, *as* has several meanings.

3) *That* is also a pronoun.

4) *How, what, which, where, when,* and *why* are also question words that can begin independent clauses that are in question form.

5) *However* can be both a conjunctive adverb and a subordinator, but it is most commonly used as a conjunctive adverb. Note that the meaning of the conjunctive adverb *however* and the subordinator *however* are quite different.

Note

The following are prepositions, not subordinators. This means that they are followed by nouns or gerund clauses.

According to	*Because of*	*By*
Considering	*Despite*	*Due to*
During	*In spite of*	

Note

What and *how* can be used as subordinators to make a special kind of reduced relative clause. *What* means *the thing that* and *how* means *the way that*.

Appendix

Appendix 6: Intransitive Verbs

abide	droop	laugh	rush in	take steps
ache	drop back	let up	rush out	taper off
account for	drop by	lie down	scream	tend
advance	drop out	limp	seize up	throb
appear	ease up	lisp	sell up	tingle
arise	ebb away	listen	set in	touch down
arrive	economize	live	settle down	trek
back down	emerge	look ahead	settle in	tremble
back off	end up	look back	settle up	twitch
back-peddle	ensue	look out	shiver	touch-type
barge in	erupt	loom up	shop	vanish
belong	evaporate	make off	shrivel up	vary
benefit	eventuate	meet up	sigh	vibrate
bleed	evolve	melt away	simmer down	wail
blush	excel	moan	sink	wait
boil over	exist	mount up	sit	walk
bounce back	expire	move off	skate	waste away
branch out	fade	move over	skid	watch out
break out	faint	nod off	sleep	water-ski
camp out	fall	oblige	slip	waver
catch on	falter	occur	smart	wear off
cease	fast	opt out	smile	weep
chatter	fidget	own up	smirk	weigh in
chip in	fight out	pass away	snarl	whimper
cloud over	flare up	pass on	sneeze	whine
club together	flinch	pay up	sniffle	wilt
collapse	flourish	pelt down	snigger	wise up
collide	fluctuate	perish	snore	work
come	fool around	persist	snort	yawn
communicate	forge ahead	play-act	snow	
concentrate	function	play around	sob	
conform	get about	plummet	sober up	
conk out	get ahead	plunge	sparkle	
converge	get along	pop up	speak	
cool off	get by	press on	speed	
correspond	get up	prosper	spring up	
cough	give in	pull through	squat	
crackle	glaze over	push ahead	squeak	
crawl	gleam	quiver	squeal	
creep	go	rain	squirm	
crop up	goose-step	range	stand back	
cry	grin	read up on	stand down	
cuddle up	grow up	rear up	stand for	
cut in	growl	rebel	stand in	
dart	hail	recede	stand out	
dash	hang back	recover	start out	
dawdle	hang together	rebel	stay	
decay	happen	relax	stem from	
depart	hesitate	relent	step	
depend	hitch-hike	relocate	stick around	
deteriorate	howl	remain	stink	
die	ice-skate	remain	stop off	
digress	immigrate	result	stop over	
diminish	interact	ring out	subside	
dine	interfere	rise	succeed	
disappear	intervene	roar	suffer	
disintegrate	itch	roll about	sulk	
dissent	kneel	roller-skate	surrender	
double back	kow-tow	roll in	swim	
doze	land up	rot	tag along	
drag on	laugh	route	take off	
drizzle	last	run	take roots	

204

Absolute clause **175-176**

Abstract nouns → nouns

Active voice 20, 34, 52-53, 72-4, 98, 169, 172, 177, 179-180

Adjective 9-10, 18-21, 28-32, 35, 38, 40, 42-43, 57, 64-66, 70, 72, 100, 114-115, 127, 129, 134, 138-140, 142, 147, 167-170

Adjective clause → relative clause

Adverb **29**, 57, 100, 103, 105, 111, 113, 114, 115, 129, 133-135, 148-154, 170, 186-187

Adverbial clause 7, 10-11, 14-15, 30-32, 37-38, 40, 45, 80, 86-89, 91, **102-130**, 133-134, 139-141, 147-148, 168-170, 173-174, **183-185**

Adverbial clauses of comparison **129-130**, 138

Adverbial clauses of concession 102, **118-121**, 138-139, 183-185

Adverbial clauses of condition 86, 87-89, 91, 102, 107, 113, 119, **121-128**, 141, 183-184, 186

Adverbial clauses of contrast 102, 118, **120-121**, 138-139, 183-184

Adverbial clauses of distance 102, **113-114**, 141, 183

Adverbial clauses of frequency 102, **113-114**, 140, 183

Adverbial clauses of manner 39, 49, 102, 103, **105**, 121, 140-141, 173-175, 183

Adverbial clauses of time 86, 102, **104-108**, 123, 140, 173-174, 183-185

Adverbial clauses of place 102, **109-110**, 183

Adverbial clauses of reason 102, 103, 112, **117-118**, 131-135, 173-174

Adverbial clauses of time 86, 102, **104-108**, 123, 140, 173-174, 183-185

Back-shifting future adverbial clauses **85-86**

Tense of conditional clauses 87-89

Appositive phrase 167, **176**

Argument language *see* refutation language

As 104, 111, 112, 113, 123, 131 **140-145**, 185

As and reported speech **47**

Aspect → tense

Bare infinitive → infinitive

Back-shifting → tense, noun clauses, *and* adverbial clauses

Cause and effect language **131-137**

Circumstances 37, 56

Clause **6-17**, 18, 19, 24, 28, 30, 31, 32, 34, 35-36, 37, 38, 42-43, 45-47, 51-52, 54-58, 59-70, 86-89, 93-93, 102-129, 132-134, 138-144, 147-166, 167-176, 179, 182-185, 189-192

Cohesion **177-193**

Adverbial clauses and cohesion **183-186**

Gerund clauses, noun clauses, and cohesion **191-192**

Theme **177-179**

Passive voice and cohesion 179, **181-183**

Pronouns **189-191**

Topic sentence and cohesion **192-193**

Transition words and cohesion **186-188**

Comma **6-8**, 37, 46, 63, 70, 102, 112, 117, 120, 139, 150, 175, 184, 187

Common errors **25**

Compare and contrast language 129, **138-139**

Complement 6, 19, 24-29, 30-37, 38, 46, 134-135, 167, 177

Coordinator **7-8**, 41, 116, 131, 133-134, 138, 186-187

Conditionals → Adverbial clauses of condition

Conjunction → conjunctive adverb, coordinator, *or* subordinator

Conjunctive adverb 8-9, 133-135, 138, 186-187

Content clause → Noun clause

Dependent clause 7-14, 18-19, 36, 40-42, 45, 47, 61, 63, 68, 86-89, 102-108, 111, 113, 116, 119-120, 123-124, 126, 133, 134, 139-142, 147-148, 150, 152-155, 157, 158, 160-163, 165, 167, 169, 170, 173-175, 183-185

Dummy subject → subject

Embedded clause 10, 102, → *also* Noun clause

Finite 6-7, 9-11, 13-14, 18-20, 22-24, 28, 35-36, 38, 40, 45, 91-95, 97, 99-101, 103, 123, 127, 134, 147, 167-170, 172-73, 175, 191, 194

Finite Clause 6, 9, 11, 13, 19, 24, 28, 35, 38, 45, 91-92, 95, 103, 134, 167-168, 170, 175

Finite verb → verb

Fragment 8, 63, 132

Gerund 6, 9, 10, 13-17, 18-27, 28-30, 32-34, 35-40, 43, 66, 72, 92-93, 103, 127, 134, 138, 167-168, 191-192, 195-197

Gerund clause 13-19, 24, 28-30, 34-38, 66, 93, 103, 134, 138, 167, 191-194

Gerund tense 93-94

Future simple → tense (simple aspect)

Future continuous → tense (continuous aspect)

Future progressive → tense (continuous aspect)

Future perfect → tense (perfect aspect)

Future perfect continuous → tense (perfect continuous aspect)

Future perfect progressive → tense (perfect continuous aspect)

Hedging 94-95, 97, 99-101

Imperative 6, 18, 70, 87

Independent clause **7-10**, 14, 18-19, 36, 40-42, 45, 47, 61, 63, 68, 86-89, 102-126, 133-134, 139-142, 147-165, 170-175, 183-185

Indirect object 29, 32, 35, 41, 47, 52, 68, 165, 180

Infinitive 6, 9, 10, 14-15, 18-19, 23-25, **28-35**, **38-44**, 52-53, 60-61, 62-66, 69-71, 72, 92-94, 97-98, 116, 127, 134, 140, 162, 167,

Bare infinitive 6, 10, 18-19, 23-24, 30-32, 38-39, 43, 70-72, 96, 97, 98, 162, 167

Infinitives after semi-modals 43

Infinitive clause 14-15, 19, 28-35, **38-44**, 52-53, 60-61, 62-66, 69-71, 116, 134, 162

Infinitives instead of relatives 43, 162-163

Infinitives instead of reported speech 41-42, **52-54**

Infinitives showing more detail about abstract nouns and adjectives 42, 63-64

Infinitives showing purpose 40

Infinitives showing result 40

Infinitives showing that something needs to be done 41

Infinitives with linking verbs 42

Infinitive tense 53, **92**

Linking verbs *see* verbs

Modals 10, 18, 23, 38, 43, 55-56, 59-62, 69, 71-75, 78, 88-89, 92-93, **94-101**, 111, 119, 123-124, 143-144, 162, 170, 180, 192, 194-196

Modals of ability 96

Modals of certainty/probability/hedging 97, 100-101

Modals and hedging → Hedging

Modals of obligation/advice 96

Modals of permission 95

Modals of politeness 95

Modal verbs → modals

Negatives 22, 61, 70, 94, 96, 110, 170

Non-finite verb **9-10**, 13-17, 18, 24, 28, 35, 92-94, 95

Non-finite tense 24, 92-94

Non-finite clause **13-17**, 19, 24, 28-30, 34-38, 35, 66, 91, 92-94, 95, 103, 134, 138, 167, 167-176, 191-194

Nouns 38, 43, 64, 67

Nouns formed from reporting verbs 64

Index

Nouns formed from adjectives 65
Abstract nouns 38, 43
Noun clause 7, 9-17, 19-35, 37, 38, 39, 40-42, **47-71**, 85,
102, 122, 133, 143, 147-148, 163, 191-192
Adjunct noun clauses 45, **63-64**, 68
Back-shifting reported speech **84-85**
If/whether noun clauses 31-32, 45-46, 57, **59-61**, 122
Indirect object **47-48**, 52, 68
Infinitive noun clauses **62**
Negatives 61, 70
Noun clauses as complements to nouns **63-64**
Noun clauses as complements to adjectives **65-66**
Omission of subordinator *that* **67-68**
Prepositions **66-67**, 68
Reporting how something should be done 63
Reporting orders and instructions **70-71**
Reporting uncertainty **62** *That* noun clauses 29-32,
46, 64-66, 69
Reporting verbs 28-32, 34-35, 28-39, 41-42, 45, **46**,
47, 49, 51-52, 54, 59-63, 68, 71, 101
Subjunctive noun clauses 70-71
Wh-word noun clauses 28, 31-32, 37, 46, **54-59**, 67
Parallel structure 12-13, 58-59, 68, 144-145
Participle 9, 10, 14, 18, **20-22**, 53, 70, 72-74, 92, 98, 127,
138, 167-170, 172-173, 175, 180, 194-196
Participle clause 14, **157-176**
Adverbial participle clauses **173-175**
Continuous aspect in participle clauses **172**
Perfect aspect in participle clauses **172**
Progressive aspect in participle clauses → continuous
aspect in relative clauses
Omission of subordinator in participle clauses **174**
Relative participle clauses **169-173**
Passive voice 15, 20, 22, 29, 32-35, 41, 52-53, 56, 59,
72-74, 92, 98, 101, 111, 127, 164-165, 168-169, 172,
179-183
Passive voice and reported speech **52-53**
Past continuous → tense (continuous aspect)
Past perfect → tense (perfect aspect)
Past perfect continuous → tense (perfect continuous aspect)
Past perfect progressive → tense (perfect continuous aspect)
Past progressive → tense (continuous aspect)
Past simple → tense (simple aspect)
Prepositions 6, **13-15**, 17-19, 25, 28-30, 32-34, 37, 43,
46-47, 52, 65-67, 68, 103, 105-106, 111, 113, 129,
131, 133-135, 138-142, 148-149, 154-159, 162, 165,
180-181, 185
Prepositional phrase 6, **14-15**, 17, 29, 28-34, 37, 43,
52, 65, 106, 129, 134-135, 149, 154, 180-181, 185
Present continuous → tense (continuous aspect)
Present perfect → tense (perfect aspect)
Present perfect continuous → tense (perfect continuous aspect)
Present perfect progressive → tense (perfect continuous aspect)
Present progressive → tense (continuous aspect)
Present simple → tense (simple aspect)
Pronouns 18, 28, 36, 111, 142, 150, 152-153, 172, 177,
189-191
Pro-verbs **111**
Punctuation → semicolon *or* comma
Questions 7, 22, **54-60**, 69, 72, 75, 80, 95, 122, 126
Circumstance questions 56
Classification/intensity/quantity questions 57
Object question 55
Polite language questions 57
Question word order 7, 22, **54-60**, 126
Subject question 55
Wh-word questions 54-55
Yes/no questions 22, 59-60, 122
Reduced Adverbial clause → Participle clause
Reduced relative clause → Participle clause
Refutation language 143-146

Relative clause 7, 10-11, 13-15, 20, 28, 37-38, 42-43,
45, 52, 54, 63, 69, 109, 126, 129, 133-134, **147-166**,
169-176
Defining vs. non-defining **150-151**, 152-153, 155, 170
Describing people 152
Describing quality and quantity **159-161**
Describing the whole clause 161-162
Describing things 152
Infinitival relatives **162-163**
Object of a preposition **155-156**
Omission of subordinator **152**
Position in clause **149-150**
Reduced relative clauses → participle clauses
Relative subordinators **147**
Relatives using subject or object of a noun clause
163-164
Restrictive vs. non-restrictive 14, 45, 63, 147-149,
150-151, 152-153, 155, 157, 159, 161, 170, 176
That/which 147-148, 150-151, **152**
Transitivity and relatives **164-166**
When/where **156-159**
Who/whom **152-153**
Whose **153-154**
Reported speech → noun clauses
Reporting verbs → verbs
Rheme → cohesion
Semi-colon **8**, 43, 75, 78, 92, 95, 97, **187**, 193
Sentence 6, 7, 8, 18, 22, 35, 45, 96, 100, 110, 122, 124,
127, 133, 134, 142, 145, 151, 177, 192-193
Signpost word → Transition word
Small Clause 30
Subject 6-7, 9-11, 13-14, 18-20, 22-23, 28-36, 39-45, 47,
52-57, 59, 63, 65, 68-70, 72-74, 79, 81, 88, 94-95,
97, 101, 111, 116, 120, 126, 132-134, 140-141, 147-
149, 152-159, 161-165, 167, 169-170, 173, 175-181,
184, 186, 189-191
Dummy subject 29-30, 32, 42, 52-54, 65, 70, 101,
190
Subjunctive 70-71, 88, 123-124
Subordinator 7-9, 11, 13, 28, 40-43, 45-47, 55, 63, 66,
68, 70, 87, 103-123, 129-130, 133-134, 138-142,
144, 147-149, 152, 155-157, 159, 161-163, 165, 169-
170, 172-174, 176, 184
Tense 22-23, **72-94**
Aspect 22, **72**, 94
Back-shifting future tense in adverbial clauses **85-86**
Back-shifting reported speech **84-85**
Construction of the different tenses 22, **72-74**
Continuous aspect 73
Events 75-76
Events with duration & events with no duration 76
Future continuous 73, **77-79**
Future perfect 73, **79-80**, 81
Future perfect continuous 74, **80-81**
Future perfect progressive → Future perfect continuous
Future progressive → future continuous
Future simple 72, **77-79**
Future tense 72-73, 77-84, 85, **89-90**
Past continuous 73, **77-79**
Past perfect 73, **79-80**, 81, 84-85, 91
Past perfect continuous 74, **80-81**
Past perfect progressive → Past perfect continuous
Past progressive *see* past continuous
Past simple 72, **77-79**, 84-85
Perfect aspect 73
Perfect continuous aspect 74
Present continuous 73, **77-79**, 90
Present perfect 73, **80-84**, 91
Present perfect continuous 74, **80-81**
Present perfect progressive → Present perfect continuous
Present progressive → present continuous
Present simple 72, **77-79**, 90

Progressive aspect → continuous aspect
Repeated events 76
Simple aspect 72
States 75, 90
Temporary states 90
Tense and conditionals → adverbial clauses (conditionals)
Using the tense-aspect system 77-84
Waxing and waning 90
Theme → cohesion
To infinitive → infinitive
Topic Sentence 177, 192-193
Transition signal → Transition word
Transition word 8-9, 133-135, 138, 177, **186-187**, 189
Verb 6, 9-10, 18-24, 28-35, 47-48, 51, 54, 59, 61, 62, 68, 70, 75, 76, 101, 131-134, 138, 164, 167-168, 179-180
  Ambitransitive verbs 28-29, 34, 179
  Ditransitive verbs 28-29, 31-32, 34-35, 47, 164-165, 179-180
  Ergative verbs 35, 179-180
  Events 6, 14, 16, 26, 34, 40, 46, 72, 75-87, 89-91, 96, 98, 103-108, 116, 120, 122, 125, 127, 136, 141-142, 147, 150, 160-161, 167, 188
  Finite verbs 6-7, 9-10, 13, 19-20, **22-23**, 28, 35, 36, 38, 40, 45, 92, 134, 147, 167, 169, 172, 173, 191
  Infinitive verbs → infinitive
  Intransitive verbs 21, 29, 47, 164-165, 179

Linking verbs 19, 28-29, 35, 140, 179
Modal verbs → modals
Reporting verbs 19, 28-29, 31-32, 34-35, 38-39, 41-42, 45-47, 49, 51-52, 54-55, 59-63, 68, 71, 101, 133, 144
States 34, 75-78, 80-82, 84, 85-86, 90-91, 96, 104-107, 122, 125,
Strong states 90
Timeless Events 90, 126
Transitive verbs 179
Verbs of motion 33, 37
Verbs complemented by gerunds 24, 29, 34-36, **38-39**
Verbs complemented by infinitives 24, 29-31, 34, **38-39**, 39-44
Verbs complemented by noun clauses 29, **31-33**, 46, 51, 54, 59, 61, 62, 68, 70
Weak states 90
Verbs as complements of verbs **24-25** *also* → gerund *and* infinitive
Voice → passive voice, active voice, *and* writer voice.
Word form **18-27**, 131
Word order 7, 20, 55, 56-57, 59, 69, 126-127, 154
  Question word order 7, 55
  Statement word order 55-59
Writer voice **50**

Answers

Chapter 1
1.1
1) dependent	3) independent	5) dependent	7) independent	9) independent
2) independent	4) dependent	6) independent	8) dependent	10) dependent

4.1
1) adverbial	6) relative	10) noun	15) a) relative b)	19) a) adverbial
2) noun	7) a) noun b)	11) adverbial	noun	b) adverbial
3) relative	noun	12) noun	16) noun	c) noun
4) noun	8) relative	13) noun	17) adverbial	20) a) noun b)
5) adverbial	9) relative	14) relative	18) relative	relative
21)				

5.1
1) Kapetanos claims that Einstein's theories of relativity are wrong **and that** long distance space travel is, therefore, possible.
2) Others argue that long distance space travel is not possible because the nearest galaxy is one million light years away **and that** Einstein's theory of relativity dictates that it would take at least a million years to travel there.
3) Some experts have argued that living in the long term without gravity in a spaceship would be bad for the body, **but that** this problem could be resolved by spinning the space ship as it travels though space to generate a gravitational field.
4) There are two remaining problems with such an expedition. **They are that** we don't have the technology for such an expedition **and that** we don't have the finance.
5) Finally, if we were to send an expedition to another galaxy, **we need to ask whether we should send** humans **or whether we should send** robots?

6.1
1) a) adverbial clause b) infinitive clause
2) a) noun clause
3) a) relative clause
4) a) gerund clause
5) a) noun clause b) gerund clause
6) a) relative clause b) gerund clause c) prepositional phrase (containing a gerund clause)
7) a) infinitive clause b) adverbial clause c) prepositional phrase (containing a gerund clause)
8) a) adverbial clause b) infinitive clause
9) a) prepositional phrase
10) a) participial clause b) prepositional phrase
11) a) infinitive clause
12) a) adverbial clause b) infinitive clause c) gerund clause
13) a) noun clause b) prepositional phrase c) prepositional phrase
14) a) adverbial clause b) infinitive clause
15) a) prepositional phrase (containing a gerund clause)
16) a) relative clause b) infinitive clause
17) a) noun clause b) prepositional phrase
18) a) prepositional phrase b) adverbial clause
19) a) noun clause b) infinitive clause
20) a) participial clause
21) a) prepositional phrase
22) a) noun clause b) prepositional phrase c) noun clause
23) a) noun clause b) adverbial clause c) noun clause

6.2
1) c		
2) d	5) h	8) g
3) f	6) b	9) j
4) i	7) e	

Chapter 2
1.1
1) We have postponed looking into this.
2) Preparing for writing tests is important when students are failing writing classes. (Note: *writing* is a participle (adjective) in both cases.)
3) Carlo rejects investigating the possibility of reworking this.
4) The reading that the students were given yesterday was not interesting to them. (Note: *interesting* is a participle (adjective).)
5) Shipping times are being reduced resulting in customers gradually becoming less dissatisfied. (Note: *shipping* and *resulting* are both participles (adjectives).)

6) <u>Intending</u> to do your homework $\boxed{\text{is}}$ not the same as <u>doing</u> your homework.

2.1

1) The <u>interesting</u> teacher $\boxed{\text{explained}}$ grammar to the <u>disinterested</u> students.
2) Some <u>complicated</u> aspects of <u>writing</u> $\boxed{\text{include}}$ <u>paragraphing</u> and <u>breaking up</u> sentences into clauses.
3) <u>Reading</u> books $\boxed{\text{can be}}$ an <u>exciting</u> way of <u>entertaining</u> yourself.
4) <u>Working</u> on a <u>troubling</u> problem $\boxed{\text{is}}$ what a <u>dedicated</u> student does.
5) A student who $\boxed{\text{studies}}$ all night $\boxed{\text{is being}}$ a <u>hardworking</u> student.
6) The <u>worrying</u> effects of global <u>warming</u> $\boxed{\text{are causing}}$ concern.

2.4 Africa is suffering from many **alarming** problems. First, some African countries are governed by **disgusting** governmental systems which are totally corrupt and which destroy their **complicated** economies. For example, Zimabawe's **troubled** economy is being destroyed because of such a corrupt dictatorial governmental system (Stewart 2004, p2). This **bewildering** government has sent Zimbabwe into a **disturbing** bankruptcy, rendering Zimbabwe's **distressed** people even more poor (Stewart 2004, p3). **Exasperating** poverty has accompanied Africans for a long time. In Sub-Saharan Africa, GDP per capita is $US790 (Collins 2005, p67). The **alarming** percentage of Africans who live in **shocking** poverty increased from 42% to 47% across the last two decades (Stewart 2004, p4). Moreover, Africa has experienced several **confounding** humanitarian crises. For instance, in Sudan 50,000 people have died, more than 1.4 million have been forced from their homes, and up to 10,000 people, most of them **exhausted** children, were dying each month because of **sickening** violence and **devastate** disease (Stewart 2004, p1). Disease strikes Africans daily, causing many to die. It has been estimated that 130,000 Africans die from **debilitating** disease every week (Laberge 2008, p21). AIDS itself kills about 44,000 Africans weekly, and unsafe water kills another 14,000 (Laberge 2008, p21).

3.1 Viking success in the pre-mediaeval period can **be attributed** to four factors. Firstly, the Vikings **established** long distance **trade** routes, the profits from which **were used** to finance the vast armies and navies that were raised by the Scandinavian kings during this period. Secondly, the Vikings **maintained** naval superiority. Thirdly, their **frightening** appearance and methods of attack **encouraged** the peasants of Europe to believe, at least at first, that they **were being attacked** by demons. The peasants believed that they could **not fight** them; as a result, they **did not fight** them. And, lastly, **advanced** battle techniques and **interesting** tactics helped the Vikings **(to) overwhelm** their **selected** enemies. The decline of the Vikings after their rapid ascent to power **was brought about** by **changing** weather patterns, by the conversion of Viking **occupied** areas and Scandinavia itself to Christianity, and by the gradual assimilation of the Vikings into 'Western' culture.

3.2 Throughout history, the country that has **controlled** the seas and oceans has **become** a major super power. The Portuguese built their empire from their position as the leading sea-faring nation in Europe in the Fifteenth Century. The Spanish Empire, too, was **created** from control of the seas; control which **lead** to the discovery of America. The British Empire **became** the largest in the world through naval superiority. The Vikings, too, came to dominate most of Europe and parts of America because they **controlled** the seas. Except for pirates, who **were** outlawed Vikings anyway, the Norsemen had almost complete control of the seas of northern Europe and the Atlantic Ocean. Since none of the northern European countries of England, Ireland, Scotland, France, or Germany **had** been threatened from the north seas before, their naval defences were poor. Thus, the Vikings were able sail out of the oceans at high speeds right up the rivers, before any warning could to be given and could **complete** their raids with lightning speed. The Vikings had an ancient history of sea-faring, dating back to pre-historic times. They had **developed** the art of sea-faring to powerful levels, they were not afraid to take to the sea during storms, and they had good methods of navigation, which included using the altitude of the sun to calculate their latitude. Some Viking raids **were conducted** over land, especially later, when Viking forts and colonies had **been established**, and particularly in Russia. But, apart from Russia, such colonies and forts could not **have** been established without first gaining control of the seas.

4.1 In the 960s Erik the Red, a fiery Norwegian, was sent from his home in Norway **to explore** the oceans. He chose **to go** to Iceland, where he convinced Thjodhildur **to marry** him. He later ended up **being** banished from there for three years. Erik kept on **going** west and spent his time **exploring** a land with inviting fjords and fertile green valleys. He described **being** greatly impressed by the land's resources, and he hastened **to return** to Iceland and convinced some Icelanders **to come** with him to this land, which he called "the green land". In 986 he planned **to take** 25 ships out from Iceland back to Greenland. He convinced 500 men and women **to join** him. Of the 25 ships, the Greenlanders documented only 14 **reaching** their destination. The Vikings evaluated **settling** in several locations, before founding Brattahlid and the two hamlets of Vesterbygden and Østerbygden. Viking records around the year 1000 claim 3,000 people **to have been living** in 300-400 farms on Greenland. This small community managed **to survive** for 500 years. Why they failed **to survive** beyond that time is still a great mystery.

4.2 It was not just control of the seas that **lead** to the Vikings **dominating** northern Europe. The Vikings also **used** their frightening appearance **to help** them. When they first **arrived** on the shores of England, Ireland, and Normandy, the troubled locals **thought** that they **were** demons in league with the devil and **were** too **scared to fight**[1] and **offered** them gifts **to be left alone**[2]. The **appalling** methods of attack which **were used** by the Vikings **helped** them **(to) believe** that these warriors **were** supernatural beings. The Vikings **raped** the women and **cut** the throats of all the children, women, and priests. They **were** even **known to**

Answers

gather[3] entire townships together in their cathedrals and **burn** them. They particularly **hated** monasteries, and **raided** and **burned** every church building they **came across** , making sure they **killed** the monks and nuns. It **is thought** that the attacks on monasteries and cathedrals **were** revenge for the Catholic Church's denunciation of the Viking Gods such as Thor. Nevertheless, the brutality of **killing unarmed** monks and nuns, as well as their other uncivilized tactics **scared** the local folk into **believing**, at least at first, that these men were receiving help from the devil whom no ordinary man could **fight**[4]. Thus, resistance was probably weaker than it might **have been**[5] , which **allowed** the Vikings **to gain** control of large parts of northern Europe and Russia. The Vikings **had** other advantageous tactics. For example, they always **attacked** by surprise, and quickly. Due to their ships **being** speedy, the Vikings could **attack** before any warning could be given. They regularly **attacked** on wet stormy nights when everybody **was** inside, and visibility **was** low. They **had** little regard for the promises that they **made** . For example, they **accepted** gifts and peace treaties, then **rebuilt** their armies and **attacked** again when the enemy let down their guard. These were such highly **developed** battle tactics, that the Germans, one thousand years later, **used** these same tactics in their blitzkrieg attacks during World War II. Scandinavia **was** a battle ground for many centuries and the art of battle **developed** there, more than anywhere else in Europe. It **is** even **thought** that the knights of mediaeval Europe **learned** their art from the Vikings. The rise of the power and wealth of the Vikings thus can **be attributed** , amongst other reasons, to battle skills that were far more **advanced** than those **employed** by other Europeans.

Notes:

(1) For more on infinitives as complements of adjectives, see Chapter 3, page 42

(2) For more on infinitives showing intention or intended result, see Chapter 3, page 40

(3) For more on dummy subjects, passive reported speech, and infinitive clauses, see Chapter 3, pages 41-42 on verb types and Chapter 4, page 52 on noun clauses.

(4) For more on modals, see Chapter 6.

(5) For more on tense and aspect, see Chapter 5.

4.3 The Viking conquests were **funded** not only by plunder from previous expeditions, but also from **trade**. Just as naval superiority has always **been** a key ingredient in establishing global power, so too has trading. The far-reaching Islamic empires of the mediaeval times **were built** on trade, as were the Dutch, British, French, and American Empires. The Vikings had a vast trading pattern; they **traded** with such far away places as Tashkent in central Asia, Baghdad, Jerusalem, Alexandria, Byzantium, Russia, France, Germany, Poland, Britain, Iceland, Greenland, and America. The revenues from this trade must **have** contributed greatly to the **financing** of the voyages of conquest.

Thus, the Vikings were able to **spread** out across the knowing world. They established trading posts at Novograd and Kiev in modern day Russia, and in fact, the modern day Russian state owes, at least in part, its establishment to the Swedish Vikings. As well, the Vikings gained control in all of England, in Normandy, parts of Germany, Ireland, Scotland, Wales, Iceland, and Greenland. Viking settlements have also been **discovered** in Newfoundland in North America, and less certain evidence has **been** found in Massachusetts, Florida, and even Brazil. Attacks were made on Spain and northern Africa, and attempts were made to **capture** Rome and Byzantium. The colonies of Greenland and America were eventually abandoned as the strength of the Vikings **declined**.

The colony in Newfoundland was attacked by Eskimos and since the settlers were too far from Greenland to receive speedy assistance, and due to **being** out-numbered, the colony was abandoned, and the colonists returned to Greenland. The Vikings had **spread** out too far. The Greenland colony fell to **changing** weather patterns. Europe, and indeed all of the north Atlantic suffered from a mini ice age between about 1350 AD and 1800 AD. The colder weather meant that Greenland was no longer inhabitable and the colony there died out. It is probable too, that this colder weather played some part in the decline of the power of the Scandinavian countries themselves. Colder weather implies that less food could **be** produced; hence, there **was** a smaller population, which **meant** less young men to fill the Viking armies. Thus, it can **be** argued that to at least some small extent, the change in weather patterns was responsible for the decline of the Vikings.

Chapter 3

1.1 The fact that hamburgers make **us** fat is true, but they also appear **to be** addictive. If there was **proof** for this, it seems to be fast food companies would prove liable. Are fast food companies purposely making their hamburgers **addictive**? If so, **there** seems to be no reason why we should not treat them in the same way as we treat cigarette companies who knowingly made cigarettes addictive despite the health hazards. We know that fast food companies have teams of scientists making hamburgers **taste** perfect; they add food colouring to the food to make it **look** delicious. Studies have shown that if you eat fast food, you will grow **obese**. They have also shown that food high in fat and sugar actually alters the brain, harnessing natural pleasure systems in the brain to make us want to eat more. Thus, it is becoming obviously that altering fast food to make it smell appetizing, taste delicious, and look mouth-watering, is not so different from what cigarette companies are doing.

2.1

1) ***Bognar believes that*** if we look at the carbon footprint of each human on earth, we can see some interesting statistics.

2) *Borzillo maintains that* interestingly, the size of the carbon footprint generated from car use is considerably smaller than the carbon footprint generated by food production.

3) *It has been revealed that* on average, each person in the western world generates about 4 tonnes of carbon a day t

4) *We are pointed out to be able to do* more to stop global warming by eating more environmentally friendly foods than by stopping driving cars.

5) *Richards explains* which food products generate the largest carbon footprint.

6) *We are told that* the largest carbon footprint is from meat and dairy products, chicken products, and greenhouse grown vegetables.

7) *The reason that dairy and meat products generate such a large carbon footprint is suggested to be* that firstly

8) *It has been noted that* organic foods require more energy and must be produced in larger quantities to feed the same number of people, so they are actually worse for the environment than non-organic foods.
(*Note*: for more similar exercises, see Chapter 4, page 52)

4.1

1) Many people like *going* out and have fun.
2) My wife enjoys *washing* the clothes.
3) The government is contemplating *making* health care reforms.
4) The government *has finished* working on these problems.
5) The incoming government is questioning *the government having* stopped its aid programme for the poor.
6) The government put off *getting* involved in the debate over abortion.
7) *People burning* fossil fuels will cause global temperatures to rise.
8) The president *acting* crazily resulted in the party *losing* the election.
9) *Being* a good president involves *listening* to others.

5.1

1) Commodity prices rose *in* many countries during the last year *due to/because of* increased transportation costs.
2) This led to lower consumer spending *in* those countries *in/during* the current financial year *due to/because of* consumers not being able to afford to buy many products *in* the way that they have in the past.
3) Lower spending led to layoffs *in* March and April *in* the United States *due to/because of* companies not being able to afford to keep their employees.
4) Lower spending has also led to lower profits *since* the beginning of this crisis even *in/at* the largest companies *because of /due to* lower revenue *like* what happened in 1929.
5) Unlike in 1929, the crisis has not led to countries increasing trade tariffs *in* 2008 *throughout* the world *due to/because of* increasing trade tariffs being seen as unhelpful these days.

6.1 The American diet of fatty meats is helping **(to) ruin** the environment and is making people in the third world **starve**. This is because we keep on **eating** mostly meat that comes from cows, and cows are helping **(to) do** three things to the environment. Firstly, cows spend their time **creating** an incredible amount of the global warming gas methane through their excrement. Their excrement also manages **to create** a lot of pollution by being washed into rivers and lakes. Secondly, they happen **to consume** a massive amount of water. In fact, the main reason why the Murray River, Australia's largest waterway, appears **to be dying**, is not the on-going drought, but over-farming of cattle. Thirdly, cattle in Australia and North America are causing deserts **to spread**. The Australian outback cannot endure hard hoofed feet of cattle **walking** all over it, slowly killing the grasses. Without grasses, the good topsoil tends **to blow** away and nothing is left but infertile bottom soil. Thus, when rains come, the grass struggles **to grow** back. Lastly, cattle to continue consume a massive amount of food. It is estimated that for every meal we get from a cow, we have **to feed** that cow eight meals. It is also estimated that in 1900, 95% of the world's crops went to feeding humans. Today. 45% of the world's crops have been demonstrated **to feed** cows. This, in turn, is guaranteeing food prices throughout the world **to rise**. Demand for grain has increased and thus so have prices. This has lead to people who are surviving on two dollars or less a day being now unable to buy enough food.

7.1

1) They plugged in the computer *to test* it.
2) They had several jobs *to do* before they could relax.
3) She drove the car very fast *to see* how it performed at high speeds.
4) We were *too* upset *to speak*.
5) He is crazy *enough to do* it.
6) There is a new law *to protect young people*.

8.1

1) In a democracy, we all have the freedom *to say* whatever we want as long as it does not harm others.
2) The global economy seems *to be headed* for total meltdown.
3) The economy, which some analysts believe *to be going to improve* in about 12 months, is currently in a downward spiral.
4) Major car companies have asked for a government bailout *to improve* sales and to help with fiscal restructuring.

Answers

5) Cycles of economic depression and boom ***are argued to be inevitable*** in capitalist democracies.
6) ***There seems to be going to be*** many more layoffs before this crisis is solved.
7) ***It was scary to surpass*** previous stock market losses.
8) Many governments have agreed ***to work*** together to solve this current crisis.
9) I was sad because ***to see*** so many people lose their jobs.
10) The economist Ashley Davis is interesting ***to listen to***.

Chapter 4

1.1

a)	4	d)	5	g)	7
b)	6	e)	9	h)	1
c)	2	f)	8	i)	3

1.2

1) To ***inform*** means to tell or share knowledge.
   We are ***informed*** that Marge Simpson's character is based on the mother of the creator of the show.
2) To ***imply*** means to suggest indirectly.
   The producers of the Simpsons have ***implied*** to viewers that the show will continue to be produced next year.
3) To ***contend*** means to argue a position.
   Christian groups have ***contended*** that the Simpsons is anti religious; the creators deny this.
4) To ***hold*** means to maintain your position.
   Jones ***holds*** that the Simpsons is the greatest TV show of all time.
5) To ***mean*** means to signify or to convey a significance.
   Homer Simpson's relaxed attitude ***means*** that he has had many jobs.
6) To ***agree*** means to not be opposed to an opinion.
   The creators of the Simpsons ***agree*** with critics that it is ridiculous that Bart and Lisa Simpson have stayed in the same class at school for over twenty years.
7) To ***respond*** means to answer a challenge or a question.
   To criticisms of declining quality, the creators of the Simpsons have ***responded*** that their show is still the number one rating cartoon on US television after over 20 years of episodes.
8) To ***indicate*** means to direct someone's attention to something.
   The creator of the Simpsons has ***indicated*** that the character 'Bart' is based on himself.
9) To ***maintain*** means to make a claim or a statement. This word is often used negatively to show that you disagree with the person making the claim.
   Grandpa Simpson ***maintains*** that he knew Thomas Edison.
10) To ***insist*** means to continue to make a claim even though others may disagree.
    The creators of the Simpsons ***insist*** that the town of Springfield, where the Simpsons live, is a fictional town.

1.3

1) The creators of the TV show King of the Hill ***inform/tell*** us that the show is not based on real people.
2) They have ***told/informed*** their viewers that the show is not based on real life characters.
3) They ***contend*** that rivalry between their show and the Simpsons does not exist; however, outsiders ***assure*** us that this simply isn't true.
4) They have ***disclosed*** to media sources that show will continue to be produced next year.
5) Viewers have ***observed*** that the show is not set in any real town.
6) Most viewers ***agree*** with critics that the coolest character in the show is Boomhauer.
7) The producers of the show have tried to ***convince*** the viewers that the lead character, Hank Hill, cannot show any emotions, except to his dog.
8) Differences between Hank Hill and his son, Bobby Hill, ***remind*** us that a father and a son can be quite different from each other.
9) Christian groups have ***reassured*** viewers that the show is not anti religious.
10) Critics have ***written*** that the shows continued popularity is due to its excellent script and fine acting.
11) Hank Hill once ***stated*** that he could never vote for George Bush.

1.5

1) Carlson stated that unlike height or weight, which can be measured, intelligence is not an absolute.
2) The reporter said that the new building would be named after the entrepreneur who donated money for it to be built.
3) In yesterday's paper, it was stated that one point two million people live in Auckland.
4) She mentioned that she had frequently got lost when she had gone out when she was young.
5) He said that he was considering the situation and would get back to me tomorrow about it.

1.6

1) ***According to an article by Wallis, Thompson, and Galvin (1983)*** modern humans suffer much more stress than their ancient ancestors did.

2) ***According to the*** article 'Stress and its affects on modern society' (Wallis, Thompson & Galvin 1983), ancient humans had to worry about where to find each day's food, about wild animals, and about keeping their sleeping place safe.

3) ***According to Linden (1984),*** modern humans have considerably more to stress about.

4) ***According to Peterson (1988),*** modern humans have to worry about the traffic on their way to work, about being late, about meeting deadlines, about doing a good job, and about the cost of living.

5) ***According to Linden (1984),*** modern humans also have to worry about family stresses, more complex friendship stresses, and the pressures of conformity to an increasingly complex web of interrelated cultures and subcultures.

6) ***In*** the article 'Stress: Can we Cope?' (Peterson 1988), the author states that all of these pressures are taking an increasing toll on our society.

7) ***As Wallis, Thompson and Galvin (1983) state,*** what was originally evolved as a mechanism to assist us in our fight for survival in the wild has become one of the biggest health problems in a world that we have created ourselves but from which we cannot escape.

2.1

1) Therefore, understanding the effect of fast food on humans is crucial.
2) Movies can make the world a better place.
3) Szalavit's article appears to be correct; fast food causes addiction.
4) Szalavitz's (2003) claims that people misunderstand what fast food addiction is because they misunderstand the word 'addict' and that we cannot regard fast food as addictive are dubious.
5) In conclusion, Stewart's (2004) claims seem correct. Africa has many problems that need to be blamed on African leaders not on the West or on colonialism.
6) Johnson would seem to be incorrect when he argues that we can treat animals however we want. Kraig is right when she says that the way we mistreat animals on farms is unethical and immoral.
7) What she states is that the research that has been done recently is superficial and not accurate and this statement is based on two general issues: changes in the brain fast food is consumed and the evolution of humans to desire fat. (***Note:*** the second point in this paragraph is not something that she stated, it is an evaluation of what she stated by the author.)

3.1

1) Smoking is alleged to cause cancer.
   It is alleged that smoking causes cancer.
2) 80% of people who got cancer last year are argued to have smoked.
   It is argued that 80% of people who got cancer last year smoked.
3) The tobacco companies are claimed to not be helping the situation.
   It is claimed that the tobacco companies are not helping the situation.
4) Tobacco companies are suggested to have been covering up the effects of nicotine on cigarette addiction.
   It is suggested that tobacco companies have been covering up the effects of nicotine addiction on cigarette addiction.
5) Tobacco companies are mentioned to be covering up this issue.
   It is mentioned that tobacco companies are covering up this issue.
6) High paid lawyers are stated to have had a vested interest in protecting these companies last year.
   It is stated that high paid lawyers had a vested interest in protecting these companies last year.
7) New laws to be introduced next year are warned to be going to have some effect.
   It is warned that new laws to be introduced next year will have some effect.

3.2

1) Smoking amongst teenagers has been noted to have declined in recent years.
2) During the same period mobile phone use has been observed to have increased
3) Mobile phones and smoking have been pointed out to have much in common.
4) The cost of mobile phones has been proven to have led to a lower rate of smoking.
5) This is believed to possibly be the reason for recent declines in rates of smoking. (***Note***: change the modal to an adverb – infinitive clauses cannot contain modals).

3.3

1) It is reasoned that games and messaging are more important to teenagers than smoking.
2) It has been remarked that independence is another reason for the popularity of the mobile over smoking.
3) It is reported that this information is important for planning future anti-smoking campaigns.
4) It is stated that mobile phone use is going to be important for future anti-smoking campaigns.
5) It was shown that smoking was the cause of countless deaths last year alone.

4.1

1) She asked what the only word in the English language that begins and ends with und is.
2) They wonder how much money there is in the world.
3) George wants to know where the city of Ouagadougou is.
4) We are just discussing why so many people in the world feel sad.
5) She explained how much wood a woodchuck could chuck if a woodchuck could chuck wood?

Answers

4.3

1) She asked me why I was wearing that silly hat.
2) I inquired whom you went to the party with.
3) He wondered when the next bus came.
4) I wanted to know how many people went to class today.
5) David asked how much that dog in the window was.

4.4

1) The student enquired which the best university is in the world and how much it cost to attend.
2) Audrey asked where you will spend your next holidays and how you will get there.
3) The explorer stated that the Gobi desert is in Asia and that he/she had been to the Gobi desert.
4) She asked how you get to school and how you get home again.
5) I would like to know why you are studying English and what you hope to use English for in the future.

5.1

First, Dr. Minogue asked the patient if they had any pain; the patient replied that they had quite a lot of pain. The doctor asked where the pain was, and the patient said that it was on the left, around their heart, so the doctor asked if it was in the chest, and the patient said that it was. The doctor then asked what part of the chest it was in; the patient replied that they thought it was in the upper part. The doctor asked the patient to describe what kind of pain it was, but the patient said that it was a bit hard to describe. The doctor then wondered whether it was a sharp kind of ache or whether it was a dull kind of ache; the patient stated that it was pretty dull. The doctor asked how the pain had started, and the patient said that it had started when they were coughing. Next, the doctor asked if it hurt a lot when the patient breathed deeply, and the patient replied that it hurt quite a lot. Finally, the doctor asked whether the pain was always there or whether it came and went. The patient replied that it came and went.

6.1

1) I cannot believe that he is the president.
2) I don't suppose that you know what time it is?
3) I can't imagine what have you been through.
4) We didn't intent that it be done. (See Chapter 4, page 69, for more on the use of 'be' in the noun clause)
5) They didn't expect that he would win.

6.2

1) She explained that we should do our homework.
2) He indicated that the crazy man might kill somebody.
3) I guess that I will probably be able to do it.
4) She wondered whether it would rain tomorrow.
5) The boy enquired whether he might go home early.

6.3

1) I guessed how it should be done.
2) He suggested how to do it.
3) I understood what I should do.
4) He revealed what to do.
5) He did not say how to do it.

7.1

1) The author makes the admission that television is partially responsible for violence amongst children.
2) Karlsson makes the claim that because difficult children are often put in front of the TV to quieten them down, it seems as though the TV is making them violent.
3) Gribble's assertion that there are many quality TV shows for children that contain little violence is correct.
4) Lee puts forward the argument that by the time a child is 10 years old in America, the child has seen over 10,000 murders on television.
5) Uchiro's assumption, that TV desensitises children to violence is probably incorrect.

7.2

1) The media gives the impression that TV *is* responsible for all crime in America.
2) A logical response is often given *that* many children's fairy tales also contain violent story lines but that fairy tales are rarely blamed for violence amongst children.
3) *The* evidence that violence on TV causes violent children is limited.
4) Recent news that violence in America has decreased in recent years *suggests* that TV is not making Americans more violent.
5) The likelihood that violence on TV will be reduced in the near future *is* very low.
6) *Cunningham reasons* that TV appears to make children violent because violent children like to watch violent TV shows.

8.1

1) Most people find it interesting that Australia has so many poisonous creatures.
2) Many new migrants to Australia fear that they will be bitten by a poisonous creature.
3) It is unlikely but not impossible that an Australian spider will kill an adult human.
4) Most people are conscious that the Redback is deadly poisonous.
5) Many people also believe that the Whitetail is deadly poisonous.

6) These people are often amazed that there is little evidence supporting this claim.

7) Nevertheless many people are still afraid that they will be bitten by a White tail.

9.1

1) Cornish told the story of how he became interested in astrophysics.

2) Smerdon discussed the question of who should be in charge of the project.

3) Gilbert considers the issue of whether everybody in the world should be forced to become vegetarian.

4) Despite how Eaton does not smoke, he advocates a more liberal attitude towards smoking.

5) Due to how the situation is hypocritical, Gilbert advocates making it illegal.

6) Several papers on what happened during the prohibition period in America have highlighted the idiocy of such an approach.

10.1 The fact that time has not been decimalised is quite incredible. The way that[1] the current model of time works is quite antiquated. Firstly, that there are twelve months in a year is quite ridiculous. It has been argued *(that)* we could just as easily have ten months. Many people *insist* this would not be possible, but they have to *admit* there could be five months with 35 days each and 5 months with 36 days each. Furthermore, that there are 24 hours in a day is extremely odd. Many fans of decimalisation of time agree that we could have ten hours in a day and that we could have 100 minutes in each hour. It would obviously be better that we had 100 minutes in an hour than that we had 60 minutes in an hour. Although this may seem strange, fans of decimalisation of time say that if we had 10 hours in a day, then each of these decimalised hours would be equivalent to 2 hours and 24 minutes of the hours that[1] we currently have. They also *say* decimalised minute would equal 1 minute and 24.6 seconds of current time. However, the main obstacle to decimalisation of time is the simple fact that changing all the clocks in the world to a new time system would be too expensive.

(1) *Note*: these subordinators begin relative clauses, not noun clauses. For more information about omission of *'that'* from relative clauses, see Chapter 9, pages 148-152.

11.1 First, the recipe says to cut up some onion and to dice some garlic; it says to put the onion and garlic into a fry pan and to fry it for five minutes. Next, it says to add a tin of diced tomatoes. Then it says to stir the mixture well and to cook it for another 5 minutes. Lastly, the recipe says to boil some water and to cook the pasta for ten minutes.

11.2 First, the recipe says that you should cut up some onion and dice some garlic; it says that you should put the onion and garlic into a fry pan and fry it for five minutes. Next, it says that you should add a tin of diced tomatoes. Then it says that you need to stir the mixture well and to cook it for another 5 minutes. Lastly, the recipe says that you have to boil some water and cook the pasta for ten minutes.

11.3 First, the recipe recommends that you cut up some onion and dice some garlic; it recommends that you put the onion and garlic into a fry pan and fry it for five minutes. Next, it advises that you add a tin of diced tomatoes. Then it advises that you stir the mixture well and cook it for another 5 minutes. Lastly, the recipe suggests that you boil some water and cook the pasta for ten minutes.

Chapter 5

1.1

1) It was caused
2) This will be affecting
3) Services have been disrupted
4) I will have been going
5) We had had
6) It has been being done
7) You contrasted
8) The disk had been corrupted
9) These programmes will be uploaded
10) You will have disregarded
11) The author claims
12) They had been considered
13) It will vary
14) The company will have been restructured
15) Johnson was responding
16) A cure had been being researched
17) A payment has been required
18) These events were occurring
19) The judge has sentenced
20) The results have been being interpreted
21) Several researchers have been involved
22) Many products will have been being exported
23) The practice is being established
24) The project will be being financed

2.1

1) a) state
2) a) event
3) a) event
4) a) event
5) a) eventb) state
6) a) event
7) a) eventb) event c) state
8) a) eventb) event
9) a) state b) event
   c) eventd) event

3.1

1) When we *arrived* at the theatre, several subjects *were waiting* to be tested on. We always *begin* by testing on animals and then *move* on to humans. When we *tested* on animals this time, the animals *had* no negative symptoms, so we *were* able to move on to humans.

2) A study which *was done* in 1996 *showed* that there *were* a lot of differences between cultures with regard to attitudes towards plagiarism. Western universities always *treat* plagiarism as if it *is* a serious crime. Eastern universities always *do not treat* it so seriously. Students who *were studying* at Hong

Answers

Kong University at the time of the study ***appeared*** confused. They ***did not understand*** why teachers ***wanted*** them to write the same thing in words that ***were*** not as good as the original.

3) While I ***was writing*** this dissertation, I ***got*** help from a number of different people. The foremost source of assistance ***was*** my supervisor, who ***helped*** me understand good research methods and ***helped*** me to find excellent resources to back up my arguments. In the future, I always ***will remember*** her help and I hope that some day I ***will be*** able to offer similar help to my own postgraduate students.

4.1 When a UN envoy visited the Darfur region of Western Sudan in 2004, they (**found** / ~~had found~~) that several hundred thousand locals (~~were murdered~~ / **had been murdered**) and almost a million people (~~were made~~ / **had been made**) homeless. The war there started in 2003 when the SLA (**attacked** / ~~had attacked~~) an airport in Darfur and (**captured** / ~~had captured~~) the head of the Sudanese Air Force. The SLA (**was made** / ~~had been made~~) up of Durfurian locals who (**were dissatisfied** / **had been dissatisfied**)[1] with their government. They (~~suffered~~ / **had suffered**) through many years of drought and (~~saw~~ / **had seen**) their land invaded by Arabic nomads who were also escaping the drought. All of this (~~was ignored~~ / **had been ignored**) by the Sudanese government. After the attack on the airport, the Sudanese government (**organised** / ~~had organised~~) a militia group to control the SLA. This militia group (**was called** / ~~had been called~~) the Janjaweed. By the time the UN envoy (**visited** / **had visited**)[2] Darfur in 2004, the Janjaweed (~~ran~~ / **had run**) riot, killing and murdering the Darfurians. The Sudanese government claimed that they did not sanction the actions of the Janjaweed, but aid workers (**told** / ~~had told~~) the UN that they (~~saw~~ / **had seen**) Sudanese government helicopters and air force planes supporting the Janjaweed.

Notes:

1) Here either tense is okay: they were dissatisfied when they formed the SLA, or they had been dissatisfied before they formed it.

2) Here again, either tense is okay, but the meaning is somewhat different. *Visited* implies that the UN visited Darfur in 2004; *had visited* implies that the UN visited Darfur before 2004,

4.2 Einstein went to school in Germany and did well. He was introduced to science by Max Talmund, when he had moved to Italy. When he had gone to university in Switzerland, he got a job at the Swiss patent office and wrote a paper on the theory of relativity

5.1 Earth ***has*** an amazing variety of life on it. There ***are*** huge trees, tiny bugs, intelligent ocean living creatures, and furry dogs. There ***have been*** living creatures on Earth since 3 billion years ago. Since then, it ***has evolved*** in weird and wonderful ways. For the last millennia, however, homo sapiens ***have dominated*** the Earth. Homo sapiens now ***have*** the largest brain of all the land creatures. Yet, with that power there ***is*** responsibility; something that human kind ***has been abusing*** since the beginning of the industrial age.

5.2 I ***had been*** interested in the subject since I was a teenager. I ***had had*** research tools since my 16th birthday, which I ***used*** regularly until I was in university. Surprisingly, though, there ***had not been*** very many developments in the field for about 30 years until the publication of my Phd Thesis. People ***had been studying*** related topics when this influential paper ***was published***, but did not focus on the exact issue that my paper focused on. I ***wrote*** it in 1966 and 1967 when I ***was studying*** at Vatalia University.

6.1

1) Computers ***have changed*** people's lives. In the past, people ***had*** to do calculations on a piece of paper or with an abacus. Today's children, however, ***have grown up*** without needing to use computers and as a result, often ***have not learned*** to do calculations in their heads.

2) Military conflicts have changed over the last 2000 years. Roman military conflicts ***were fought / used to be fought*** with swords and wooden shields. Medieval military conflicts ***were fought*** with swords, metal shields, and catapults. Since the 1500s, conflicts have been fought with guns. Now, however, military leaders ***have learned*** to use a wide array of computer-assisted weaponry. In fact, weapons ***have been developed*** that can remotely send missiles to a target pin-pointed by a satellite.

3) The invention of the automobile ***has revolutionised*** the way of life in many countries. People who ***had*** to walk for days to reach a city can now reach the city in hours, while people who ***lived*** on the edge of cities can now get to the city in less than an hour. This ***has led*** to a massive boom in the number of people living on the edge of cities and ***led*** to the phenomenal growth of sprawling cities like Los Angeles, Sydney, and Tokyo.

4) Unfortunately, I ***have been asked*** to switch off the wireless router by the university because it ***has caused*** some problems campus wide. I ***have logged*** a request for the wired points to be activated throughout the building, but ***have not*** yet ***received*** a response from them. I ***did not realise*** that this would happen if we used a wireless router as the university ***did not tell*** me that such problems could arise.

7.1

1) c	4) b	7) b	
2) b	5) b	8) c	
3) a	6) a	9) a	

7.2

1) 1	3) 1, 1	5) 4, 1	7) 1, 1, 3	9) 2
2) 4, 1	4) 3, 4	6) 1	8) 1, 1	10) 1, 2

216

7.3 So that we _**understand**_ future weather patterns, we _**need**_ to look to the past. For the last few million years, the world _**has been moving**_ in and out of glacial periods. Most people _**call**_ glacial periods ice ages, but actually an ice age _**is**_ a period during which ice _**covered**_ at least a part of the earth. At the moment, ice _**covers**_ parts of the north and south poles; therefore, the earth _**is**_ currently in an ice age. During a glacial period, ice _**extends**_ much further south. During the last ice age, ice sheets _**extended**_ almost as far south as Italy in Europe, and as far south as the great lakes in North America, which that ice age _**created**_.

As we _**said**_ before, the earth _**has been moving**_ in and out of glacial periods for over a million years. Glacial periods usually _**last**_ around 100,000 years; the warm periods in between, which scientists _**call**_ interglacial periods, usually _**last**_ around 10,000 years. The longest that an interglacial period _**lasted was**_ 12,000 years. The current interglacial period _**lasted**_ 10,000 years. This _**means**_ that a glacial period _**will begin**_ very soon. If this _**is**_ true, in the future, the world _**will not heat**_ up, it _**will cool**_ down.

Temperatures _**do not remain**_ constant during glacial periods. During the last glacial, temperatures sometimes _**spiked**_ at temperatures much the same as today's temperatures. These warm periods sometimes _**lasted**_ for a few years. During the last glacial, primitive humans _**spread**_ out across Europe and Asia. They _**hunted**_ the mammoths that _**had evolved**_ for that cold weather. At the same time, Homo Neanderthal, a creature that _**was**_ very similar to humans, _**lived**_ successfully throughout Europe. Both the mammoth and Homo Neanderthal _**died**_ out when the last glacial _**ended**_ because they _**were**_ unable to cope with an environment which _**was changing**_ rapidly.

When the next glacial comes, it _**will be**_ difficult for humans. The cities that we _**have built built**_ heavily on large-scale agriculture. Farms across the world _**will fail**_; without food, there _**will be**_ no food in shops. Millions of people _**will starve and die**_. People who survive _**will live**_ in a world in which society _**will have broken**_ down. There _**will be**_ no police and no armies, and people _**will have**_ to scavenge for food. By the time that the glacial ends, 100,000 years in the future, humans _**will have evolved**_ again into quite different creatures to what we are today.

8.1
1) Einstein said that we only use 10% of our brain in our lifetime.
2) Eisenhower said that the Russians were developing a nuclear bomb.
3) Al Gore said that the world has limited resources and that we should use those resources wisely.
4) Einstein said that anyone who had never made a mistake had never tried anything new.
5) A priest said that they had not known that child abuse had been a crime.
6) Kennedy said that communism had never come to power in a country that had not been disrupted by war or corruption, or both.

8.2
1) Hitler said that the Third Reich would last 100 years.
2) Walt Disney said that nobody would want to hear people talk in movies.
3) The IPCC said that the world will run out of oil in 2030.
4) Matlock said that the Earth will experience another glacial period (ice age) within the next couple of thousand years.
5) Kennedy said that they would commit themselves to sending a man to the moon.

9.2
1) _**As soon as**_ the law _**is**_ passed, there will be more civil liberty.
2) _**When**_ the world's oil supplies _**are depleted**_, there will be no more plastic.
3) The university will have a graduation ceremony _**once**_ you _**complete**_ your degree.
4) _**After you**_ write your first draft, re-write your essay making sure you find all the errors.
5) _**When you**_ write your essay, try to include as many references as possible.

10.1
1) If you _**add**_ Omega 3 to a child's diet, it helps the synapses in their brain strengthen.
2) If Hitler _**had stopped**_ when he invaded Czechoslovakia, World War II would probably not have happened.
3) If I _**were**_ president of the world, I would bring an end to poverty and hunger.
4) If a female _**wins**_ the next election in the USA, it will be a great victory for women's right's.
5) If the nuclear bomb _**had not been invented**_, there might have been many more intense wars in the latter half of the 20th century.
6) If humans _**settle**_ on the moon, they will need to find a reliable source of water and oxygen.
7) If this movie _**were made**_, we would be able to make a lot of money.
8) If children _**are exposed**_ to more than one language as an infant, they are often slow to learn to speak.
9) If you _**had done**_ all of the readings, you would have known that this issue has been researched at length.

Chapter 6

1.1
1) broadening   to be broadening
2) having enlarged   to have enlarged
3) having deteriorated   to have deteriorated
4) having been deteriorating   to have been deteriorating
5) being going to modify   to be going to modify
6) being confined   to be confined

Answers

7)	having been restricted	to have been restricted
8)	having been emphasised	to have been emphasised
9)	being going to be speculated	to be going to be speculated
10)	Having been being generated	to have been being generated

1.2 It is said ***to be*** ten thousand years since the last ice age. Since then, temperatures ***have been fluctuating*** quite significantly. We can see rises and falls in temperature of several degrees. During a warmer period four thousand years ago, humans ***began*** to build the first farms and cities, and we ***have tracked*** temperatures from that time by looking at the price of food crops. Prices ***going up*** for a significant period in the past ***indicates*** temperatures ***being*** colder at that time; with prices ***having gone*** down at certain points in the past, temperatures are understood ***to have been*** warmer. To map temperatures prior to the onset of these ancient civilisations, we ***look*** at tree rings and ice cores drilled in the Greenland ice sheet. Tree rings are also known ***to tell*** us a lot about temperatures in ancient times. Rings ***having been*** thicker tells us that temperatures ***were*** warmer; thin rings resulted from temperatures ***having being*** cooler.

Of course, much more information about temperatures in the last 1000 years ***is known***. Around 1000 years ago, temperatures are known ***to have been*** significantly warmer than today. This is thought ***to have allowed*** the Viking people of Scandinavia ***to increase*** their populations and ***to spread*** out across the world. Historians ***believe*** the Vikings not only ***settled*** in Greenland and ***farmed*** land too cold to farm today, but also ***settled*** in Canada, which they ***called*** Vinland, or land of vines, even though today Canada ***is*** too cold to grow vines. This period ***referref*** to as the Medieval Warm Period. The Medieval Warm Period ***was*** a time that ***enjoyed*** great prosperity. Crops across Europe and Asia ***were*** bountiful; cities ***expanded***, and people ***were*** wealthy.

2.1

1) Could I use your phone?
2) You can do any of the first three questions, but not the fourth.
3) You have to complete an outline of your essay before Monday.
4) You should make a reference list at the end of your essay outline.
5) You cannot pass this session unless you complete your essay.
6) You will not pass if you do not make an outline of your essay first.
7) You probably think you can pass without doing an outline, but it is harder than you think.
8) As you can't speak English as well as native speakers, the outline of your essay is very important.

2.2

1) Could understand / was able to understand
2) Could be going to lead to problems
3) May be meeting with difficulties
4) Might have been at risk
5) More information will be required
6) Would like to have be consulted
7) Must have been their priority
8) Should have jailed
9) Ought to have been doing better
10)

2.3

1) 1	4) 5	7) 2	10) 3	13) 2
2) 3	5) 2	8) 4	11) 4	14) 4
3) 3	6) 3	9) 4	12) 5	15) 5

3.1

1) No hedging
2) No hedging
3) The Sudan government ***could be said to be*** responsible for the war in Darfur.
4) Humans ***might*** go crazy travelling the vast distance from Earth to Mars.
5) No hedging
6) Robots will ***probably*** soon be developed that will be able to do housework.
7) No hedging
8) No hedging
9) ***It is probably that*** a meteorite that crashed into the earth killed all the dinosaurs.
10) ***It seems likely that*** life once existed on Mars.
11) There ***are likely to be*** other life-supporting planets in the universe.
12) ***It could be argued that*** women are smarter than men.
13) No hedging
14) If a country changes the side of the road that people drive on, it ***may*** cause lots of accidents.
15) If a superstore opens in this town, the small shops ***could*** go broke.
16) No hedging
17) English ***appears to be*** more complex than Korean.
18) The Australian government ***seems not to care*** about refugees.
19) No hedging
20) ***The likelihood is that*** the dollar will remain stable for the foreseeable future.
21) No hedging
22) Aliens ***may have come*** to Earth before humans developed towns and farms.

23) African leaders say that colonialism is to blame for their problems. However, *it could be argued that they are* wrong.

Chapter 7

1.1

1) As you write a plan of your essay, check to make sure that your writing is logical.
2) Begin to make a first draft when you have written plan of your essay. (When)
3) Do not begin your final draft until you have got somebody to check over your first draft for you.
4) After you finish your final draft, use a grammar checklist to make sure that your writing is as grammatically accurate as possible.
5) Before you submit your essay to your lecturer, check one more time for any grammar mistakes.

1.3

1) The president was waiting **when** we arrived.
2) **When/while** I was a new employee at the company, I never got to take important trips like this.
3) **While/when/as** I was sitting in the aeroplane, I thought about the speech I would give.
4) It will be a relief **when** the speech is over.
5) The president was watching me **when/while/as** I was giving the speech.
6) I was worried that people would notice **when** an sms message arrived on my phone during the speech.
7) **When/as** the speech came to an end, I realised that it had been a success.
8) It was great **when/while** I was the star of the conference, but of course my stardom soon faded.

2.1

1) You can't buy burdock **everywhere** you go in Britain.
2) You can find Asian supermarkets almost **everywhere/anywhere** you go in British cities.
3) **Wherever/anywhere** a big Asian community is living, there are many Asian shops and restaurants.
4) You can buy Asian groceries in most parts of Britain, but you can't buy them **everywhere** you go.

3.1

1) The dog raised his paw **as I had taught him to**.
2) She did CPR on the child **as she has been advised to in such a situation**.
3) Do these exercises **as the instructions tell you to**.
4) She walks **as a model walks**.
5) She makes pasta **as her mother made pasta.**

3.2

1)	M	4)	R	7)	T	
2)	R	5)	M	8)	M	
3)	T	6)	T	9)	R	

3.3

1) He looks **as if/as though** he is a pirate.
2) He talks **as if/as though** he is our boss.
3) You should act **as if/as though** you are not scared.
4) He sounded **as if/as though** he did not want to come.
5) You drive **as if/as though** you have the road to yourself.

3.4

1) The roads were not **as** busy today **as** they usually are.
2) The palace is ten times **as** big **as** my house.
3) I did not do **as** well in the test on adverbial clauses **as** I had thought I would.
4) The student answered the questions **as** quickly **as** she could.
5) Try to finish these exercises **as** quickly **as** you can.

4.1

1) I carried the box **as far as** I could.
2) Everyone should have **as much** fun **as** they possibly can.
3) Buses in this city don't run **as often as** they should.
4) I walked **as quickly as** I felt able to walk.
5) She uses a taxi **as often as** she has the money to.

5.1

1) Taipei 101 is **so** strong **that** it can withstand strong typhoons and earthquakes.
2) Burj Dubai has been built **so** secretively **that** nobody knows how many floors it will have.
3) Burj Dubai will be **such** a tall building **that** it will be more than twice the height of Taipei 101.
4) The world's longest suspension bridge, the Akashi Kaikyo bridge, has **such** a strong structure **that** it can withstand an earthquake of 8.5 on the Richter scale.
5) Tokyo, the world's largest city, is built on **so** many earthquake fault lines **that** a major earthquake catastrophe is inevitable.
6) The world's largest country, Russia, has **so** much unused land **that** much of it still remains unexplored.

6.1

1) People use slang **so that** outsiders will not understand them.

Answers

2) Slang allows people to create and reinforce identity, **so** we can say that slang reflects the speaker's experiences, viewpoints, and principles.
3) Slang is not understood by everybody, **so** people don't tend to use it outside of their social group.
4) People use slang **so that** hey appear knowledgeable.
5) Historically, slang was originally used by gangsters **so that** nobody would understand their secret code.
6) Similarly, people tend to use swear words **so that** they fit into a group.
7) Swear words have changed over time, **so** the words that our parents thought were swear words are no longer swear words.

6.2

1) Not possible
2) Monkeys know how to hide food from other monkeys **in order to** eat it themselves.
3) People have taught some chimpanzees sign language **in order to** communicate simple requests to the monkeys.
4) Not possible

7.1

1) Attempts to teach chimpanzees to speak in the past have failed **because** chimpanzees physically cannot speak.
2) **Because** they do not have a pharynx, chimpanzees cannot speak.
3) Researchers have had much more success through teaching chimpanzees to use sign language **because** the chimpanzees do not need to speak.
4) **Because** chimpanzees that have learned sign language have managed to teach that sign language to their babies, researchers have been impressed.
5) **Because** chimpanzees have been able to communicate using sign language., researchers have had to re-evaluate just how intelligent these creatures are.

8.1

1) The football manager will loose his job **even if** his team wins.
2) The desalination plant will go ahead **even if/even though** the dams are full.
3) **Even if/even though** you have been on an aeroplane many times before, you should still keep these points in mind.
4) **Even if** it were not illegal to use drugs, I still wouldn't use them.
5) **Even though** farmers are rejoicing, it is too early to know if it will be a good harvest this year.

9.1

1) **Although/even though** he hated the president, he decided to vote for him anyway.
2) **While/whereas** Bill Gates has a lot of money, I have only a little money.
   Bill Gates has a lot of money, **while/whereas** I have only a little money.
3) **Although/even though** the official death toll stands at only 20,000, there is little doubt that the real figure is closer to 100,000.
4) **While/whereas** she was always cheerful, she was very unwell.
5) **While/whereas** I have written many books, my sister has written none.
   I have written many books, **While/whereas** my sister has written none.
6) **While/whereas** Gilling claims that global warming is not a serious problem, Hardy claims that global warming is a serious problem.
   Gilling claims that global warming is not a serious problem, **while/whereas** Hardy claims that global warming is a serious problem.
7) We went to the beach **although/even though** it was raining.
8) **Although/even though** I didn't get the job, I was the best qualified person.
9) **While/whereas** PCs are the best computers to use for programming, Apples are the best computers to use for computer graphics.
   PCs are the best computers to use for programming, **while/whereas** Apples are the best computers to use for computer graphics.
10) **While/whereas** it is surprising that he passed, there is no proof that he cheated.

10.1

1) European domination of the world was inevitable; if we started world history over again from the start, the Europeans will still win.
2) However, this has nothing to do with the genetic make up of Europeans; they are not somehow better people; if we put Africans or Indians or Chinese or Incans in Europe 10,000 years ago, the people in Europe would still win.
3) This is because of the flora and fauna of the continent; if a tribe of people wants to settle down and build cities, they need plants and animals that can be domesticated.
4) Africa has plants that can be domesticated, but it doesn't have animals that can be domesticated; if the Zebra could be domesticated. Africa might be the continent that dominates the whole world.
5) North America has one plant (maize) that can be domesticated, and animal (the turkey); the North American Indians might have conquered the whole world if North America had had horses or cows.

6) South America has one plant and two animals that can be domesticated (the llama and the guinea pig); farming cannot progress if a country does not have horses or cows.
7) If Australia had had plants or animals that could be domesticated, it might have developed farming.
8) If the emu could be domesticated, it could be used to pull ploughs.
9) Eurasia had plenty of plants that could be domesticated (wheat and rice), and it had plenty of animals that could be domesticated (pigs, cows, sheep, horses, chickens); if a continent does not have these plants and animals, it will not develop farms and cities.
10) Farming of these animals and plants easily spread east and west from the Middle East into Europe, India, and China; it is easy for farming methods to spread to other countries if the countries are on roughly the same latitude.
11) It is very hard for farming to spread if a continent has a north south axis, like the Americas.
12) If all of this is true, why was it Europe, not the Middle East, China or India that conquered the whole world?
13) The answer is geography; many small kingdoms can exist to compete with each other over technology and exploration if a continent is mountainous like Europe.
14) It is easy for one kingdom to conquer the whole continent if a continent has vast flat areas, like China and India.
15) If one country controls a whole continent, the country does not need to compete with other countries to defend itself, and it will not emphasise the development of technology.

10.2
1) If it rains tomorrow, I'll have to cancel my appointment.
2) If sea levels **rose**, most cities in the eastern region **would** be under water.
3) If aliens **came** to Earth, we **would** be ready to great them.
4) If aliens **had come** to Earth 4000 years ago, we **would** not know if they came or not.
5) If the people of 1938 **had known** what we know now, they **would have known** to stop Hitler before his evil atrocities really started.
6) The sea level in the Atlantic might start to rise. In this case the flow of warm water from the Pacific to the Atlantic **would** stop. This **would** cause Europe to become cooler than now.
7) If Canada **invaded** the USA, they **would** not win.
8) The Republicans may win the next election. Should this happen, they will try to stop stem cell research.
9) If a monkey **won** the next election, it **would** be a better president.
10) If I **worked** in Antarctica, I **would** go skiing everyday.

11.1
1) Were I more careful when I write in English, I would get higher marks.
2) Had he taken more time to investigate the side-effects, this problem would not be occurring.
3) Had they taken the time to read other research on the same topic, this problem would not have arisen.
4) Were they more careful when they do their research, this sort of problem wouldn't arise.
5) Not possible

11.3
1) Should you see my George, tell him that him that I want to speak to him.
2) Can you tell me should you find an article on 'work ethic' while you're looking.
3) Should they have been late, they would have been excluded from the study.
4) Not possible
5) Should the professor be busy, his secretary is available.

11.5
1) If taking this medicine daily, make sure you should make sure you drink plenty of water too.
2) If studying English, you will need to buy this grammar book.
3) Take two copies of each of these documents if studying nursing.
4) Not possible
5) Try to improve the coherence in your writing if trying to pass the IELTS test.

12.1
1) I am happier now than I have ever been happy before.
2) I am not as young as my sister is.
3) She is the same age as I am.
4) Richard has the same IQ as Albert Einstein had.
5) He wears the same sunglasses as I do.
6) PCs are not as good computers as Apples are.
7) Portsmouth is not an as interesting a place to live as London is.
8) I find relative clauses easier to understand than adverbial clauses.

Chapter 8
1.1

1) strokes / blockages in arteries → blockages in arteries cause strokes.
   (effect)   (cause)

Answers

2) blocked arteries / blood not getting to part of the brain
   (cause)   (effect)

   → Blood not getting to part of the brain arises from blocked arteries.

3) most strokes / blood clots in the arteries supplying blood to the brain
   (effect)   (cause)

   → Most strokes are the consequence of blood clots in the arteries supplying blood to the brain.

4) arteries that are narrowed by a long-term build up of cholesterol and other fats in the artery wall / blood
   clots
   (cause)   (effect)

   → Arteries that are narrowed by a long-term build up of cholesterol and other fats in the artery wall result
   in blood clots.

5) a heart attack if it occurs in the arteries supplying the heart / the same process
   (effect)   (cause)

   → The same process gives rise to a heart attack if it occurs in the arteries supplying the heart.

6) rupture of an artery in the brain / a haemorrhagic stroke happens
   (cause)   (effect)

7) → Due to rupture of an artery in the brain, a haemorrhagic stroke happens
   rupture of an artery in the brain / there is bleeding and squashing of the surrounding tissue
   (cause)   (effect)

8) → Because of rupture of an artery in the brain, there is bleeding and squashing of the surrounding tissue.
   rainforest destruction / agriculture and in drier areas, fuelwood collection
   (effect)   (cause)

   → The causes of rainforest destruction **are** agriculture and in drier areas, fuelwood collection.

9) forest degradation / logging
   (effect)   (cause)

   → Logging results in forest degradation.

10) rainforests / mining, industrial development and large dams also
    (effect)   (cause)

    → Mining, industrial development and large dams also affect rainforests.

11) a larger threat to the forests / tourism
    (effect)   (cause)

    → Tourism generates a larger threat to the forests.

12) the timber industry's method of 'selective' logging / natural forest regrowth (the outcome of)
    (cause)   (effect)

    → Natural forest regrowth is the outcome the timber industry's method of 'selective' logging.

13) autism / it is still unclear what
    (effect) (cause)

    → It is still unclear what gives rise to autism.

14) a child with a genetic problems being exposed to one or more problems / recent research suggests that
    Autism   (effect)   (cause)

    → Recent research suggests that Autism results from a child with a genetic problems being exposed to
    one or more problems.

15) these problems / a series of poor interactions between Genes and Nutrients
    (cause)   (effect)

    → These problems result in a series of poor interactions between Genes and Nutrients.

1.2

1) l	3) e	5) j	7) f	9) c	11) k
2) h	4) a	6) b	8) g	10) d	12) i

2.1

1) Lightning strikes are the cause of almost all natural bushfires
   (noun phrase)   (verb) (noun phrase) (prepositional phrase)

2) On January 7, 2003 over 120 bushfires started as a consequence of lightning from thunderstorms in
   south-
   (prepositional phrase)   (noun phrase)   (verb)   (prepositional phrase)   (prepositional phrase)   (prepositional
   phrase)

   eastern Australia.

3) In late November 1997 over 100 fires in East Gippsland were caused by lightning within a 24-hour period.
   (prepositional phrase)   (noun phrase)   (prepositional phrase) (verb)   (prepositional phrase) (prepositional phrase)

4) All other bushfires on public land are started as a result of human activity.
   (noun phrase)   (prepositional phrase) (verb)   (prepositional phrase)

5) The reason for approximately 74% of all bushfires on public land is human activity.
   (noun)   (prepositional phrase)   (prepositional phrase) (prepositional phrase) (verb) (noun phrase)

6) On average, approximately 10% of the bushfires that start on public land are due to campfires.
   (prepositional phrase) (noun phrase)   (prepositional phrase) (relative clause) (prepositional phrase) (verb) (prepositional phrase)

7) Fires on public land can arise from farmers burning vegetation.
   (noun) (prepositional phrase) (verb)   (prepositional phrase)

8) Any equipment or machinery that generates heat or sparks is a potential cause of bushfires.
   (noun phrase)   (relative clause)   (verb) (noun phrase)   (prepositional phrase)

9) Other bushfires result from deliberately lit fires, often by children who are playing with matches.
   (noun phrase)   (verb) (prepositional phrase)   (prepositional phrase) (relative clause) (prepositional phrase)

2.2

1) **Cause:** People earn more money.
   Effect: Prices for goods and services increase because people have more money to spend.
   Since people earn more money, prices for goods and services increase because people have more money to spend.

2) **Effect:** Everybody likes pop music.
   Cause: The regular beat of pop music sounds very similar to the heartbeat in the womb.
   Because of the regular beat of pop music sounding very similar to the heartbeat in the womb, everybody likes pop music.

3) **Cause:** People do not understand the clothing, manners, and customs of new migrant groups.
   Effect: People always dislike new migrant communities.
   Due to not understanding the clothing, manners, and customs of new migrant groups, people always dislike new migrant communities.

4) **Effect:** More and more people are opting for plastic surgery to improve their looks.
   Cause: Magazines and television make people increasingly more aware of their self-image these days.
   As a consequence of magazines and television making people increasingly more aware of their self image these days, more and more people are opting for plastic surgery to improve their looks.

5) **Cause:** During the past 100 years, many Pacific island people saw foreigners from Europe, Japan, and America come to their islands. A short while after the foreigners arrived, aeroplanes would come with cargo for the foreigners. The Pacific Islanders thought that this cargo came from gods.
   Effect: The Pacific islanders started worshipping these cargo gods, hoping that the cargo gods would send them cargo too.
   During the past 100 years, many Pacific island people saw foreigners from Europe, Japan, and America come to their islands. A short while after the foreigners arrived, aeroplanes would come with cargo for the foreigners. The Pacific Islanders thinking that this cargo came from gods gave rise to the Pacific islanders starting to worship these cargo gods, hoping that the cargo gods would send them cargo too.

6) **Effect:** Some people go crazy and start to murder people.
   Cause: These days there are increasing problems with overpopulation. Humans only recently evolved from being scavengers, hunters and gatherers. Many humans are not able to adjust to this new environment.
   These days there are increasing problems with overpopulation. Humans only recently evolved from being scavengers, hunters and gatherers. Many humans not being able to adjust to this new environment has resulted in some people going crazy and starting to murder people.

7) **Effect 2:** Today there are many fewer wars.
   Cause: In the past countries wanted to show off how strong they were.
   Effect 1: Countries had wars. However, today, countries can show off how strong they are at international sporting events such as the Olympics and the World Cup.
   In the past countries wanted to show off how strong they were, so countries had wars. However, today, countries can show off how strong they are at international sporting events such as the Olympics and the World Cup; as a consequence, today there are many fewer wars.

8) **Cause:** People have inadequate cooling off or rest periods at work.
   Cause: People do not consume enough water at work.
   Effect: Heat-related health problems happen at work.
   The causes of heat-related health problems happening at work are people having inadequate cooling off or rest periods at work and people not consuming enough water at work.

9) **Effect 2:** People who play computer games too much sometimes do crazy things like killing people.
   Effect 1: They think that they can turn off life and start it again.
   Cause: People play computer games too much.
   The effect of people playing computer games too much is that they think that they can turn off life and start it again; therefore, people who play computer games too much sometimes do crazy things like killing people.

10) **Cause 1:** Human minds have evolved to understand how things are created.
    Effect: People tend to believe that the universe must have a creator.
    Cause 2: People tend to believe that everything must have a creator.

Answers

The upshot of human minds having evolved to understand how things are created is people tending to believe that everything must have a creator; thus, people tend to believe that the universe must have a creator.

11) **Effect 2:** They began to make grunting noises to each other. After time, these grunting noises became words, and the first languages had begun.
Cause: Human-like apes long ago needed to make tools.
Effect 1: The need to exchange information about making tools.
Human-like apes long ago needing to make tools gave rise to the need to exchange information about making tools; hence, they began making/to make grunting noises to each other. After a time, these grunting noises became words, and the first languages had begun.

12) **Cause:** Since the 1950s, the number of women working has increased dramatically.
Effect: The unemployment rate has not gone up during that time.
Since the 1950s, the number of women working having increased dramatically, had not caused the unemployment rate to go up.

4.1

1) Many people claim that French is as difficult to learn as English is.
2) The English and French languages are similar.
3) Although there are many differences in English and French pronunciation, there are also some similarities.
4) Several sounds in the English language are similar to sounds only found in French.
5) French has many accented letters, whereas English does not have many accented letters.
6) English has many irregular verbs just like French.
7) French writing looks like English.
8) The meanings of many French words are the same as the meanings of many English words.
9) For example, the meaning of the word *ballet* is the same in both languages.
10) Hotel means a place to stay in English just as it does in French.
11) Often the nuance of the vocabulary in English can differ from its French meaning.
12) However, some similar words have actually come into both English and French alike from one foreign language. For example, 'pajama' is the same in both languages because it actually comes from the Hindi language of India.
13) On the other hand, despite there being similarity in vocabulary between the two languages, grammatical structures are often quite different.

5.1

UFOs are an **as yet** unexplained phenomenon; in recent times there has been a massive proliferation in the number of alleged sightings and abductions. However, it is not **as if** UFOs are an entirely new phenomenon. A UFO was reportedly sighted **as long** ago **as** 1878, when 'a black disk flying at incredible speed' was seen. Most sightings, nevertheless, have been post world war two. However, **as** is often pointed out, many have been sightings of US and Russian test planes and experiments. **As well as** being man made objects, some have been hoaxes, and some psychological phenomena; however, there has been some unexplainable evidence. Sightings by notable persons such as former US presidents and NASA astronauts **such as** mass sightings in which whole towns or cities have seen objects that can't be explained remain mysteries, **just as** photographic and video footage do.

Sceptics have pointed out that there are several reasons to doubt these sightings. Firstly, why would aliens travel across the universe **as far as** Earth to observe us for just a few moments and then leave without contacting us? And secondly, modern physics deems long distance space travel near impossible. For instance, **as** the maximum speed that an object can travel at is slightly below the speed of light, if a spacecraft were to travel at the speed of light, it would take 8.6 years to travel **as far as** the nearest star and back again; it would take 30,000 years to travel to the centre of the Milky Way, and it would take 2,000,000 years to travel to the nearest galaxy. Thus, **as long as** modern physics is right, it seems unlikely that aliens would ever be able to travel between universes.

Still, UFOlogists have pointed to other evidence **such as** signs of aliens having come to earth in ancient times. One popular idea is that the ancient ideas of gods visiting earth is based on UFOs visiting earth. More compelling, however, is evidence **such as** the Piri Reis Map, a map whose depiction of the earth is **as good as** modern maps, but which was drawn before mankind mapped the earth.

On the other hand, **as** UFOlogists or sceptics debate, with the recent proliferation of mobile phones with video recording functions, very hard to explain video footage of of UFOs is being uploaded to the internet. Once such piece of footage is a 28 minute video from Turkey in 2008, in which a security guard videoed a UFO hovering above the earth on two consecutive nights. This evidence does not appear to be a hoax and cannot easily be explained.

5.2

1) Statements *such as* that always upset people.
2) He describes UFOs *as if* he has seen one.
3) Not possible
4) Nobody believes hysterical claims *such as* Gibson's.
5) Not possible
6) James talks about UFOs *as if* he is an expert.

7) Most people describing Carter write about   him *as if* he is insane.

Chapter 9

1.1

1) Adverbial	4) Noun	7) Noun	10) a) Noun clause
2) Noun	5) Adverbial	8) Relative	b) Relative clause
3) Relative	6) Relative	9) Relative	

1.2

1) Subject	3) Subject	5) Subject
2) Object	4) Subject	6) Object of a preposition
7)		

2.1

1) Correct	4) Correct	7) Incorrect	9) Incorrect
2) Incorrect	5) Incorrect	8) Correct	10) Incorrect
3) Correct	6) Correct		

3.1

1) Ronald Reagan, who was president of the United States in the 1980s, suffered from Alzheimer's. [NR]
2) George Bush Senior was the president who succeeded Ronald Reagan. [D]
3) Being president of the United States was a position that the next president, who was named William Jefferson Clinton, did not take seriously. [D] [NR]
4) One of the presidents in the 1970s, who was considered weak by many due to his failure to handle the Iran Contra Scandal properly, was Jimmy Carter. [NR]
5) Presidents that are involved in corruption should resign and that is what happened to Richard Nixon, who was forced to admit involvement in Watergate. [R] [NR]
6) The president that came between Nixon and Carter was President Gerald Ford. [D]
7) Prior to Nixon, the United States' presidency, which is a very powerful position, was held by Lyndon Baines Johnson, who was also known as LBJ in the years after Kennedy's murder, which is thought by many to have been a conspiracy. [NR] [NR] [NR]

4.1

1) South Korea has several large companies, which are called *Chaebol.*
2) LG, which is a large South Korean Company, produces electronic and petrochemical goods.
3) Goldstar, which the company was originally just called, began in 1947.
4) In 1995, the company changed its name to Lucky Goldstar, which the letters LG represent.
5) Samsung, which means three stars, is another *Chaebol.*
6) Samsung telephones are excellent quality as are the cars that they also make.
7) Samsung, which People often mispronounce as sæmsʌŋ, is pronounced sʌmsɒŋ.

5.1

1) Sir Isaac Newton, who wrote *Philosophiæ Naturalis Principia Mathematica*, was a mathematician and a physicist.
2) Sir Isaac Newton, whom many modern scientists idolise, was a physicist.
3) Physicists are scientists that investigate the laws that govern the physical world.
4) Albert Einstein, whom many people believe to have been a genius, was also a physicist.
5) Chemists, which history is also full of, are another kind of scientist.
6) Michael Farraday, who was famous for his work on magnetic fields, was a chemist.

6.1

1) Apple is a computer company whose logo is recognised by everyone.
2) Apple, whose products have immense popularity, make products such as the i-pod and i-phone.
3) Customer loyalty is important to Apple, whose products millions of people across the world use.
4) My great grandfather, whose name was Frost, started a company called Holden & Frost with a man named Holden.
5) Frost later sold his share in the company whose name people now know as Holden.
6) Holden is a company whose cars are owned by almost a quarter of the Australian population.
7) Holden, whose cars are exported to many countries, is now owned by General Motors.
8) The Commodore is a car whose shape people can see all over the world from South Korea to Saudi Arabia.
9) The company whose success the people of Adelaide depend on is trying to build more fuel efficient cars to cope with changing demand.

7.1

1) Finding a language school at which you can satisfy your learning needs can be a challenge these days with so many to choose from.
2) English schools at which good language programmes are run are rare.
3) Programmes before going on to university through which all students must pass are common.
4) Schools from which all students graduate with satisfaction are rare.
5) Schools in which textbooks are not routinely used are even less common.

Answers

6) Students need to choose schools at which they will study carefully.
7) Many students prefer schools to which students from many different countries go.
8) Other students choose schools at which they prepare for university based on the location of the school within the city.

8.1

1) Britain is the place where the English language originated.
2) English later spread to many countries including the United States, where two major accents of English are spoken.
3) The southern United States, which has a proud history, is the home of one major accent.
4) The northern United States, which is the home of the 'Yankies', is where the other major accent is spoken.
5) Canada, where an accent blending British and United States pronunciations is spoken, is home to another regional dialect of English.
6) Then, there is India, which is regarded as having the most marked accent.
7) Lastly, there is Australia, where people speak with a mixture of different accents.

9.1

1) In 2002, when Brazil won the World Cup, it was held in Japan and South Korea.
2) 2008 was the year when Spain won the European Cup for the first time in 44 years.
3) The year which had the most exciting World Cup was 1966.
4) 1966, when England beat Germany to take the World Cup, was the year that the cup was held in England.
5) South Africa will host the World Cup in 2010, which will be the first time an African nation has hosted it.
6) The year when an Asian or African nation wins the world cup will be the beginning of a new era.

10.1

1) Australia has five major cities, most of which are located along the east coast.
2) The people of Sydney, some of whom Australians from the countryside don't always like, believe that their city is the best.
3) On the other hand, this is not what the people of Melbourne, many of whom were born overseas, believe.
4) Melbourne is the home to many sporting events, the most exciting of which is the Australian Football League Grand Final.
5) The beaches around Brisbane, the most popular of which people across the world have heard of, are popular with tourists.
6) The smaller cities of Australia, a few of which are also popular tourist destinations, vary in size and in the services they provide their populations.
7) The cities of Australia, the fourth most populous of which is Perth, are all in the top 100 best cities in the world.
8) Unfortunately, these cities, the largest of which economists are now also listing in the top ten most expensive cities in the world, are becoming expensive to build a house in.

11.1

1) Cows are left outside in the cold during winter, which means that many of them die.
2) Many cows die, which is not a serious problem for farmers.
3) Chickens live in small cages, which suggests that they do not have enough room to move.
4) The animal rights movement has been upset about this for a while now, which has resulted in some action being taken.

12.1

1) They are the people to whom to give it.
2) I am the person to whom to sing it.
3) These are the books into which to delve.
4) The director is the person to whom to write.
5) This is a subject about which to write.

12.2

1) Johnson, who write that we need to remain cautious about hasty judgements in these situations, raises several new issues in his latest paper.
2) The paper mentions phase two, which it is thought might eliminate a lot of the earlier problems.
3) The Bull Offensive, which Ostapuk mentions that Syahputra planned, has been studied extensively.
4) Much has been written about the causes of this, which Mifuni believes are of little significance anyway, but little focus has been made on the results.
5) An overpowering need for accompaniment, which Joachin states has been witnessed in many different people of all ages and from all cultures, is a natural side effect of situations like this.

13.1

1) Aliens, which have probably visited the earth, no doubt exist somewhere.
2) The Darfur crisis that had the worst violence in Africa was genocide.
3) Some scientists that have found a strong relationship between levels of blood-sugar addiction and addiction to fast food are working to change the taste of the food.
4) Some amino acids such as the essential amino acids that must be obtained from diet are needed to meet body requirements.

5) The second graph explains that the US uses the largest amount of minerals such as phosphorus, of which 8322 tonnes is used in one person's life.

13.2

1) Several assignments that the professor has given us are due next week.
2) The letter that we have written to Johnson to protest his recent actions has not arrived yet.
3) Everyone was surprised at the truth that Johnson's behaviour tells us about his beliefs.
4) They are waiting for a result, which we hope to deliver to them by the end of the week.
5) The ministry is awaiting answers, which we do not guarantee.

Chapter 10

1.1

1) f	5) p	9) nf	13) nf
2) f	6) p	10) f	14) f
3) nf	7) nf	11) f	
4) f	8) nf	12) nf	

2.1

1) Claims for autonomy by many groups in Europe have been hindered by factors including 'internal colonialism', economic dependence, and world wars.
2) Ethnic minorities demanding autonomy usually have a long history of independence.
3) For this reason, many ethnic minorities in Europe preferring autonomy have lagged well behind in their claims.
4) Ethnic minorities being seen to be economically dependent on the 'parent country' have little hope for independence.
5) On the other hand, some ethnic minorities can be richer than the 'parent country', possibly leading to feelings of resentment.
6) A 'brain drain', happening in many poorer ethnic groups over the last 50 years, meant less effective nationalist leaders in such areas.
7) Scotland, having experienced a 'brain drain', is an example of a poorer ethnic group.
8) Catalonia, not suffering from the same phenomenon, is considerably wealthier than its 'parent country'.
9) In many cases, ethnic groups given a considerable degree of autonomy over the past 100 years were less vocal in demands for independence.
10) Independence movements in the United Kingdom, affected by the euphoria of victory after World War 2, have progressed less towards autonomy than groups in other countries.

3.1

1) Wales is an example of a region having been diluted with colonists from the 'parent country'.
2) Western Europe, moving closer to becoming a federation of states has many ethnic minorities which are asserting autonomy without risk of economic isolation.
3) Tibet, having been demanding autonomy from China, is another ethnic minority.
4) Ethnic minority rights, being ignored by the media and government throughout China, are also a concern for the southern Mongol people.
5) The Islamic minority in Western China is another ethnic group having had trouble with issues of autonomy.
6) Russia is another country having been struggling with ethnic groups which have been demanding autonomy.
7) Ethnic autonomy, even being considered for the Lapp people of Northern Scandinavia, is an issue affecting both rich and poor countries alike.
8) Australia, the United States, Canada, and New Zealand are all examples of countries having been affected by struggles for recognition by aboriginal ethnic minorities.

4.1

1) In 1945, a man called Vannevar Bush first dreamed up internet websites when imagining a desk with screen projecting books and a keyboard to access them which he called a Memex.
2) Before being able to create the first web page in the early 1970s, they had to connect together all of the computers at the Pentagon, which weighed over 100 tonnes each.
3) No change
4) Since starting with this page in the early 1970s, the internet has come a long way.
5) While working at CERN in Switzerland in 1989, Tim Berners-Lee invented the first real web page using html.
6) No change
7) Before being called 'the internet', it was called APRANET; the name 'internet' was thought up in 1990 to make it sound more exciting.
8) After coming into being in 1992, web browsers started receiving the first SPAM messages
9) If not invented in 1996, instant messaging would not have made the internet the interactive chatting device that it is today.
10) While now struggling to cope with e-mail overladen with SPAM, we are also now able to access the internet on our mobile phones.

Answers

5.1

1) The rules about voting have gradually changed over the last century, women having been demanding more rights since the late 1800s.
2) The western world being a largely patriarchal society, men hold the best and highest paid jobs, and the vast majority of the positions of power in the world.
3) France, the United States, and Japan have never had a female leader, it is clear that it is difficult for women to ascend to the top of patriarchal societies.
4) There are several examples throughout history of societies run by females, proving that societies do not *have* to be run by men, the Indian tribes of North America were often run by the females of the tribe.
5) Women having won many rights, including the right to vote over the last 100 years, many men predicted that the increase in women working throughout the last few decades would lead to greater unemployment; however, this simply has not been so.

6.1

1) Mozart, a famous composer, is considered to have been a musical genius by some.
2) Classical music, which differs from pop music in a number of aspects, does not put as much emphasis on the player as on the composer.
3) Pop music, the most popular form of music today, tends to be played by groups of musicians that both like to take credit for their work, and shun changes in their line up.
4) Music heard regularly on the radio today is often a re-make of previous works.
5) John Coltrane, considered one of the greatest jazz musicians of all time, is a musician whose music is often covered by other artists.

Chapter 11

1.1

a) 2
b) 2
c) 1
d) 2
e) 1
f) 1
g) 2

1.2

1) America has an insatiable appetite for meat. This appetite for meat has been imported by China and India as they gradually become richer. However, this diet has a number of problems. First of all, when we eat meat, we waste money because it takes 7 bowls of cow food to get one bowl of human food (meat) from the cow. Eating a bowl of meat is equivalent to wasting 6 bowls of food.
2) A second problem with the meat diet is that it is causing incredible damage to the environment. It results in a massive over consumption of water to feed the animals. It also results in a massive amount of methane being released into the atmosphere. Methane is a global warming gas, much stronger than CO_2. It is released from the belches and excrement from cows. The volume of methane being released is almost double the amount of gas being released by cars.

2.1

1) am/is/are investigated
2) not possible
3) is being kept
4) was/were caused
5) not possible
6) has been produced
7) have been being used

2.2

1) The current of warm, salty water that is moved up the African coast by ocean currents is called the Great Ocean Conveyor Belt by scientists.
2) European temperatures are affected by this flow of water being joined by the Gulf Stream.
3) Temperatures in Europe are kept considerably warmer than those of comparable latitudes in Asia, Russia, and North by this flow of warm water.
4) Once the warm water reaches Greenland, it is rapidly cooled by the cooler weather.
5) Because the water is encouraged to sink by cold temperatures and high salinity, it *descends* to the bottom of the ocean once it reaches Greenland and *freezes.*
6) The water is then carried back out to the Indian and Pacific oceans along the ocean floor by ocean currents along the bottom of the Atlantic.
7) The flow of the Great Ocean Conveyer Belt is thus affected by seawater around Greenland, which global warming *is making* warmer and less salty.
8) If this flow of water *stopped*, significant cooling would be experienced by Europe.
9) Thus, ironically, major cooling rather than warming could be caused by current climate change trends.

2.3

1) This is because it had already consumed everything.
2) Prior to 10,000 years ago when almost all parts of the earth were covered by ice, the temperature fluctuated slightly between -52°F BS -50°F.
3) An ice age has continued from millions of years ago until now.
4) Some scientists have found a strong relationship between levels of blood-sugar addiction and addiction to fast food
5) We have already lived for 10,000 years in a warm period called an interglacial.

6) The U.S. uses the largest amount of minerals such as phosphorus, which is 8322 tonnes in one person's life.

2.4

1) Our solar system and galaxy could quite suddenly come to an end without us knowing it due to a gamma ray burst. A gamma ray burst can explode across 8 billion light years of space. About three hundred of these blasts each year are detected by scientists. A burst like this would wipe away our galaxy before we even knew what had hit us.

2) Lord Kelvin, who was born in 1824 in Belfast, was the son of a professor of mathematics. He was admitted to the University of Glasgow at the age of ten. By the age of 20, he had completed studies in both London and Paris, he had been elected a teacher and researcher by Cambridge University, and he had written several mathematical papers.

3) Plague is a disease. It is carried by Rats. It is carried by Fleas from one rat to another, but it can be caught by human beings if they are infested by fleas. In crowded medieval cities, this happened quite frequently.

3.1

1) Tchaikovsky's family educated him to become a civil servant even though music was his love as a child. He ignored this education as an adult and began a musical career at the St. Petersburg Conservatory although his family didn't want him to. Tchaikovsky wrote many different types of music from symphony as his musical ability developed. Although he was very successful, personal crises and emotional trouble followed him throughout his life. Because of this, depression was a common problem throughout his life.

2) Winston Churchill coined of the term 'iron curtain' to describe Eastern Europe after World War II. While World War II had been raging, the USSR and the West had been allies, but the USSR had not forgotten that the Western Allies had tried to bring down the USSR during the Russian Civil War. Because of this, the USSR remained wary of the Allies and they tried to set up a buffer zone between them and the West. This buffer zone had its beginnings before World War II had really started. In 1939, after negotiations on a military, economic, and political agreement had been finished, the USSR and Germany signed a trade and non-aggression agreement. After this agreement was signed, the Baltic States and Eastern Poland were invaded by the USSR. This was the beginning of the buffer zone. While the USSR and Germany were friends at the start of the war, their friendship had deteriorated into a bitter war by 1945. Because firstly the Allies and then Germany had betrayed them, the USSR became even more determined to create a buffer zone around their country. Thus, after the war, the USSR decided to keep and expand control of Eastern Europe.

4.1 Recently civilization marked the end of another century. In 1900 many predictions were made about the year 2000. Some of these came true, such as the prevalence of cars, electric trains, air conditioners, and refrigerators, but others were way off the mark, for example floating fortresses above cities, the extinction of all animals, and the extermination of all insects. However, other events and inventions, such as the two world wars, aeroplanes, man walking on the moon, television, and computers, were simply not imagined. This essay will try to make as accurate predictions as possible about the year 2100. It will look at the fields of technology and will look at the field of transportation.

Firstly, lets look at three aspects of technology: computers, mobile phones, and robots. Firstly, Computers will of course become smaller and smaller. It is quite possible that advances in nanotechnology will allow computers to become almost invisibly small, but there are practical limitations to how small a computer might become; for instance, keyboards need to be a reasonable size for people to use them, and computer screens need to be a reasonable size. Furthermore, it is possible that computers could be voice, or possibly even mind activated and could talk to us although there will still be times when we want to work in silence with our computers. Similarly, mobile phones will become smaller but will be limited in size by issues of practicality. Nevertheless, one possibility is that mobile phones and computers will be implanted in our brains. Whenever we want to call somebody or take a photo of something, we will be able to do so using a device directly connected to our brains. On the other hand, robots appear ever more allusive. Many predictors in the 1900s imagined that by 2000, we would have robots helping us with housework, but this simply hasn't happened yet. Robots remain bulky, inefficient, and very expensive. There is, however, one exception: robot vacuum cleaners that move around the floor automatically sensing furniture and other objects, cleaning as they go. Thus, robots will probably be no more common in 2100 than they were in 2001.

Secondly, lets imagine what transportation will be like when petrol supplies will have been virtually depleted and electric, ethanol, and hydrogen fuelled cars will prevail. It is certain that by 2100 AD, much of the world's oil supplies will have been depleted. There will still be oil available, but will be produced by an expensive extraction process from peat and from nearly empty oil wells. Nevertheless, public transportation will no longer rely on petrol. Aeroplanes will probably be fuelled either by ethanol, a biofuel produced from plants, or from super-cooled hydrogen, but the problem with widespread use of biofuels is that if today all the crops in the world were switched to ethanol production, we still wouldn't have enough fuel for all of our cars, so biofuels will probably be the domain only of aeroplanes. On the other hand, supercooled hydrogen could also be used for aeroplanes. It could be used for vehicles, probably those needing more energy, such as trucks and tractors. However, as battery technology improves, it is more and more likely that the future will see an abundance of small electric cars, fitted with an amazing array of electric devices, which no doubt will not have

Answers

keys. They will instead be started at the press of a button which will recognise the owner's fingerprint. They will be fitted with advanced GPS systems that will know where traffic jams are, and the GPS systems will guide the cars around the traffic problems. Cars will also be fitted with sensors that will prevent cars from hitting each other and even other objects. Finally, it is quite possible that these cars will become fully automatic. They will be able to drive themselves to a given destination, and park themselves at the end.

5.1 Proponents of global warming need better perspective. Firstly, the statistics that they are using are very questionable; secondly, they fail to see the big picture, and thirdly, they are searching for evidence to prove the hypothesis that global warming is correct rather than testing the hypothesis scientifically.

The proponents' statistics are questionable for several reasons. If a scientist wants to determine temperatures from more than a hundred years ago, he or she must resort to tree rings. Although rings provide a broad picture of what has been happening, they are nowhere near as accurate as statistical data from satellites and should not be used in the same graph. The inaccuracy of rings is why the statistics used to create the 'hockey stick' graph are so easily discredited; the statistics are not based on hard data. On top of the inaccuracy of rings, the temperatures taken by meteorologists in the first half of the 20th century are questionable because the data was not taken under strict enough conditions. For example, some data were taken in sheds, and some under trees. Moreover, the urban heat island effect also calls this data into question. Many people know that many of the weather stations that were once located in countryside are now located in cities. When a person records temperatures in urban areas and the countryside, there is always a considerable difference. Cities are hotter. Take Orange County for example. It is now located in the Greater Los Angeles urban area, but in 1900 was a small fruit-farming region. Data showing that temperatures have risen there since 1900 merely show that it has evolved from a farming area to an urban area.

5.2 Proponents of global warming fail to see the big picture because whether you consider **the climate change trend** to be warming or cooling really depends on when **we** start from. Lets take seven different possible starting points: 100,000,000 years ago, 10,500 years ago, 3000 years ago, 1000 years ago, 150 years ago, 20 years ago, and 10 years ago. 100,000,000 years ago, the dinosaurs still roamed the earth. At that time, the earth was considerably warmer than **it** is today; there were no polar ice caps; in fact, Antarctica was covered in rain forests. If one makes this point in time a starting point, it is clear that **the earth** has undergone a massive cooling. 10,500 years ago, the last ice age was coming to an end. During this time, the earth was considerably cooler than **it** is today; the polar ice caps spread as far south as the great lakes in North America and northern Italy in Europe. If **we** take this time as a starting point, it is clear that **the world** has undergone massive warming. 3,000 years ago, global temperatures were somewhat warmer than today. **They** had just peaked at one of the many high points that we have experienced in the period since the last ice age. During this warm period, the first cities and civilizations began to flourish. If we take this point in time as a starting point, we can see a slight cooling in **global temperatures**. 1000 years ago, the earth was in yet another warm **period**, somewhat warmer than today. It was during this period that the Vikings were able to settle and farm the now snowy and inhospitable lands of Greenland. Again, taking **1000 years ago** as a starting point, we can see a slight cooling in global temperatures. 150 years ago, the world was in a significantly cooler period. **This** was known as the 'little ice age'. Taking **it** as a starting point, the world appears to be going through a period of rapid warming. 20 years ago **it** was about half a degree cooler than today; it has been through **this time** that scientists have observed the so-called global warming effect; however, 10 years ago in 1998, world temperatures peaked at record highs. Since **this time** temperatures have declined. Thus, if we take **1998** as a starting point, we can see a clear trend of global cooling. Therefore, it is easy to argue that whether the world is warming or cooling all depends on your perspective.

6.1

1) *Scientists having been searching for a vaccine* is a good thing because they may succeed a lot quicker than anyone had hoped since it turns out that people have an unexpected degree of immunity to the pandemic.

2) *Scientists believing this virus had not created any immunity* had resulted from the current virus spreading faster than would be expected if there were widespread immunity to it.

3) *Contact lenses being able to contain tiny microchips and tiny screens* would lead to a wide range of new technological possibilities, including instant sub-titles for foreign language speakers in front of our eyes.

6.2

1) *That the last ice age or glacial period probably began in just a few months, rather than taking decades to start* is proof that we should not be complacent about how soon another ice age may start.

2) *That they could avoid repaying debts* is a common reason for migrants to leave the country.

3) *That submitted sites cannot currently be edited or deleted* is a problem with the programming and not a fault of the website owners.

6.3 It can be difficult to hear what is being said at noisy parties. But hearing what is being said seems to be easier for people who are good at music. Playing an instrument appears to improve how well we can pick up emotional signals when we are talking. Musicians use their brains in a way that helps them distinguish between speech and background noise. Whether musicians use their brains in the way was tested by scientists. They asked musicians and non-musicians to listen to people talking in quiet and noisy environments while their brain activity was being monitored. The brain was slower to respond if there was background noise, but it was found that musicians were less slow to respond than non-musicians. Musicians being less slow to respond than non-musicians is undoubtedly partly genetic, but the scientists have suggested that musical training will help even the very non-musical. Thus, musical training could really assist both children with autism and with language difficulties, who often find that it can be difficult to hear what is being said at noisy parties.

7.1

1) *Dogs and cats were both domesticated because they are useful.* Dogs were first domesticated by humans around 15000 years ago. They were domesticated from wolves who either were friendly to humans, were attracted to the warmth of human fires, or were found as babies by humans. It did not take humans long to realise that these animals were both useful hunters and good companions. Cats, on the other hand, were probably domesticated almost 10,000 years ago. Again, cats were probably attracted to the warmth of human fires or were found as babies. Their usefulness to humans largely centred around their ability to catch mice and rats and other undesirable rodents.

2) *There are a number of differences between classical music and popular music.* In classical music, the emphasis is on the composer of the music, not on the players. In fact, classical music groups frequently change members with few people raising an eyebrow. Popular music places emphasis on the players. Bands frequently become headline news with few people even noting the fact that they are playing an interpretation of another person's work. Perhaps as a result of this, the changing of members of a pop group frequently becomes headline news or leads to the demise of the music group.

3) *Buddhism, which has two 'paths' is not really a religion.* Theravada, which is the oldest type of Buddhism, is popular in Sri Lanka and Southeast Asia; it is stricter form of the Buddhism, in which adherents attempt to live as pure and honest a life as possible. Mahayana, which is known as the 'lesser path' is popular in East Asia; adherents believe that the path to Nirvana is long and unachievable in one lifetime. Buddhism is not really a religion, but rather, a way of life. One semi-religious aspects of Buddhism are its belief in reincarnation; however, mostly it is a philosophy about life.

Information Sources

Ideas have been sourced from the following articles and books for academic use in this publication:

Bill Bryson 2003, *A Short History of Nearly Everything*, Broadway Books, New York.

Charles Flowers 2002, *Instability Rules*, John Wiley & Sons, New York.

Charles Van Doren 1991, *A history of knowledge*, Ballantine Books, New York.

Diamond, J. 1997, *Guns, Germs and Steel*, Random House, London.

DSE, 1996-2010, *What Causes Bushfires on Public Land in Victoria?*, viewed 07/02/2009, http://www.dse.vic.gov.au/dse/nrenfoe.nsf/FID/-90A4796345F5395F4A25679300155A40?OpenDocument.

Matlock, B. 1998, 'Cool Heads on Global Warming', *The Australian.*

Pearson, A. 2009, 'Noisy parties no problem for musical brains', *New Scientist*, viewed 13/11/2009, http://www.newscientist.com/article/dn18147-noisy-parties-no-problem-for-musical-brains.html

Stevenson, R. 1997 'Rurik & the Vikings', *Nordic Notes* online Journal for *Centre of Scandinavian Studies*, ISSN1442-5165 Vol 1

The Norse History of Greenland 982-1500, n.d., viewed 12/7/09, http://www.greenland-guide.gl/leif2000/history.htm.

Wikipedia contributors 2009, 'Iron Curtain', *Wikipedia, The Free Encyclopedia*, viewed 07/02/2010, http://en.wikipedia.org/w/index.php?title=Iron_Curtain&oldid=324764522, page Version ID: 324764522

Wikipedia contributors 2009, 'Pyotr Ilyich Tchaikovsky', *Wikipedia, The Free Encyclopedia*, viewed 07/12/2009, http://en.wikipedia.org/w/index.php?title=Pyotr_Ilyich_Tchaikovsky&oldid=324645182, Page Version ID: 324645182

Grammatical information sourced from:

Celce-Murcia, M. & Larsen-Freeman, D. 1999, *The Grammar Book*, 2nd Edition, Heinle & Heinle, USA.

Collins Cobuild English Grammar 1990, HarperCollins Publishers, Glasgow.

Huddleston, R. & Pullum, G. K. 2002, *The Cambridge Grammar of the English Language*, Cambridge University Press, Cambridge.

Printed in Great Britain
by Amazon.co.uk, Ltd.,
Marston Gate.